CAMBRIDGE TEXTBOOKS IN LING

General Editors: B. COMRIE, C. J. FILLMORE, R. LASS, D. LIGHTFOOT,
P. H. MATTHEWS, R. POSNER, S. ROMAINE, N. V. SMITH, N. VINCENT

SECOND LANGUAGE ACQUISITION

SECOND LANGUAGE ACQUISITION

WOLFGANG KLEIN

MAX-PLANCK-INSTITUT FÜR PSYCHOLINGUISTIK

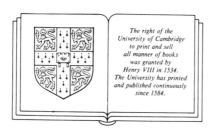

The right of the
University of Cambridge
to print and sell
all manner of books
was granted by
Henry VIII in 1534.
The University has printed
and published continuously
since 1584.

CAMBRIDGE UNIVERSITY PRESS

CAMBRIDGE
NEW YORK   PORT CHESTER
MELBOURNE   SYDNEY

Published by the Press Syndicate of the University of Cambridge
The Pitt Building, Trumpington Street, Cambridge CB2 1RP
40 West 20th Street, New York NY, 10011, USA
10 Stamford Road, Oakleigh, Melbourn 3166, Australia

Second Language Acquisition is a revised and up-dated translation of
Wolfgang Klein: *Zweitspracherwerb: eine Einführung* (Athenäum
Verlag, 1984) by Bohuslaw Jankowski

First published 1986
Reprinted 1986, 1988, 1990

Printed in Great Britain at The Bath Press, Avon

British Library cataloguing in publication data

Klein, Wolfgang
Second language acquisition
1. Language and languages – Study and teaching –
Social aspects   2. Sociolinguistics
I. Title   II. Zweitspracherwerb. *English*
401'.9   P53.8

Library of Congress cataloguing in publication data

Klein, Wolfgang, 1946–
Second language acquisition.
(Cambridge textbooks in linguistics)
Translation of: Zweitspracherwerb.
Includes index.
1. Language acquisition,   I. Title   II. Series.
P118.K5413 1985   401'.9   85–9703

ISBN 0 521 26879 6 hard covers
ISBN 0 521 31702 9 paperback

CONTENTS

Contents

PREFACE

Benedetto sia 'l giorno e 'l mese e l'anno
E la stagione e 'l tempo, e l'ora e 'l punto,
E 'l bel paese e 'l loco ov'io fui giunto
Da duo begli occhi, che legato m' hanno

The acquisition of a second language, be it by everyday communication or by instruction, follows certain principles, which stem from various properties of human language processing, from the learner's specific motivation and, finally, from the way in which samples of, or information about, the language to be learned are made accessible to the learner. The objective of second language acquisition studies is to uncover these principles.

Above and beyond the genuine interest which any human activity as common as learning and using a second language excites, there are two reasons why the study of second language acquisition is an important and sometimes rewarding enterprise. First, for foreign language teaching to be maximally effective, it must be tuned to the principles outlined above. To the extent to which we do not explicitly know them, successful language teaching can only be a matter of practical experience, of individual pedagogical gifts, or of luck. Second, the study of how the human mind builds up fragmentary linguistic systems from limited input, how it re-organizes them if new input becomes available, and how it uses them for communicative purposes for which they may still be inadequate, can tell us something about how human language processing functions in general. The study of second language acquisition opens a window on the nature and function of human language to an even greater extent, perhaps, than have aphasia studies, with their many methodological problems, and studies of first language acquisition, where linguistic and cognitive development are so difficult to tease apart. The present introduction is not so much a comprehensive survey of all of the research done in the field over the years; rather, it attempts to give the reader an idea of what the relevant problems are, of how they were and are approached, and of what the results so far obtained can contribute to the practical and theoretical issues mentioned above.

The present version is a revised and extended translation of the German original; some of the changes were suggested by Suzanne Romaine and

John Trim. Bohuslaw Jankowski undertook the tedious task of rendering my sometimes very idiosyncratic German into readable English; Clive Perdue and Julia Harding worked through the English translation and suggested many changes both of style and presentation. The manuscript was typed and retyped by Marlene Arns. Many friends and colleagues helped me with critical comments and advice: Rainer Dietrich, Willem Levelt, Clive Perdue, Christiane von Stutterheim and Jürgen Weissenborn commented on the original manuscript; Michael Clyne, Norbert Dittmar, Jane Edwards and Bohuslaw Jankowski pointed out some shortcomings in the printed German version and suggested improvements.

The basic content of the book was presented in seminars at Brighton, Heidelberg, Frankfurt and Salzburg where I profited a great deal from the discussions. To all the people I have mentioned I am very grateful.

A final note: There are female and male learners and researchers. For simplicity's sake, I have chosen to use the pronoun *he* when referring to them generally.

PART I

The process of language acquisition

This part comprises three chapters. The first offers a panoramic view of language acquisition research. Various types of language acquisition are considered, some fundamental facts are stated, a number of issues which have been the focus of discussion in recent years are reviewed, and several important theories are outlined. This overview is not meant to be complete; rather, it should give the reader an idea of what researchers in second language acquisition were mainly concerned with during the past decade. It also includes a brief look at other forms of language acquisition. Although this book is essentially devoted to second language acquisition, the subject matter itself as well as the way in which the research field has developed over the last fifteen years make it imperative to consider the problems in a broader framework.

It is not easy to convey a picture of the state of the art in second language research, given the heterogeneity of issues, research methods, interpretations, and, last but not least, of terminology. An attempt is made in the second chapter to impose a uniform – psycholinguistic – perspective on this complex field. From this perspective second language acquisition appears to be a process which

> exhibits certain regularities,
> is constrained by a number of factors determining its course, rate of progress, and final outcome,
> is subject, within certain limits, to external influences such as (methods of) instruction.

The focus throughout is the *learner*, who is seen as being obliged by social circumstances to apply his language learning capacity to the available linguistic material. Much, but not all, of what is treated globally in the second chapter of Part I will be elaborated on in some detail – to the extent that current research permits – in Part II (chapters 4 to 8). In many areas of second language research there is still very little evidence to rely on. There are good reasons however to start off with a cohesive overall picture, even if it proves impossible to fill in all the details.

The third chapter of Part I briefly explores the possibilities of methodically influencing the process of language acquisition; thus, we examine the points at which systematic intervention into the acquisition process becomes effective, and the limits of such instruction. This is not a book about teaching, and little is said about how to streamline instruction in the concrete case. (See, for an excellent treatment of this matter, Els *et al.*, 1984.) But it seems important to put instruction into perspective right from the beginning. As chapter 3 demonstrates, we cannot build up instructional methods from a scientific foundation so long as we remain ignorant of the regularities that govern the process of acquisition.

I

Some forms of language acquisition, some fundamental facts, some focal issues, some well-known theories

Every normal child acquires a language, his first language (or 'native tongue'), in the first few years of life. There are exceptions, on either physiological (e.g. deafness) or social grounds (e.g. 'wolf children'[1]); but usually a child can communicate freely by the time he goes to school. Beyond puberty, our command of language shows little progress, though in some areas – the vocabulary, for instance – learning continues throughout our life span. First language acquisition is thus *primary* in at least two ways: in terms of sequence ('first') and in terms of (mostly life-long) importance.[2]

Most people learn more than one language, however. There are various ways in which this may happen, and the transitions between them are gradual. A child may be exposed to two (or even more[3]) languages right from the beginning, for example if his parents use different languages. In this case, we may still speak of 'first language acquisition' – except that not one but two languages are 'first'. In other words, a language is 'first' – and so is its acquisition – if no other language was acquired before; otherwise, it is second. The distinction is neat if acquisition of the second language begins when acquisition of the first is over, as is typically the case after puberty. But since the acquisition process extends over a long period of time, there are all sorts of intermediate cases.

It may also be that a language acquired once has to be acquired a second time – because it has been forgotten or is inaccessible due to aphasia. Thus we have three basic kinds of language acquisition: first language acquisition (FLA), second language acquisition (SLA), re-acquisition (RA).[4] This is a first distinction which helps us to classify the phenomena. But in reality it is somewhat hazy, and, in addition, we must be prepared to consider further differentiation.

At this point we come to the distinction between first and second language acquisition. If a second language is learned before the acquisition of the first is completed, the distinction becomes blurred. And a further complicating factor arises when a language is re-learned after a lapse of years or is gradually recovered. The first and foremost question in language acquisition research is the extent to which all three types are governed by universal laws of language learning.[5]

1.1 First language acquisition

First language acquisition occurs when the learner – usually a child – has been without a language so far and now acquires one. If it is one language, we speak of *monolingual* FLA. The less frequent case – in Western European societies at least – of a child learning two languages in parallel is known as *bilingual* FLA.

Monolingual first language acquisition is by far the most thoroughly investigated form of language learning. This is not the place to enlarge upon the issue.[6] However, there are a number of points which are also important for second language acquisition; we now turn to some of these.

1.1.1 *Cognitive, social, and linguistic development*

First language acquisition is intimately bound up with the child's cognitive and social development. To use the antique terms: the 'wordless' *infans* develops into the *zoon logon echon* and a *zoon politikon*: the child becomes a 'carrier of both word and concept' and a 'social creature'. This makes for a number of essential differences between first and second language acquisition, which will be illustrated by a series of examples.

A.   Cognitive development

In languages like English, French, or German, practically every sentence carries some tense marking effected by a finite verb. Correct tense marking presupposes that the learner has acquired temporal concepts such as present, past, future, and the like. This in itself is an intricate and laborious process; many children tend to confuse 'yesterday' and 'tomorrow' right into their early school years. Even if four-year-olds are found to form grammatically correct sentences, we cannot be certain – short of misunderstandings and communicative failures – that their use of, say, the past tense is that of the adult language. Two important conclusions can be drawn from this. First, the production of grammatically well-formed utterances does not imply that the speaker has mastered the language; he may endow these utterances with quite a different meaning. Secondly, a speaker must have acquired the *cognitive categories* which underlie the various expressive means of natural languages – categories such as time, space, modality, causality, etc. Whereas this condition is usually met in second language acquisition, it is not necessarily so in first language acquisition.[7]

Now consider another, less obvious but particularly instructive example. An essential feature of any natural language is its context-dependency: a clear illustration is offered by the existence of *deictic terms*. Whereas terms such as *Napoleon, in Brighton*, and *before the First World War* carry a relatively stable meaning, deictic terms such as *I*, *here*, and *now* may refer to totally different things or circumstances, depending on who is speaking, where the speaker is, when the speaking is taking place, etc. The implementation of deixis varies from language to language. For example, place is indicated in English by two terms, *here–there*, and in German by three, *hier–da–dort*. What is identical however is the underlying principle of change of reference in relation to speaker, place, time, and several other phenomena.[8]

It is not an easy task for the child to master this principle of 'deictic shift' (cf. E. Clark, 1978; Wales, 1979; Tanz, 1980). But once acquired, the concept is available for one's whole life; when learning a second language the subject need not learn the underlying mechanisms of contextuality anew; he merely has to learn the particular words referring to the 'particular speaker', the 'particular place of speaking', etc.

To summarize, there are crucial elements of language mastery that are interrelated with the child's development; these are mastered in the course of first language learning, and are then available for SLA. This is not to say that there is absolutely no need to develop some new concepts in order to master a second language; in fact, there is usually a need to modify and readjust some existing cognitive concepts, and this may prove a particularly exacting task for the learner. For example, a native speaker of English or German has had no need to develop the category of 'aspect' in the same way that a native speaker of Russian has had to acquire it; when learning Russian as a second language, however, the English or German native speaker is obliged to develop the category in an appropriate fashion.

All in all, the cognitive prerequisites of language mastery are more readily available in second language acquisition than in first language acquisition, and this makes first and second language acquisition different in at least one important aspect.

B.   Social development

Learning the first language is but one part of the young child's overall development into a fully-fledged member of society. Language enables the child to express feelings, ideas, wishes in a socially accepted manner; the child learns that it is not advisable to speak one's mind at all times, in any way, or to anyone; he comes to realize that words can serve to make friends as much as foes and that it is not always possible to tell the truth. Language is the medium through which the child acquires the cultural, moral, religious, and other values of society. In the drive to acquire language a child is guided by the principle: 'Become – with small differences – like others.' Or else, 'Acquire a social identity and within its framework, develop your personal identity.' All this does not apply to most types of SLA. The social identity of the second language learner is more or less fixed. In fact, the desire to preserve one's identity may become a major obstacle in mastering a second language. The apparent facility with which children learn a second language is often attributed to biological factors, but an alternative explanation might be that, unlike adults, children have no need to fear the loss of their social identity. Leaving the matter for further consideration, we may conclude at this point that first language acquisition is closely linked with the child's social development; and hence, to the evolution of a social identity; this does not apply to second language acquisition to the same extent.

1.1.2 *The language acquisition device*

First language acquisition is widely believed to proceed both quickly and easily. This conviction gave rise to what must be seen as the most momentous development in language acquisition research of the past thirty years: Chomsky's 'language acquisition device' (Chomsky, 1959, 1965, 1975). Any normal child, exposed to mostly inadequate and often defective language data, Chomsky argues, comes to know the grammar of his native language within an amazingly short time span. This cannot be accounted for in the framework of behaviouristic learning theories of the kind postulated by Skinner (1957) for verbal behaviour (an orientation which dominated in the USA at the time), so one has to assume that humans are endowed with a language device which

(a)   is *species-specific*, i.e. distinguishes man from other primates,
(b)   is specific for *language* learning as opposed to the acquisition of other forms of behaviour or knowledge,
(c)   prestructures the properties of grammar to a large extent (consequently, many structural properties of grammar are innate and need not be learned).

There is no need to quarrel with the thesis that human beings possess what might be called a language acquisition device (LAD) if this only means that they have the capacity to acquire language. What is more disputable is the exact nature of LAD, in particular, the validity of the claims under (a–c). Most important in this context is (c) – the claim that certain structural properties of grammar are innate: the language data available to the child serve to activate latent components of grammar, just as the specifically human system of visual perception develops according to a predetermined biological programme whose activation is contingent upon external stimulation. A child raised in complete darkness could never learn to see; by analogy, a child deprived of speech input could not build up a grammar. Just as it is wrong to say that the characteristics of the human visual system – compared with those of the ant, for example – are constructed, through inductive learning, from what catches the child's eye, it is equally unreasonable to assume, argues Chomsky, that a child's language derives from the verbal behaviour of other people. Thus, for Chomsky, the study of mother–child interaction (cf., for example, Snow and Ferguson, 1977) is as illuminating in the context of first language acquisition as would be an inspection of the cradle, the nursery, or of grandma herself for an understanding of the development of the child's visual perception.

Evidence suggests that each newborn baby is capable of acquiring any human language. The obvious conclusion is that the innate structures of language must be common to all languages, and these constitute what Chomsky calls Universal Grammar. However, the *specific features* of each language, as for instance those that distinguish Chinese from English, must be inferred from the data made available to a child in the course of first language acquisition. These specific features cover:

> the entire vocabulary,
> the entire morphology,
> the entire syntax (to the extent to which it is treated in conventional descriptive grammar books),[9]
> most of the phonology;

in a word, practically everything. What qualify as components of Universal Grammar are for Chomsky a number of general principles which need not be discussed in detail here since the validity of Chomsky's views in this respect are still highly tentative and are constantly being developed (see Chomsky, 1981, for the current state of his theory; and Hornstein and Lightfoot, 1981, or Baker and McCarthy, 1982, for its relevance to first language acquisition).

It is interesting, on the other hand, to consider their implications for second language learning. Chomsky himself has not elaborated on the issue, and there is little in the literature on this subject (but see, for example, Schmidt, 1980; White, 1983; Mazurkiewicz, 1984). Suppose for the moment that the following statements hold true:

(a)   Language acquisition is, in the case of the child, easy, quick, and – to use Chomsky's nice phrase – 'hopelessly underdetermined' by the accessible language data, whereas for the adult learner it is an extremely arduous, time-consuming, and imperfect quest.

(b)   This discrepancy is due to the beneficial effect of Universal Grammar.

The inevitable question is, why should Universal Grammar not benefit an adult? An immediate suggestion is that a human being's learning capacities are radically reduced with age for biological reasons (more on this in section 1.1.3). But this could not put Universal Grammar completely out of action as it is present all the time and in every language; there is even no need for the learner to activate it in the process of second language acquisition. We might speculate that due to the influence of Universal Grammar on first language acquisition, 'some open parameters are fixed' – to use Chomsky's formulation – and have to be weakened before a second language can be fully acquired; until this is done, they act as impediments. If this were so, second language acquisition should be as troublesome for a child as it is for an adult. Although the problem has not been investigated in depth, current evidence points in the opposite direction; children learn without difficulty two languages in succession, the second one on the whole presenting even less difficulty than the first. We therefore have to conclude that the relatively quick and effortless first language acquisition of the child (and such has been our assumption, till now) is the result of something other than the simple presence of some Universal Grammar.

1.1.3   The 'critical period'

A first language is normally acquired in childhood. So we might ask whether there is an age beyond which first language acquisition is impossible. A preliminary question here would be: how long does the learning of the first language last? There seems to be no clear-cut answer as long as there are doubts as to what comprises a language and what complete language mastery means. If we consider the babbling of the newborn, or the crying of the infant to express wishes and needs or to give vent to feelings, as the beginnings of language development, then we must time birth as the onset of first language acquisition (on this see Kainz, 1959, Part II, chapter 4; Weir, 1962; Fletcher and Garman, 1979, Part I). If we were to regard an active mastery of the second subjunctive or of the dative–accusative distinction as essential for a command of German, most people would not complete the acquisition of their first language in their lifetime.

In general, it is reasonable to assume that little progress is made after the age of puberty. Even though a child is usually quite fluent in his first language in the early school years, the language problems facing the young child are of a limited scale and there are many structures that are acquired at a later age (C. Chomsky, 1969; Karmiloff-Smith, 1979; Lindner, 1983). From this it follows that first language acquisition is neither as easy nor as quick as one tends to assume at the outset. Assuming a child is exposed to language for something like five hours a day, also practising speech in the process (those who have children will agree that this is probably an underestimate), we arrive at a total of about 9,100 hours of active language learning in a child's first five years (cf. Burke, 1974). In spite of this enormous time expenditure, the child is still a long way from being in command of very many structures (such as the much-discussed 'easy' construction, as in 'John is easy to please'). By contrast, many second language schools offer total-immersion programmes where learners are taught a language twelve hours a day for periods of four to six weeks. In a six-week course, the time expenditure amounts to as little as 500 hours, yet this intensive training results in most cases in a reasonable command of the language, albeit limited in terms of vocabulary and syntactic variations. Comparing the two time scales, it is clear that the view of first language acquisition being quick and easy compared with the labour of second language learning is nothing but a myth. Naturally, if first language acquisition is assumed to be completed only at the age of puberty, the contrast is even more striking.

The ill-advised notion of quick and effortless first language acquisition led the neuropsychologist Penfield to the view that this had something to do with the development of the brain in childhood (Penfield and Roberts, 1959). This idea was revived by Lenneberg (1967), who developed it into the widely discussed theory of the critical period for language acquisition. He suggested that between the age of two and puberty the human brain shows the plasticity which allows a child to acquire his first language. This unique capacity is gone once the particular functions of the brain – notably the localization of most speech functions in the left hemisphere

– have been 'wired in' for good. If it is possible to acquire another language after the critical period, this is accomplished in a physiologically different, and more difficult way. In view of this biological distinction, first and second language acquisition (after puberty) must be seen as two different processes.

There can be no question that the critical period theory is of considerable relevance for second language learning, and even more so for second language teaching. If it holds true, we are obliged to employ largely different methods of instruction before and after the age of puberty. But there are serious doubts as to whether it is true. Firstly, the strictly biological evidence is by no means conclusive (for a discussion see Lamendella, 1977; Ekstrand, 1979; Paradis and Lebrun, 1983). Secondly, the notion that second language acquisition becomes more difficult and is less effective after the age of puberty rather than before, is indeed corroborated by everyday observations as well as by some empirical investigations. Nevertheless, the biological explanation can be replaced, or supplemented, by arguments of a social nature. It may well be, for example, that the adult is much less willing to give up his well-established social identity. Even in the case of phonology – including intonation – where adult second language learners often seem to encounter special difficulties, investigations by Neufeld (1979) have shown that suitably motivated adults are capable of mastering to perfection the pronunciation of the (for them) most exotic languages, as revealed by the fact that native speakers could not recognize any 'foreign accent' in their speech. This shows that ideal second language acquisition is biologically feasible even after the age of puberty. Nothing can be said on this evidence, however, about relative ease or difficulty, or indeed about what kind of learning may be involved at this stage.

The three issues – cognitive, social and linguistic development; the language acquisition device; and the critical period – have some bearing on bilingual as well as monolingual first language acquisition. A number of peculiarities of bilingual acquisition will be discussed below. Cases of bilingual (i.e. parallel) language acquisition are, admittedly, not very frequent in Western European societies as there is rarely perfect synchrony in the acquisition of the two languages; and here we come to the transition from bilingual first language to second language acquisition. A number of well-documented case studies of the former are available, among them the classical works by Ronjat (1913) and Leopold (1939–49).[10] Our discussion here will be restricted to three issues: compound and coordinate bilingualism, the domination of one language over the other (possibly in specific areas), and possible side effects on development.

1.1.4   *Compound and coordinate bilingualism*

Bilingual first language acquisition ('compound bilingualism') means that two languages (say, English and French) are being learned in parallel. Any two language systems, no matter how different they are, have some features in common. For instance, they may employ the same categories, such as time, modality, person; many of their words may have equivalents in the other language; some syntactic rules may be quite similar; and so on. It is therefore conceivable that the learner might have developed *one* system with a number of variable components between which he may switch at will. This assumption seems particularly plausible in the case of the vocabulary: the learner gets to know that the notion 'chair' may have two phonological realizations, i.e. [tʃɛəʳ] and [ʃɛzə], and when speaking he chooses the one that fits the communicative situation.

A bilingual person who, in addition to a first language, has acquired another as a second language ('coordinate bilingualism'), initially develops one system (maybe not an entirely separate one, depending on how early he has started to learn the second language). Subsequently, he builds up another system and can then operate the two in parallel. Changing from one language to the other, he switches from one system to the other, rather than switching over within one, compound system. If one of the two languages is dominant, we can infer that much of the person's language processing is effected in the dominant language, and that the other language is used only at a superficial level of production or comprehension. In extreme cases the use of the second language may involve merely the substitution of second language phonological structures for the first language structures within an otherwise unified system that provides for a suitable correspondence of sound and meaning. It may well be that such is the outcome of the old-fashioned vocabulary drill (associating the foreign word with its native counterpart).

The first to formulate this distinction was U. Weinreich (1953), who identified three kinds of bilingualism with reference to the structuring of the vocabulary (lexicon). His system is illustrated in Table 1.

The distinction became extremely influential over the following twenty years: not in its original form, but rather in the revised version, proposed by Ervin and Osgood (1954), which distinguished merely between compound and coordinate bilingualism, and incorporated Weinreich's third type into their coordinate type. What distinguishes the two types of bilingualism is the way the languages are acquired. Coordinate bilingualism emerges when the two languages are acquired in different contexts, as for instance one at home, the other at school. All other ways result in

Table 1. *Three kinds of bilingualism (according to Weinreich)*

Compound	Coordinate	Subordinate
'chair–chaise'	'chair' 'chaise'	'chair'
tʃɛəʳ ʃɛzə	tʃɛəʳ ʃɛzə	tʃɛəʳ
		ʃɛzə

compound bilingualism. Nevertheless, certain segments of a bilingual's lexicon may be compound, and others coordinate. These two modes of acquisition entail distinct modes of semantic representation. Ervin and Osgood described these semantic representations in terms of a modified stimulus–response schema. Subsequently, the distinction between two types of bilingualism was reinterpreted on several occasions, primarily in work by W. Lambert (e.g. 1969). Summing up this work, Macnamara (1970, p. 31) concludes, 'Any clarity which the coordinate–compound distinction seemed to have was deceptive.' Nevertheless, it is still cited as a firmly established research finding up to this day. One reason for the doubtful validity, but perhaps also for the attractiveness, of the distinction could be its heterogeneous composition (we will mention three phenomena):

(a) The mode of language acquisition: it is assumed, for example, that acquisition in one and the same context results in compound bilingualism while other modes of learning lead to coordinate bilingualism (though there is some disagreement among researchers on this issue).

(b) The linguistic characterization: we referred above to one 'system with variable components' as opposed to two relatively independent systems. The distinction is not easy to capture in strictly linguistic terms, even with respect to vocabulary, where it originated and ought to be applied. The notion, 'one meaning – two phonetic realizations', is questionable if only because the lexicon of each language reveals an intrinsic structure conditioned by the fact that any word's meaning is determined by the word's relationship to other words of the same language.

(c) The neurophysiological realization: coordinate bilinguals may well have their linguistic knowledge stored in a different manner from compound bilinguals. For instance, the first language – or languages, if there is more than one – is localized in the left cerebral hemisphere while any second language(s) could reside in the right hemisphere. Hypotheses of this kind have recently received much discussion.[11]

It is not inconceivable that the distinction between compound and coordinate bilingualism is of some relevance, but for the time being it has proved more confusing than beneficial.

1.1.5 *Relative dominance*

Bilingual first language acquisition means, ideally, that two languages are acquired in parallel at an even pace. This kind of symmetry is rarely achieved in practice. Typically each of the two languages is used in relation to either a particular person, or environment, or activity. In effect, it seems almost impossible to avoid one language gaining a certain advantage over the other. The dominance may extend to all areas of communication and may eventually result in the decline of one language. Alternatively, the 'secondary' language may be reserved for certain uses only. In the most thoroughly documented case so far, that of Leopold's daughter Hildegard, the language of the mother as well as of the broader environment (English) gradually became dominant over the language of the father (German).

Second language acquisition entails an even stronger dominance and functional specialization. Throughout the world today English is predominantly spoken as a second rather than as a first language (Smith, 1983), which suggests that it is used in a restricted manner in the face of dominance by the respective native language. However convincing and significant this may seem, it is very difficult to determine the role of the relative dominance of a language in the process of acquisition and in the neurophysiological basis of such acquisition. Could it be that the second language learner begins by constructing the given sentence in the dominant language, then translates it into the second language, before he is finally able to articulate the utterance? This suggestion seems to be confirmed by the extent of *interference* from the dominant language. Speakers of German, for instance, have a strong tendency to use the pronoun *it* when referring to a child in English, even though they well know that *it* should be either *he* or *she* (they hasten to correct themselves moreover as soon as they are challenged). The notion of interference implies that in order to generate the sentence in English the speaker had begun to form a German sentence. Similarly, there is a tendency for experienced speakers of a second language to rely on comprehension strategies that have their source in their use of the first language (cf. Bates *et al.*, 1982). However, one must qualify this suggestion by the fact that interference seems to be less pronounced when each of the two languages is used in a specific area of communication, i.e., has its specific uses.

1.1.6   *Side effects on development*

A child who acquires two languages in parallel might be considered to be facing a double task. Even if we assume – in line with the notion of coordinate bilingualism – that he need not develop two complete systems, there remains the task of learning all that distinguishes the two languages, and the child has to be able to keep the two linguistic inputs separate so that elements of one language are not incorporated into another. Thus one might expect massive contaminations to occur, and also that first language acquisition would take appreciably longer than the acquisition of a single language. The facts have not confirmed these expectations. Admittedly, contaminations do take place, chiefly in the early phases; but they are quite limited in extent, and there is scarcely any evidence that the two systems could not be separated in principle; rather, these contaminations give the impression that the individual occasionally may draw on two sources, if the need arises. It is hard to tell whether a bilingual child needs more time to complete first language acquisition, firstly because there are considerable individual differences in acquisition time amongst individual children (both bilingual and monolingual), and secondly because it is difficult in any case to define completion of FLA. If any generalization can be made, then we must state that bilingual FLA does not take *appreciably* longer than monolingual FLA, nor does it appear to be more cumbersome to the child in any clearly noticeable way.

The question of possible adverse effects of bilingualism on the child's cognitive or social development has not been studied extensively. Some researchers claim to have found such effects, others deny this or even point out positive effects. But at present, all claims of this sort are scarcely supported by convincing research findings. McLaughlin (1978a, p. 206) concludes his careful discussion of the whole issue as follows:[12]

In short, almost no general statements are warranted by research on the effects of bilingualism. It has not been demonstrated that bilingualism has positive or negative consequences for intelligence, linguistic skills, educational attainment, emotional adjustment, or cognitive functioning. In almost every case, the findings of research are either contradicted by other research or can be questioned on methodological grounds. The one statement that is supported by research findings is that command of a second language makes a difference if a child is tested in that language – a not very surprising finding.

In other words, there is no evidence that bilingual children differ in their development from other children, except that they know two languages.

14

1.2   From first to second language acquisition

As we have already noted, no sharp dividing line can be drawn between first and second language acquisition for the simple reason that the latter is frequently initiated before the former has come to a close. In many cases, the decision to use the terms 'second language learning' or 'bilingual first language acquisition' is a matter of personal preference. Following common usage, we will use the term 'second language acquisition' if acquisition starts at or after the age of 3 or 4 (i.e. at a point when first language acquisition is in fact still in progress). If a finer distinction is needed, we will speak of either child or adult second language acquisition. We do not want to go into the particular aspects of the transition from first to second language learning in this book since it is impossible to tell in general terms what effect the *partial* acquisition of the first language might have on the learning of a second one. Some of these issues will nevertheless be taken up in chapters 5 and 6.

Before passing on to second language acquisition itself, it might be useful to summarize the four modes of language acquisition discussed so far (see Table 2).

Table 2. *Basic modes of language acquisition*

Age	Acquisition of language		Designation
	A	B	
1–3 yrs.	+	−	monolingual FLA
	+	+	bilingual FLA
3–4 yrs. up to puberty	+	+	child SLA
after puberty	−	+	adult SLA

1.3   Second language acquisition

A second language can be acquired in a variety of ways, at any age, for different purposes, and to varying degrees. Accordingly, we may distinguish different types of second language learning. Traditionally, a fundamental distinction has been made between tutored and untutored (spontaneous) language learning. It is not at all certain if this distinction corresponds to different modes of language learning (for a critical discussion, see Felix 1982, chapter 15), but, because of its practical significance, we find it useful to distinguish at this stage between *spontaneous* and *guided* (usually by a tutor) language acquisition.

1.3.1 *Spontaneous learning*

The term 'spontaneous learning' is used to denote the acquisition of a second language in everyday communication, in a natural fashion, free from systematic guidance. A prototypical case is that of a Turkish worker who settles in a West European country not knowing a single word of the local language and who manages to acquire – through his sporadic and unsystematic social intercourse with the broader society – some knowledge of the language. A 'purer' example of spontaneous learning would be the missionary or social anthropologist who attempts to master the language of a hitherto unknown tribe, relying on his (possibly somewhat pathological) social intercourse without the benefit of any sort of guidance.

Spontaneous language acquisition is anything but uniform. The person who learns a language independently in order to translate the Bible into that language does so in quite a different way from someone who arrives in a strange country in order to seek employment for an unspecified period of time and throughout that time lives there, relatively cut off from the native population, preferring the company of his compatriots.

In the following sections we discuss briefly two crucial characteristics of spontaneous second language acquisition, namely that it (a) takes place in the course of *everyday communication*, and (b) is free from any *systematic and intentional intervention*.

A. Everyday communication

The case of a spontaneous learner has an ingredient of paradox: in order to communicate, he must learn the language, and in order to learn it, must communicate. Of course the paradox is only apparent, for communication can be effected in a variety of ways and may vary in depth and scope. There are situations where a few gestures or an odd phrase will often suffice: with the cards he has in his hand the player (or rather the speaker) must do the best he can, but unlike the (honest) card player he is in a position to improve his hand. In other words, the spontaneous learner can avail himself of different means of communication at any point; initially, his repertoire may chiefly consist of nonverbal means and, to a different degree, means which allow him to enter communication – though at a very reduced level. But it is this communication which allows him to start learning, and learning in turn allows him to make progress in communication. Whatever his actual communicative competence at a given point in time, the learner is faced with two related, but clearly different tasks:

16

to utilize his actual and (for a long time) quite limited repertoire in
an optimal fashion, in expressing himself as well as in understanding
others (*his communication task*),

to approximate to the target language – i.e. the language as used by
the environment (*his learning task*).

The two tasks are closely interconnected, but it would be wrong to
confuse them. The communication task is a stabilizing factor in that it
encourages the learner to develop an optimal language variety in the interests of efficient communication. The learning task, while inciting the
learner to abandon the means he has developed thus far in favour of more
efficient ones, is a dynamic factor in that it pushes the process of acquisition
along. A convenient illustration is offered by the avoidance strategies
employed by the spontaneous learner (cf. Kleinmann, 1978; Faerch and
Kasper, 1983). What is avoided by the learner are those words or constructions he is not certain of; these are replaced by paraphrases, and if none
are available, the learner tends to avoid the particular topic, or even the
situation in which the missing elements of language might prove necessary.
Far from being an acquisition strategy, this kind of avoidance behaviour
must be seen as a strategy of language use; as such it may be considered
part of the communication task. As far as acquisition is concerned, an
avoidance strategy is more of an impediment in that it serves to reduce
the pressure exerted by the environment; it is like taking aspirin rather
than going to the dentist.

A further essential aspect of learning a second language through contact
with everyday situations is the marginal attention paid to the language
itself. The learner focusses instead on communication, and is prepared
to use any means to serve that end. Being concerned with effective communication rather than with 'proper language', the spontaneous learner takes
a different attitude to the means of verbal communication than is customary
in a language teaching setting. At the same time, there is little need or
opportunity for metalinguistic reflection: little if any thought is given to
linguistic forms and rules, which are the domain of tutored language learning. The extent to which the metalinguistic component may influence
language acquisition is an open question. Krashen's 'monitor theory'
(Krashen, 1981) focusses upon this issue; we deal with this much-discussed
hypothesis in section 1.5.3, also reserving some comments on metalinguistics for section 8.1.4.

B.   Absence of systematic and intentional intervention

Any language acquisition is 'guided' by some factors, as for instance the scope and kind of linguistic data available to the learner. Some kind of 'guidance' will obviously occur even in the most spontaneous language learning, whenever someone cares to correct an error made by the learner, prompts the latter with the word designating an object, or casually explains a puzzling construction. However, the term 'guided' (as opposed to 'spontaneous') refers here to learning that is open to *systematic* and *intentional* influence. Typically, this takes the form of regular language instruction in school, but 'teach yourself' methods would also be included.

Although the terminological distinction between 'guided' and 'spontaneous' learning is still valid, it is worth considering the advantages of alternative terminology. A number of terms have been proposed for what we call spontaneous learning, for example 'naturalistic second language acquisition', 'second language acquisition in a social context', and the like. None of these can be accepted without reservations. What would be the opposite of 'naturalistic'? Why should the school setting not come under 'social context'? So there are good reasons to abide by our terminology. (In any case, it does not actually make any difference.)

Until a few years ago, spontaneous language acquisition remained a side issue in research; even today the bulk of second language investigations are addressed to guided learning. Moreover, students of spontaneous learning are chiefly preoccupied with child second language acquisition; very few of them deal with spontaneous learning in adults, or at an age when a first language is fully established. An obvious reason for this is the accessibility of data and hence the relative facility of empirical research in the case of guided second language acquisition: schoolchildren or students attending language courses can be tested much more readily than migrant workers or immigrants. There exists furthermore the natural expectation that the study of guided learning (i.e. language instruction) would yield evidence of considerable value to the language teacher – more so at least than the study of spontaneous acquisition ever could. Hence the temptation to restrict investigations in SLA to the learning of a second language in the context of instruction.

This is a deplorable fallacy. It appears that any attempt at aiding the process of language acquisition must be based on a sound knowledge of the underlying mechanisms, or the laws that govern the process. It seems quite problematic to try to identify these mechanisms when their operation is modified by the application of a particular method of instruction (no matter whether its effect is positive or negative). The human mode of language processing – including first and second language acquisition – has evolved over millennia; organized instruction is a recent innovation historically. Human beings have thus acquired the ability to learn a language and, as a special case, a second language in actual communication, and we have no reason to assume that this ability can be freely manipulated, although there are surely points at which successful intervention is possible. Granted this, we may also assume that the human language learning ability resists the various methods of instruction to varying degrees.[13] Be that as it may, spontaneous second language acquisition ought to be granted some 'logistic priority' in research; which is not to say that there is no need to investigate guided language learning (cf. Heidelberg Research Project, 1976, ch. 1). We will take up this point in chapter 3.

1.3.2   *Guided language learning*

We have referred above to the relationship between guided second language acquisition and spontaneous learning. The former ought to be seen as a derivative, rather like the domestication of a natural process. Its practical importance cannot, however, be overestimated, although many people would doubt the validity of second language acquisition research except with regard to its significance for language teaching.

As in spontaneous SLA, guided second language learning research shows little agreement on questions of terminology or substance. Two twin concepts are crucial here: 'foreign' vs. 'second language' and 'learning' vs. 'acquisition'. There is considerable variation in usage. Attempts have been made in recent years to keep them terminologically apart (e.g. Richards, 1978, Introduction; Bausch and Kasper, 1979). The term 'foreign language' is used to denote a language acquired in a milieu where it is normally not in use (i.e. usually through instruction) and which, when acquired, is not used by the learner in routine situations. Latin is a classic example and a living language which simply forms part of the schoolchild's curriculum is another. A 'second language', on the other hand, is one that becomes another tool of communication alongside the first language; it is typically acquired in a social environment in which it is actually spoken. Examples are French among the German-speaking Swiss population, English among many Hindus, Russian among many Georgians in the Caucasus, etc. There are, of course, many intermediate cases. In our terminology, 'second language' also covers 'foreign language' as defined above. Ultimately, the distinction between foreign and second language tends to coincide with that between guided and spontaneous acquisition (of a second language) and we therefore retain our terminology as it rests on an obvious criterion. Nevertheless, we will occasionally refer to 'foreign language instruction' in the limited sense indicated above.

A parallel distinction is that between 'learning' and 'acquisition', the former referring to guided, the latter to spontaneous learning. Krashen's monitor theory, for instance, assumes the operation of two basically different processes labelled in this distinctive way (Krashen, 1981; see also section 1.5.3). We do not, however, intend to follow Krashen's distinction since there is no clear evidence that the processes are basically different, and since it is unsatisfactory to have no superordinate concept. Thus we prefer to use the term 'acquisition' (and 'acquisition process'), reserving the term 'learning' as a purely stylistic variant. What is important is that both terms refer to the *perspective of the learner*, not the teacher or the social environment.

Many methods have been developed to exert a systematic influence on the progress of second language acquisition. This is not the place to review them in any detail (for this, see Corder, 1973; and for an excellent, also theoretically very insightful discussion, see Els *et al.*, 1984). We will discuss only two ways in which the various methods seem to differ substantially: (a) the way in which the material of the target language is presented to the learner, and (b) the opportunities offered for an application of the repertoire available to the learner.

A. Presentation of material

In spontaneous language acquisition, the learner has access to the target language in the course of everyday communication with the environment; the sounds of the language are embedded in a relevant situational context and the learner's task is to extract from this material the rules for the use of the language. In guided learning, such material is supplied in 'digested' form. At one extreme, the learner is initially offered no more than a description of the material. This was the approach of the traditional grammarians, and it dominated foreign language teaching from Donat's time until the late nineteenth century, and is still very much alive. The other extreme is marked by 'communicative instruction' with very little grammar and a tendency to use role play in imitation of real-life communication (see, for example, Müller, 1980). Its most radical and perhaps most successful form could be described as *guided* second language acquisition in which the learner is guided to learn in a *spontaneous*, and – so the assumption – very efficient, manner. Between these two extremes – the predominantly metalinguistic orientation and an optimal imitation of spontaneous learning – there are innumerable intermediate stages, one of them being the now dominant single-language, grammar-avoiding school instruction.

Guided and spontaneous learning differ not only in the manner but also in the order in which material is presented. The selection and order of presentation in guided acquisition depends mainly on such criteria as the degree of difficulty and relevance of various portions of the material. In some cases glaring mismatches arise in comparison with what might be regarded as a 'natural' sequence of acquisition (as observed in spontaneous learning). To give an example, foreign-language teachers attach enormous importance to aspects of morphology such as inflection of irregular verbs, whereas in spontaneous learning this is at best a tertiary question.

This is not to say that language teachers ought to select their material and determine the manner of its presentation in close imitation of spontaneous learning; they have to bear in mind the frequently very unfavourable learning conditions of guided language acquisition. It is unreasonable, however, to present material in a manner and an order which prevents the learner from processing it. This, in turn, presupposes that we indeed know how the human language learning capacity operates in its natural form.

B.   Applying the repertoire in comprehension and production

The spontaneous learner is invariably under pressure to utilize his entire language potential in order to communicate successfully (see section 1.3.1.A). There is no such pressure in guided language acquisition. It is replaced by exercises: dictation, essays, pattern drills, etc. (Imagine the driving instructor letting the learner practise pressing the clutch and operating the gears without moving the car.) Here again language instruction attempts to approximate the modes of spontaneous learning to a greater or lesser extent, but even in role playing – which might appear to be a kindred approach – the real objective is not so much communication at any price as behaviour in keeping with a pre-established and not always fully internalized norm (cf. Trévise, 1979).

We have tried to outline above the mutual relationship of guided and spontaneous language acquisition, pointing out some crucial distinctions. It is self-evident that such distinctions do exist, and there are no grounds for assuming that the two basic modes of language acquisition are governed by exactly the same mechanisms. What we have tried to show is that in each case the human language learning capacity may have a somewhat different scale of application and pattern of action (cf. d'Anglejean, 1978; Felix, 1982, Part II).

1.4 Re-acquisition

Cases of language loss are not as rare as might at first appear, and they apply to a second as well as a first language. The loss of a language does not imply its disappearance from the brain cells where it is stored, but rather an inability to process it in comprehension or production. All manner of intermediate stages have been observed: from the forgetting of a few words or structures to complete disappearance. Any such deficit may be caused by two kinds of factors:

(a)   Lack of practice, as with people who, having moved to a different country, have not used their first language for many years (Lambert and Freed, 1982; Sharwood-Smith, 1983).

(b)   Speech pathology (aphasia) due to brain lesions or disturbances in bloodflow etc., or peripheral disorders, such as cancer of the larynx or deafness.

In many cases it is possible to recover the lost language, if only because it is not really lost, but has simply become inaccessible. For simplicity's sake this can be termed 're-acquisition', even though there can be no doubt that it differs crucially from first and second language acquisition.

As yet only recovery after aphasia has been studied in any detail (for some remarks on the recovery of a language lost through lack of use see Wode, 1981, pp. 47–53; Sharwood-Smith, 1983), and results have differed considerably, possibly because of the difference in respective deficits (cf. Leischner, 1979). Generally speaking, judging by the available evidence, the re-acquisition of language after aphasia bears little resemblance to any of the modes of language acquisition discussed so far. Comparisons could be made with the other form of re-acquisition, in the case of a 'lost' language. It is generally thought that a 'lost' language can be recovered much more quickly than when it was first learned. This may be so, but no evidence is currently available. Moreover, it is difficult to tell to what extent such re-learning could be based on the 're-discovery' of 'lost' elements, or on their re-learning, or on both. In each case different processes of re-acquisition would be at work; but for the moment we can only speculate.

A few words may be in order on the relationship between first and second language in re-acquisition. Bilingual aphasics have often been found to recover either only or primarily their first language, even if they had used predominantly, or exclusively, a second language prior to aphasia, and as long ago as 1882 the French aphasiologist Ribot posited this order as a rule (règle de Ribot). Unfortunately, however, it has just as often been found that the language recovered first is the one that was dominant prior to aphasia, no matter whether first or second language (règle de Pitres, named after another French aphasiologist). The whole range of cases studied by aphasiology is reviewed in Albert and Obler (1978, pp. 143-94); an excellent discussion of the problem can be found in Paradis (1977); for a more recent comprehensive survey, see Paradis and Lebrun (1983).

At least one case has been recorded where it seems to have been possible to restore a completely forgotten language under hypnosis (Fromm, 1970). At the age of 26, a Japanese American who had learned Japanese as a child but now claimed not to understand any of it, was able to produce a number of sentences under hypnosis; these utterances were identified by native speakers as haltingly produced, child-like Japanese sentences. Attempts at a replication of this experiment have so far been unsuccessful. (On this and other cases of hypnosis, see Campbell and Schumann, 1981.)

1.5   Theories of second language acquisition

The inevitable conclusion at this stage is that second language acquisition is a process of enormous complexity in which a variety of factors are at work and which evades description, let alone explanation. Nevertheless, it is not uncommon for authors to seek to offer facile solutions to the problem. In this section a number of theories or hypotheses which have received considerable attention in second language research are reviewed and analysed, including some which have already been referred to above.

1.5.1   *Identity hypothesis*

In its extreme form, the identity hypothesis[14] asserts that it is irrelevant for language acquisition whether or not any other language has been learned before; in other words, first and second language learning is basically one and the same process governed by the same laws.

Such a radical claim has in fact never been seriously upheld, but many authors accept an 'essential identity' of first and second language acquisition (e.g. Jakobovits, 1970; Wode, 1974, 1981; Burt and Dulay, 1980; for an insightful discussion see especially Ervin-Tripp, 1974). Although less impressive, the 'essential identity' version is definitely more plausible, but it all depends on what one would regard as the 'essential', as opposed to the non-essential elements of language acquisition. Five points will be examined in this connection:

1. As pointed out in section 1.1.2, one difference between first and second language acquisition is that the former is an intrinsic component of a child's overall cognitive and social development, whereas in second language acquisition this development has already been more or less completed. A child must acquire, for instance, the principle of deixis (viewed by all linguists as a fundamental property of human language) plus the respective words of the native language. A second language learner need only acquire the respective words of the target language (cf. section 1.1.1.A). Even in its weak form, the identity hypothesis is tenable only if one is prepared to regard as non-essential those differential aspects in respect of an individual's cognitive and social development, along with all their possible consequences in the realm of language.

2. As far as the outcome of the process is concerned, there are vast differences between the two modes of language acquisition. A first language is normally acquired with perfect pronunciation (the given social environment, rather than a dictionary transcription, being the standard), whereas cases of adults acquiring a second language without any accent are very rare. This alone does not provide sufficient evidence that second language learners are in principle unable (for biological reasons for example) to attain a native pronunciation. However, it is not only important to know what is possible but also what is the norm.

3. The notion of an essential identity of first and second language acquisition rests squarely on the findings that in both modes there is a parallelism in the acquisition order of such structures as interrogatives, negation, or certain morphemes (Burt and Dulay, 1980; Wode, 1981). Nevertheless, there are substantial variations between first and second language acquisition in this respect, and even the similarities are disputed. In any case, a conclusive demonstration of a perfect parallelism in the order of acquisition of certain elements would entail nothing more than making it clear that the two modes of acquisition do have *some* features in common – which is beyond dispute.

4. In section 1.1.3 it was stressed that first language acquisition, on the one hand, and second language acquisition, on the other, are themselves amazingly variable. Consequently it does not make sense to compare the former in general with the latter in general. It is a different matter to compare the manner in which a child acquires his first language through many interactions with his mother (or whoever) with (a) the way in which Latin is learned in school and (b) the way a migrant worker acquires

the language of his host country. Again, this is not to deny that the various modes of language acquisition have many features in common, too.

5. The overall conclusion is that there are both similarities and differences between first and second language acquisition – something that is hardly surprising. So, one should try to explore both forms of acquisition in considerable detail, rather than approaching acquisition from a single perspective. Nevertheless, no discipline can develop successfully without efforts to arrive at a coherent theory of maximal generality. From a methodological point of view, therefore, we would be justified in assuming that it *might be possible* to develop a uniform theory for both modes of language acquisition. Striving towards this goal is certainly not the same as asserting their identity, albeit an 'essential identity'.

1.5.2 *Contrastive hypothesis*

The identity hypothesis asserts that the acquisition or availability of one language has little or no influence on the acquisition of another language. The contrastive hypothesis, conversely, claims that the acquisition of a second language is largely determined by the structure of an earlier acquired language. Those structures of the second language that coincide with corresponding structures of the first language are assimilated with great ease as a result of 'positive transfer'. Contrasting structures, on the other hand, present considerable difficulty and give rise to errors as a result of 'negative transfer', or 'interference' between the two contrasting languages.

The theory has a number of variants which occupy different positions along a 'weak–strong' scale. The original idea – as expressed by Lado (1957) in what was for many years the bible of foreign language teachers – was to predict from a systematic comparison of any two languages the problems likely to be encountered by learners, or even to deduce the most effective order of acquisition for the various structures of the target language. Inspired by this exciting prospect, applied linguists launched a number of contrastive analysis projects.[15] However, the results of this work, whilst interesting on purely linguistic grounds, proved to be of much less help than had been expected. (For a discussion and a résumé, cf. Els *et al.*, section 4.2.) A major reason for this relative failure lies in the fact that structural similarities and dissimilarities between two linguistic *systems* and the processing of linguistic means *in actual production and comprehension* are two quite different things. Contrastive linguistics was concerned with the former; acquisition, however, has to do with the latter. It is not the existence of a structure as described by the linguist that

25

is important, but the way the learner deals with it in comprehension and production. Therefore, comparison of *structures* may totally miss the point. A related reason is that for a learner with a given first language background, a specific second language structure may be easy to perceive but hard to produce, or vice versa. Consequently, this structure has no uniform effect on the learner's acquisition capacity.

At present, no one seriously entertains the contrastive hypothesis in its strong sense. This is not to deny, however, that the learner's knowledge of his first language influences the way in which he approaches and eventually learns a second language. The unsatisfactory results of contrastive analysis cast some discredit on the notion of 'transfer' from the first to the second language. But the existence of various forms of transfer is too obvious to be ignored, and there has recently been increasing interest in this issue. Although we cannot review the whole literature here we will briefly look at five crucial points (a good survey of the present state is given by Gass and Selinker, 1983; see also Kellerman and Sharwood-Smith, 1985; Dechert and Raupach, 1985):

1. As has been mentioned above, predictions on possible transfer should not be based on comparisons of structural properties but rather on the way in which the learner processes these structural properties. German, for example, has no [ð], as in English *that*. It is very likely that a German learner of English will realize that the sound is unusual; but he or she might be unable to produce it and consequently replace it by a sound from German. There are two candidates, namely [d] and [z], which, on purely structural grounds, are equally similar to [ð]. Now, such a transfer indeed often occurs, and the sound chosen is always [z] – in contrast to learners with other source languages or to speakers of some English vernaculars who say *dat*. This is not predictable if one compares only structural – in this case, phonetic – properties. (See, for a related, though not identical point, Kellerman's (1979) concept of 'perceived' distance.)

2. Many deviant constructions and 'errors' in learner utterances which are apparently due to transfer may have quite different causes. Turkish, for example, normally has the verb in final position. Turkish learners of German often put it into that position in their German utterances rather than into the second one – for obvious reasons, one might think. But Spanish and Italian learners often do the same, although the verb is not normally final in their languages: its position is relatively free. Thus, the alleged transfer is probably due to other, more universal constraints (for an insightful discussion of this and related problems, see Meisel 1983; cf. also section 6.2 below).

3. Transfer has been observed on various linguistic levels – mainly in phonology, and in the lexicon, but also in syntax. It is quite rare in morphology: for example it is very unlikely that a German learner of Russian would transfer a German genitive ending or the marking of the preterite to Russian. On the other hand, there is also transfer on levels where it is not immediately apparent. Here are two examples:

(a)　　English, German and Italian give different weight to the various features which mark an NP as the subject of a clause: in English, the position is dominant; in Italian, the lexical content (plus agreement with the verb) is most important; in German, the case marking outweighs all other factors. Bates *et al.* (1982) have shown that non-native speakers tend to follow their 'native' strategy even when they are quite fluent in the second language.

(b)　　Transfer may also occur on a conceptual level. During first language acquisition, speakers develop a certain concept of time, space, modality, definiteness, and the like. This conceptual imprint may deeply influence the way in which they approach the second language – for example, how they interpret its morphological system, its subordinate conjunctions, etc. It also partly determines what they think must be encoded in an utterance. If a language rigidly marks the definite–indefinite distinction of noun phrases, it seems likely that a speaker of that language will want to encode this difference in his second language, too – more so at least than a learner whose first language does not mark this distinction.

4. For a learner to recognize an error due to transfer, he must generally already know a lot about the *second language*. For example, a speaker of Basque, where the tensed element is always clause-final, might transfer this word order to German, where the position of the tensed element of a clause varies with the clause type (initial in interrogatives, final in subordinate clauses, second in declarative main clauses). But in order to do so, he must know the tensed element in German – and it is a very complex task to find this out (for a discussion of this problem see section 6.2 below). In other words, the possibilities of transfer increase as knowledge of the second language increases (for a related point, see Andersen, 1983a).

5. Whenever a learner of a second language tries to comprehend or to produce utterances in that language, he relies on all sorts of knowledge that might help him. One component of this knowledge is what he knows about his first language, and application of this knowledge leads to what is called 'transfer'. But it is crucial to remember that his first language

competence is but one of his possible resources; it always interacts with the other sorts of knowledge he may draw on. It is this interaction of different kinds of knowledge that needs to be considered in order to understand what a learner does, and why he does it. This point will be discussed at some length in chapters 5–8 below.

1.5.3 *Krashen's monitor theory*

The two theories outlined above concern the relationship between first and second language acquisition. Krashen's much-debated monitor theory[16] is addressed chiefly to the relation between spontaneous and guided learning and can be summarized as follows:

1. There are two ways for adult learners to gain proficiency in a second language: subconscious *acquisition* and conscious *learning*. The former, which is by far the more important of the two, is based on meaningful and purposeful communication with speakers of the target language. The learner is oriented not to the form but to the content and effect of his utterances, remaining unaware of the linguistic rules and structures used in the process. This kind of language acquisition tends to result in a relatively invariant acquisition order. Language *learning* as conceived by Krashen consists in the internalization of explicit rules under conscious control. Here there can be no invariant acquisition order beyond what is predetermined by the process of instruction.

2. The crucial point of the theory is that 'learning' in this sense is always effected through a 'monitor', or an effort on the part of the learner to control his language output and to self-correct it whenever necessary. The monitor controls the learner's language knowledge in the same way as a rider controls a horse.

3. The monitor can become effective in a communication situation only if (a) there is enough time to operate it, (b) the speaker is concerned with the correctness of his speech production, and (c) the speaker knows the correct rule.

As this summary indicates, the theory underlines the distinction between guided and spontaneous language acquisition. In both cases, however, the crucial element is 'acquisition' in the sense of a subconscious process governed by certain rules. The 'learning' (and, indirectly, teaching) in which the learner is involved exerts, to a certain extent, a controlling influence upon the 'acquisition' of the language.

In section 1.3.2 guided second language acquisition was characterized as an attempt to domesticate the natural process of spontaneous learning. The same idea is contained in Krashen's model with the specification that the effective control operates within the learner, although the motivation may come from outside. To put it another way, the supervision is effected by the learner's capacity to guide his speech production and comprehension, i.e. the monitor.

Krashen's monitor theory is not a model of language acquisition in general; it does not attempt to specify the rules governing the process or the factors responsible for this or that outcome, but it presents hypotheses about the manner in which language acquisition can be influenced by conscious awareness. The validity of these assumptions is open to debate. What is certain is that the theory, if correct, carries important implications for language instruction.

1.5.4 *Theories of learner varieties*

Whatever the mode of language acquisition, the learner must employ those means that are available to him or her at the time, whether it be for purposes of real-life communication (in spontaneous learning) or for dealing with exercises or simulated conversations (in guided acquisition). However imperfect from a normative point of view, these means represent the learner's current repertoire and as such form a *learner variety* of the (target) language. In the past fifteen years this aspect of language acquisition has been subject to various theoretical accounts and interpretations, focussing upon the following two concepts:

(a)   Any language variety, no matter how rudimentary, has, apart from some variable components, a certain intrinsic *systematicity*. Thus the function of any one word or construction within the given variety cannot be derived solely from the function of the corresponding word or construction in the target language.

(b)   The process of language acquisition can be construed as a series of transitions from one variety to the next, and these transitions again reveal an inherent systematicity.

Some of the relevant theories are less explicit in their assumptions, and all differ on more specific points. The first explicit proposal for construing the acquisition process and its intermediate stages as a sequence of transitions from system to system was made by Corder (1967; see also Corder, 1973). Similar concepts were subsequently developed by other authors. The most influential of these was the concept of 'interlanguage' proposed by Selinker (1972), who further defined *type of transfer* and *strategy of acquisition* as the factors determining the particular form of any interlanguage (cf. Tarone, Frauenfelder and Selinker, 1976).

29

The most comprehensive empirical research based on the concepts of learner varieties and the transition from one to the next is the Heidelberg Research Project for Pidgin German (1975, 1976, 1977, 1979; see also Klein and Dittmar, 1979). Formal grammars of varying completeness have been developed to describe the respective learner varieties, and the transitions are designated by 'probabilistic weighting'.

The various theories of learner varieties cannot be readily defined in terms of any common empirical assumptions as to the process of second language acquisition or its determining factors. They represent a specific way of looking at things, but this is not a convenient basis for an overall assessment. All in all, this approach is gaining in popularity, and the perspective of this book corresponds to it.

1.5.5   *Pidginization theory*

A pidgin is a second language which comes into being whenever speakers of a politically, socially, or culturally subordinate language try to acquire some knowledge of a dominant language for specific purposes (e.g. for trade).[17] They tend to be identified by two kinds of features:

(a)   The way in which they have developed and function: pidgins serve strictly limited communicative purposes, bridging (and possibly perpetuating) extreme social divisions, as for example between colonial masters and the indigenous population.

(b)   Their structure: pidgins display features of both the dominant and subordinate languages as well as some independent features. They are typified by such structural properties as limited vocabulary; absence of gender; by the marking of tense, aspect and mood by adverbial particles rather than by verb inflection; and by the preponderance of coordinate rather than subordinate grammatical relations between utterances.

For further information on pidgins and their properties the interested reader should refer to the literature cited in note 17. From what has been said so far it can be seen that pidgins (in terms of both structure and development) have much in common with learner varieties developed in spontaneous second language acquisition. A number of authors have drawn attention to this: the first was Clyne (1968), who discovered a number of pidgin-like structural features in the language of adult foreign workers in Germany, so he called their learner variety 'Pidgin-German'. Both idea and term were taken up by the Heidelberg Research Project

(1975), although pidginization was seen then as just one facet in the formation of learner varieties. (See also Meisel, 1975, for a critical discussion; and Ferguson 1977.)

Schumann (1978a) has gone furthest in claiming that similar sociopsychological processes underly both the formation of pidgins and spontaneous second language acquisition – at least in some cases. This argument has its empirical base in the case of a Spanish-speaking immigrant who learned English as an adult and whose language became 'fossilized' (Selinker, 1972) at a rudimentary level within the first year. The language variety of this speaker revealed many of the properties of a pidgin and Schumann attributed the fossilization of this variety to the same social and psychological circumstances that typically contribute to a pidgin's emergence. The learner feels disconcerted by confrontation with a dominant culture and language and finds it necessary to adjust to a certain extent in order to survive (communicatively!), he nevertheless avoids anything that could endanger social, cultural, and linguistic identity (for a discussion, see Andersen, 1981). The most comprehensive account in the context of pidginization is the one given by Andersen (1983a, where he summarizes a number of studies both of his own and by others). Pidginization, defined as 'language acquisition under conditions of restricted input or, where input is adequate, under conditions where intake is severely restricted due to socioaffective factors, time constraints, or linguistic complexity' (p. 8), is just one of several processes which determine the development of specific individual learner varieties and which, under specific social circumstances, may eventually lead to the emergence of a pidgin.

Another, somewhat spectacular view is Bickerton's (1981) 'language bioprogram hypothesis', according to which all kinds of acquisition processes are guided by a neurophysiologically 'wired' bioprogram. Its functioning is most clearly displayed in the creation of creoles, i.e. native languages derived from pidgins where, according to Bickerton, the result of the process goes far beyond what could be derived from the input. But it also operates in first and second language acquisition, although its effects are blurred there by other determining factors, in particular the influence of the first language in SLA (Bickerton, 1984). Bickerton's proposal has been much challenged on both empirical and theoretical grounds, but it does have the seductive charm of simple views.

There is little doubt that both in the circumstances of their emergence and in their structure, pidgins and early learner varieties share many common features. The logic of scientific investigation demands that the emergence of pidgins (and possibly their creolization) be regarded as special cases of spontaneous second language acquisition. In specific conditions language varieties emerge that are used by entire groups of people with little variability. In other words, the study of pidginization might prove less revealing for second language acquisition research than vice versa.

1.5.6 *Conclusion*

The aim of the chapter was to provide an overview of the diverse problems, hypotheses, and research approaches encountered in the field of language acquisition research. It would not be surprising if at this point, rather than seeing the vast forest spread before him, the reader felt he was lost in a jungle. In the following chapter an attempt will be made to cut a path or two through the trees.

2
Six dimensions of
language acquisition

In this chapter an attempt will be made to impose a kind of structure on the complex field of language acquisition and to organize the many different influencing factors along a number of dimensions; from an interplay of the values variously distributed along these dimensions we would expect to derive the different forms of language acquisition. The six basic dimensions of language acquisition will be introduced with the description of an imaginary case of second language acquisition and will then be discussed in greater detail.

2.1 A global view

Suppose your airplane makes a crash landing in a remote valley in New Guinea. You are lucky to survive and you manage to reach a human settlement where you find the members of a tribe, let's call them the Eipo, who evidently live in complete seclusion from the rest of the world. The Eipo turn out to be friendly people, they receive you well and are willing to incorporate you (in the more metaphorical sense of the word); so you are somewhat shocked, but not terrified, by the prospect of spending an unforeseeable period of time among them, as there seems to be no chance of crossing the wild mountains which effectively separate the valley from the world. Given the prospect of living among the Eipo for many years, you had better think of mastering their language (which we will call Eipomek) and of acquiring a number of other skills and customs which are part of the tribe's way of life.

What are the salient points at the start of the language acquisition process? First, the learner (that's you!) feels the need to learn the language, a kind of urge or *propensity*, as we shall call it. There is no reason why the learner should be clearly aware of what causes this propensity, or of the forces that propel him along the path of language acquisition, but there must be some kind of inner force that urges him to make progress.

The presence of some such propensity is a necessary but not sufficient condition. The learner must also (still) possess the capacity for language learning or, more generally speaking, the *language faculty* – a notion which encompasses the ability to process language (i.e. to produce and to comprehend utterances) and, if necessary, the ability to learn a language. It includes, for example,

> the ability to discriminate among speech sounds and also to produce them correctly;
> the ability to analyse sound sequences into the sound units of the language and to relate these units to particular things or events in the environment (e.g. the sound sequence *nup* to the object 'house' – in Eipomek);
> the ability to remember these relationships and to combine the lexical units into larger entities (sentences);

and so on, and so forth.

These two conditions, propensity and language faculty, are still insufficient: should the Eipo lock you up, or refrain from speaking in your presence, you would have no chance to learn their language. A further condition is therefore *access* to the language.

We have thus identified the three indispensable components of any language learning: propensity, language faculty, and access. Each of these may vary considerably: the propensity may be quite different from what we have seen in our example (as when a second language is learnt at school); the language faculty may undergo substantial changes in the course of life – positive, because of expanding knowledge, or negative, because of a deteriorating memory or defective hearing, for example; access need not result from actual communication, as in our example, but can be of a very limited kind, as in the study of Latin. Nevertheless, each of these three components must be present in some form for language learning to take place.

In our illustration, all three components are given: you are willing to integrate socially and hence linguistically, your language faculty has not suffered as a result of the plane crash or because of the natural food, and the Eipo gladly offer you their company. Since the three conditions are satisfied, the process of language acquisition can begin. Now this process displays a certain *structure* in the sense that the mastering of Eipomek follows a certain course: you become acquainted with the various features of the language in a certain order. Although this order may depend on, say, the frequency of occurrence, or the communicative relevance of various forms, or on the ease with which they are perceptually or cognitively processed, any process of language acquisition will nevertheless display a certain structure.

The speed at which language takes place depends on the strength of the propensity, the excellence of the language faculty (assuming human beings differ on this score), access to samples of the language, and the like. Thus although any process of language acquisition displays a certain tempo, there is no reason why this tempo should be constant: it may start high, but then slow down as you find yourself getting on socially. Later still, you become deputy chieftain of the tribe, which requires you to speak a lot, so the tempo again increases. There is, however, a point at which progress ceases: you have reached a certain *end state*, the point beyond which you are either not willing, or not able to go. Your language skills at this point may be practically the same as, or a good deal worse than, or (because of your level of intelligence) better than those of the average native speaker. You might also considerably surpass the average Eipo in breadth of vocabulary and yet lag far behind in pronunciation. Whatever the cause of such variations, a state of relative stability will be reached, the point at which the language acquisition process is, in practice, at an end.

Thus the three components which determine the process of language acquisition – propensity, language faculty, and access to the language – together with the three categories which characterize the process – its structure, tempo, and end state – comprise the six basic dimensions of language acquisition, which will be discussed in turn below.

2.2 **Propensity**

The term 'propensity' covers the totality of factors – some helpful, some detrimental – that induce the learner to apply his language faculty to acquiring a language, and it is the outcome of their interaction that determines the actual propensity of the learner. While it is not easy to systematize these factors, there are two reasons for keeping them apart: first, since they do not affect all aspects of language acquisition to an equal degree, it would be unwise to relate propensity to the process of acquisition in a general way (in fact, only *specific* elements of propensity can be sensibly related to *specific* aspects of the process); secondly, the component elements of propensity can be affected by external factors (e.g. teaching) to varying degrees.

Although the following rough differentiation of the various components may appear arbitrary at first sight, it does at least provide a provisional orientation.

Six dimensions of language acquisition

A.   Social integration

In first language acquisition social integration seems to be a dominant factor. A child unconsciously follows the maxim, 'Acquire a social identity and, in its framework, a personal identity' (see section 1.1.1.B). The relevance of this factor diminishes as we move away from child language acquisition to other forms of language acquisition. Social integration is presumably more important to a child learning a second language in overlap with his first than to a migrant worker, although this depends on how strongly the latter feels the need to become socially integrated in the wider society of the host country. The need is certainly more pressing for our imaginary Eipomek learner than for a Turk who comes to West Berlin in search of employment and finds there a relatively large group of his countrymen, especially if the migrant plans to return to his country after a couple of years. Social integration has little significance as a propensity-generating factor in second language learning at colleges and universities, especially in the extreme case of learning classical Latin and Greek, where social integration is somewhat unlikely.

The social integration factor may, on occasions, have a negative effect. If, for example, a migrant worker is well integrated in and possesses a social identity within his native community, he may shrink back from becoming integrated into a new language community for fear of losing this social identity – despite an awareness of the concomitant benefits of this new integration. This may be a likely cause of early 'fossilization' (Selinker, 1972) in the second language skills of many adult migrants (on this, see Schumann, 1978a,b).

B.   Communicative needs

This factor must be carefully distinguished from social integration, especially since the two often go hand in hand. Although social integration clearly implies the satisfaction of certain communicative needs, the two factors nevertheless differ as much as integration in a community differs from understanding utterances or indeed producing utterances in the target language. You may be learning Spanish or French or German in order to write business letters, or you may be learning it to build up a new existence in the respective country.

These two factors have been carefully separated out because they can influence language acquisition in very distinct ways, as may be exemplified in five domains: phonology, morphology, syntax, vocabulary and discourse. A foreign accent will not generally prevent a speaker from being understood, but it will quickly identify him as an *alien*. Equally irrelevant are inflectional morphology (traditionally a favourite preoccupation of second language teachers), and syntax. For example, in a bakery, *Me bread* conveys the message as well as the correct *May I have a loaf of bread, please*, but with the former the speaker gives himself away as an outsider. The vocabulary acquired by a speaker for communicative purposes is likely to belong to those domains that correspond to his needs. This is as true of spontaneous second language acquisition (an Italian waiter in Germany) as it is of guided learning (for commercial purposes, or for reading the set texts in a university-level foreign language course); the vocabulary developed for specific purposes is always more one-sided than the vocabulary required to achieve social integration. Moreover, ordinary interaction within any community is dominated by ritual conversation patterns, i.e. by standard phrases, routine expressions, figures of speech, but also by a delicate balance of explicitness and implicitness, direct and indirect speech acts, and the like. A person's mastery of these linguistic forms prejudges his integration into the given community; mere communication can do without it. Communicative needs have so far been discussed without any further specification, but it should be pointed out that there are a great variety of such needs, and their influence upon language acquisition is correspondingly varied.

The distinction made here between social integration and communicative needs as two interacting components of propensity seems to coincide with the distinction between integrative and instrumental motivation proposed by Gardner and Lambert (1972). Nevertheless, we would prefer to avoid the term 'motivation' because in foreign language teaching it is strongly associated with behaviouristic motivation theory. There is no denying that much – but not all, see below – of what has been discussed under the heading 'propensity' could be discussed with reference to motivation. But to explain 'propensity' by the term 'motivation' would be tantamount – leaving aside its unfortunate association – to calling a poor man a pauper. This is not to say that motivation research could not tell us a lot about the propensity to learn a second language. For a comprehensive treatment of the subject see Heckhausen (1981).

C.   Attitude

Learners vary considerably in their attitude to the language they are learning and to the people who speak this language, and it is generally thought to be an important factor in second language learning. (Children seem to have no particular attitude to their first language, and it is uncertain whether their evaluation of father and mother has any effect on language acquisition.) It is perfectly natural that a learner who regards a particular language as gibberish and who cannot stand any speaker of that language will prove less successful in learning it – other things being equal – than a learner with a positive attitude (except, maybe, in the training of secret agents).

These subjective attitudes can also influence language learning in less obvious ways, as, for example, in the aforementioned case of the presumably unconscious worry about the loss of social identity. (This case incidentally illustrates the intertwining of the various factors insofar as this kind of attitude represents a negative component of the 'social integration' factor.) Another example is the – conscious or unconscious – feeling that there is no real need to learn the language. A German will assume that it is much easier to learn Dutch than Italian for instance, since the similarity between the former two languages enables him to understand some of the Dutch and try to guess the rest. In fact, this language affinity might prove a trap: underrating the difficulties of the task, the learner pays so little attention to it and expends so little effort that he is unsuccessful. A further example is connected with the notion of 'ego permeability' proposed by Guiora *et al.* (1972); this term refers to the varying readiness of learners to reveal their imperfect command of a language and disgrace themselves with inappropriate, awkward, or even ridiculous utterances. Even children learning a second language were found to differ considerably in this respect (Wong-Fillmore, 1976): some plunge head-first into the cold water and talk straight away, others are extremely wary and try not to speak until they are certain how to. What is involved is presumably an attitude not only to linguistic but also to other kinds of social behaviour. Wong-Fillmore found these differences to result in different structures and rates of progress in the language acquisition of the five children she tested. (On the subject of attitude see also Oller, 1981; and Solmecke and Boosch, 1983.)

D.   Education

A second language can be learnt in the same way as set theory or biology – simply because it happens to belong to the educational organization of a particular society. In Western European countries, for instance, an educated person is one who has studied, amongst other things, Latin and one or two modern languages. In foreign language instruction in schools this is the overriding consideration, even if it is not the only one. At the same time, this educational ideal is the weakest among all the factors contributing to propensity; by itself it can drive the process of language

learning only in exceptional cases. It may be effective if it is combined
with the other propensity factors: social advancement (measured in good
marks and passed exams), avoidance of punishment, or factors A, B, and
C above. In the context of institutional second language teaching the term
'motivation' is used basically in an attempt to create positive attitudes
or to suggest communicative needs to the student – that is, to substitute
factors such as A, B, and C for the underlying educational ideal.

2.3   Language faculty

Human beings are endowed with a natural capacity for processing language, both as speaker and listener, or, to use Saussure's (1916)
term, with a 'faculté du langage'. In exercising this faculty they have
to make use of one of the socially normed systems referred to as 'natural
languages' (Saussure's 'langue'). Hence the language faculty comprises
the ability to adapt the language processing capacities to such a social
system: that is, to learn a given language. In other words, the *language
processor* – i.e. those parts of the human brain, motor system, and perceptual apparatus that are tuned to processing language – is capable not only
of producing language and comprehending it but also of adjusting its language production and comprehension to the particular linguistic material.
It is important to recognize language learning first and foremost as an
inherent ability of the human language processor, rather than as a separate
ability of the human mind. What is involved in SLA is the capacity to
reorganize the language processor to cope with another language, a capacity
that can be exercised provided there is a sufficiently strong urge in this
direction.

It should be clear from this discussion of the human language faculty
why it is indispensable to understand the workings of the language processor in order to fathom the mechanisms and laws of language acquisition.
A more searching analysis of the language processor will be made in
chapters 4–8, but in this section the rudiments of the problem will be
considered.

The functioning of the language processor is contingent upon (A) certain
biological determinants, and (B) the knowledge available to the speaker
at any one time.

A.   Biological determinants of the language processor

Among the biological components there are firstly certain peripheral organs: the whole articulatory apparatus, from the larynx to the
lips; and the auditory apparatus. Then there are some parts of the central

nervous system, namely those dealing with perception, memory, and the higher cognitive functions. All these components as well as their interplay are innate to the human being. They can vary during our lifetime within certain limits: for example, it is generally assumed that the sensitivity of the ear to the higher sound frequencies tends to decline in old age. The higher cognitive functions (roughly speaking, 'thinking') develop over many years and may then be preserved for any length of time (as we older people would like to believe).

The biological components of the language processor provide a kind of framework within which language processing can take place. How much of a straightjacket this framework is remains a matter of dispute, at least as far as the central segments are concerned. As pointed out in section 1.1.2, one of the most influential schools in linguistics, generative grammar, asserts that much of what makes up human language is innate, and needs only to be activated during the acquisition process. Although other investigators insist that the biological components are responsible for no more than a fraction of our language skills, the *existence* of biological components in language processing, and hence acquisition, is beyond dispute. There is only disagreement on how tight this biological frame is.

B.   Available knowledge
Both language production and language comprehension rest squarely on knowledge (in a broad sense). This term refers here to what are in fact two distinct varieties of knowledge: *conscious* knowledge acquired from other people, from books, at school, etc.; and *tacit* knowledge, which is unconscious and cannot normally be verbalized but which forms the basis of many skills, including verbal ones. Much of our language proficiency (e.g. the rules that define word order in a sentence, or the use of the article in English) is of the second kind. This 'tacit' knowledge can under certain circumstances be made conscious, and many textbooks, including the grammars used in language teaching, do just this. The term 'knowledge' used here refers to conscious and tacit knowledge because they are both part of what is commonly called our 'knowledge of (the) language'.

In our use of language we have to rely not only on linguistic knowledge (conscious *and* tacit) but also on nonverbal knowledge. The role of the former is obvious: in order to understand the utterance, *I'm coming round tomorrow at eleven*, it is necessary to *know*:

the phonemes of English,

English morphology,
the meaning of the individual words,
the syntactic rules of English,

and many other things about the English language as well.

However, linguistic knowledge of this kind does not usually suffice to ensure a full understanding of the utterance in its context – an understanding which would allow us to respond in a communicatively appropriate way (for instance by saying, *Okay, I'll be in all evening*). In order to do so, it is also necessary to *know*:

> who the speaker is (which does not follow from knowing the word I),
>
> what day it is, and hence what *tomorrow* means (which could be different if heard on tape, or read on an undated postcard),
>
> what *round* refers to: the house, country residence or office of the interlocutor, or any other place *known* to both speaker and listener (hearing the utterance on the telephone from a distant friend would convey something quite different from what it would mean if uttered by a next-door neighbour).

All this *contextual knowledge* is not contained in the utterance as such; but it can be constructed from our knowledge of the situation, from preceding utterances, and from our general knowledge of the world. Indeed, the share of this contextual knowledge can be so large that a fair measure of the verbal communication going on around us is comprehensible even in the absence of strictly linguistic knowledge. An utterance such as *Me bread*, heard in a bakery, could not be mistaken by anyone in his right senses as meaning 'I am a bread', notwithstanding its grammatical defectiveness and communicative inadequacy. Thus the meaning of any utterance emerges from our knowledge of the situation and our world knowledge, as well as from the utterance itself.

Communication depends heavily on a combination of contextual (implicit) and linguistically conveyed (explicit) information. Only the latter derives directly from the linguistic knowledge at our disposal, that is, our knowledge of grammar, vocabulary, etc.; the former information derives from our other knowledge. In spontaneous second language acquisition there is a gradual shift in the balance of the two kinds of information: in early learner varieties of the language, great weight is placed on contextual knowledge, since the linguistic knowledge of the learner can only take a small part of the linguistic load; later the learner will become less dependent on his nonlinguistic knowledge. This holds true not only for

41

language production but also for comprehension. A learner is apt to 'understand' utterances in the target language even if he has no knowledge of many of the words used, or of the syntactic and other rules involved – provided he can rely on his nonlinguistic, contextual knowledge. The difference between the production and comprehension of utterances is that the former depends mainly on the nonlinguistic knowledge of the (native) listener, and the latter, on that of the learner.

This fact sheds new light on a familiar aspect of second language acquisition: the apparent asymmetry in the 'active' command of a (second) language (proficiency in the production) and the 'passive' command (comprehension of the language). In theory a learner who possesses no more than 60 per cent of the linguistic knowledge needed to handle a certain utterance in the target language has a 60 per cent understanding of it if he relies solely on linguistic knowledge. (To define someone's command of a language in percentages is an obvious oversimplification which can be tolerated only for purposes of illustration.) In practice the learner may understand it completely by relying also on nonlinguistic knowledge. Now if the same learner were to construct the utterance, he would be liable to be 40 per cent unsuccessful, but even so a *native* speaker might be able to understand it, again by relying on *his* nonlinguistic knowledge. Viewed in this way, the learner's active and passive command of the language or his *knowledge* of the language, are in no way different. The difference is in the eye of the observer who tries to compare the learner's defective utterance – the product of an imperfect knowledge of the language – with what the learner (also relying on nonlinguistic knowledge) understands of the same utterance.

There is also an important methodological consequence of this incessant interplay between linguistic and nonlinguistic knowledge. If, as has often been the case in second language acquisition research, only the appearance of isolated linguistic forms in morphology, syntax or the lexicon is considered, then the whole internal systematics of learner varieties, their functioning and non-functioning and, consequently, the entire dynamics of the acquisition process must often look quite enigmatic. Any linguistic form, be it an inflectional suffix or a specific word, is dispensable to a greater or lesser extent, depending on all of the other possible ways of conveying the information which this form is supposed to express, either by other linguistic means or by the context. Verb morphology, for example, may be largely superfluous *in a given context*, because, in this particular context, it is already clear that the action is in the past (*laughed*) or that only one agent is involved (*laughs*). This is not to say, of course, that the acquisition process only advances where and when the interplay between linguistic and nonlinguistic information leads to unsatisfactory results and communication problems, but it is surely one of the seeds of the developmental process, determining when and in what order particular forms appear. This point will be developed in chapter 7.

The two components of the language processor, biological determinants and available knowledge, could be labelled metaphorically 'hardware' and 'software': the former are the wired-in mechanical and electronic elements, the latter are the programmes and operating systems. As any such analogy, this one is at the same time revealing and misleading. It is misleading, for example, in that the human language processor, in contrast to any known computer hardware, is endowed with the capacity for 'self-organization': it continuously changes and is normally able to improve its software and even its hardware (the articulators include muscles that can be trained for better performance). However, the analogy does hold for its differential modifiability. The processor's hardware is relatively invariant, the software is subject to incessant change: new knowledge is stored, old information is deleted.

From this perspective, the differences between first and second language acquisition can be pinpointed in relation to two groups of issues:

(a)   The second language learner is older, so there may have been changes in some biological determinants which bear heavily on language processing. This may certainly apply to the peripheral components such as hearing. It is, however, an open issue whether these peripheral changes and possible changes in the central nervous system (memory) can exert a noticeable influence on language processing.

(b)   The learner's knowledge is in constant flux, at least as far as nonlinguistic knowledge is concerned. But the second language learner is already in command of (at least) his first language, and it is perfectly natural for him to lean, consciously or unconsciously, on his knowledge of this language. This is where the first language may exert an influence upon the second, resulting in phenomena such as transfer, interference, etc.

This introductory discussion of the language faculty is developed in greater detail in chapters 4–8.

2.4 Access

The language processor cannot operate without access to its raw material. The term 'access' in actual fact covers two distinct components which, whilst having many things in common, should be carefully distinguished: one is the amount of 'input' available, the other the range of opportunities for communication. Let us go back to our Eipomek learner for an illustration.

A.   Input

As you may remember, you had to start from scratch when embarking upon the formidable task of learning the language of the Eipo tribe. In the beginning, there was just a sequence of strange sounds that hit your ear, or more precisely, you initially learn from a series of variations in air pressure registered by your eardrum. Stated in this somewhat odd way the magnitude of the task facing the learner is blatantly clear: with all the constraints imposed by his biological endowment and the limitations of his knowledge (in other words, his ignorance) the learner has to extract from those variations in air pressure practically everything that distinguishes this particular language from all other languages.

How could the learner possibly generate the entire knowledge of the phonology, morphology, vocabulary, syntax, and all other aspects of the language solely on the basis of the sound waves of Eipomek? Suppose you were locked in a room and were continually exposed to the sound of Chinese coming from a loudspeaker; however long the experiment continued, you would not end up speaking Chinese; at most, you might know parts of the phonological system. What makes learning possible is the information received *in parallel* to the linguistic input in the narrower sense (the sound waves): the learner must know who is speaking to whom, when and where, he must be able to watch the accompanying 'body language' (gesture, facial expression, etc.), and he must note the reactions of the listener. Eventually he should be able to establish a relationship between identifiable segments of the sound stream and particular pieces of the parallel information. He may then conclude that the sound sequence *ngaguga* uttered by people every morning as they meet for the first time means 'good morning' (although it could mean 'get lost'). Watching people point to a bird and say *haua*, he may come to the same conclusion as anyone else, etc.

Patterns of speech sounds and the parallel information about the context of this speech event jointly represent the input to the learner's language processor, at least in spontaneous language acquisition. In guided language learning the same factors will be present, in principle, but in a greatly modified form: sound sequences are presented in carefully chosen segments, and utterances are supplemented by word lists; more often than not the sound patterns are replaced by written language. Finally, the learner is relieved of the burden of inducing the rules of syntax or morphology from the linguistic material, since these are supplied ready-made as rules of grammar. Even the parallel information comes in prefabricated form: the meaning of sound patterns (words), rather than being inferred from the context, is provided, for example, in the form of a word list which draws on the learner's knowledge of his first language. This 'prefabrication' of the linguistic material may indeed assist the language processor in its work, or it may create difficulties if it violates the inherent principles of language processing. If properly looked after a lion may thrive better in the zoo than in his natural environment; or a wrong diet may cause his death.

Although the input in spontaneous language acquisition generally consists of authentic speech, cases of deliberate modification are not that unusual. In first language acquisition this occurs as 'motherese' (Snow and Ferguson, 1977), in second language learning as 'foreigner talk' or 'simplified registers', or just 'broken language' (Ferguson, 1977; Ferguson and de Bose, 1977; Clyne, 1982). The native speaker has a tendency to adjust his language to the presumed potentialities of the learner. For example the speaker will say, *You go to Mayor, office, police, understand?*, rather than *You must go to the registration office*. Such adjustments occur in every domain:

> in phonology, when speech is slowed down deliberately and articulation exaggerated,
> in morphology, when verbs are used chiefly in the infinitive,
> in syntax, when word order is modified, certain elements (copula, article) omitted, and compound clauses avoided,
> in vocabulary, when certain words are avoided or supplemented with paraphrases,
> in communication in general, when certain topics are avoided, and some ritual elements of language communication are replaced by repetitive questions on standard topics, more attention is paid to comprehension checks (e.g. 'do you understand?'), etc.[1]

Introducing these modifications into his speech, the native speaker is guided – consciously or unwittingly – by his hypotheses concerning the learner's defective language skills. In doing so the speaker may err in two ways. Firstly, his modifications may hinder comprehension if the learner is fairly advanced in the language. Secondly, the learner may interpret them as a sign of social distance and condescension, and feel insulted by being addressed in this kind of jargon (on this, see also Bodemann and Ostow, 1975).

45

B.   Opportunities for communication

As has been noted above, spontaneous language acquisition involves learning in and through social interaction. The learner is obliged to bring to bear all the knowledge available to him (i.e., his particular variety + contextual knowledge) in order to understand what others say and to produce his own utterances. He may be expected to speed up the process of language acquisition when the need for communication becomes stronger and the opportunities more frequent. The phrase 'may be expected' is used to stress that this is a highly plausible notion although it has never been verified by research. It is supported by at least two observations. Firstly, the learner is offered more linguistic input: the elements of language (speech sounds, words, constructions) come to his attention with increased frequency and in a wider range. Secondly, he has more opportunities to test his own speech production against that of his environment, in order to verify his hypotheses about the structure of the target language. This monitoring of one's own and others' language output is an important factor in language acquisition, as it is in language processing in general (see chapter 8 for a detailed discussion). The acquisition process comes to an end as soon as the learner ceases to be aware of differences between his own speech production and that of his environment, and this explains why, in the long run, those structures in which first and second language resemble each other closely may present greater difficulties than those where they are radically different. Learners tend to differ in the extent of their linguistic monitoring, which need not result from their individual disposition in this respect but could have something to do with attitudes, specifically a willingness to attend to what other people say. Children appear to be tremendously attentive, which accounts in part for the fact that they are far less likely to 'fossilize' than adults. One would expect here also a reference to the highly suggestive notion that children are faster learners than adults, but whereas scientific research often merely confirms commonplace views, the actual evidence here is that children become more efficient learners with age (see Bühler, 1972; Snow and Hoefnagel-Höhle, 1978; Chun 1981; and, for a review, McLaughlin, 1978a).

The opportunities to communicate verbally are far more restricted in guided second language acquisition and the substitutes consist of 'prefabricated' elements of language production and comprehension which succeed to varying degrees in approximating real-life communication. The best approximation to the basic function of the language processor is attained by 'acting out' in 'communicative instruction' (Piepho, 1974; Müller, 1980), and contrasts with the least interactive 'pattern drills', or translations of text units as employed in teaching Latin, where productive skills are quite inadequately tapped.

Sections 2.2–2.4 were devoted to the three major determinants of language acquisition, each having its own components. In sections 2.5–2.7 the three categories which characterize the process of acquisition will be discussed: structure, tempo and end state, the latter two in a more cursory way.

2.5   The structure of the process

There are two key questions to be asked in an inquiry into the structure of the acquisition process: (a) How are the various skills and elements of knowledge that make up language proficiency synchronized? (b) What kind of variations across learners and learner categories can be observed in the acquisition process? We discuss the two issues under separate headings, while attempting not to overlook their interrelation.

A.   Synchronization

The command of a language involves the acquisition of all kinds of linguistic knowledge (leaving aside nonlinguistic knowledge for the time being), as illustrated by the following examples, mostly taken from English or German.

To know a language, a speaker must be able to make proper use of the following types of information, as well as a multitude of others:

1. English, and even more so German, distinguishes between short and long vowels: *live–leave*, *kin–keen*, or *Mitte–Miete*, in contrast, for example, to Spanish. Unlike English, German plays down the differences between final voiced and voiceless plosives (*hat–had*, but German *Rad* and *Rat* are both voiceless). English, German and Spanish have an invariable word stress, whereas in Russian, stress can vary with inflection. French has a peculiar intonation pattern which is quite different from the Spanish, the English or the German one, which are themselves different again. All this might be described as *phonological* knowledge.

2. English verbs have a very limited inflection (*-ed* for past tense, *-s* for third person singular), with certain variations for irregular verbs, which contrasts strongly with some other European languages, where verb (and in many cases also noun) inflection is a source of endless problems for the learner. Whereas in German, noun inflection is indicated chiefly by the article, in Slavic languages there is no article and the noun assumes variable endings. Similar differences apply to adjectives. These features

47

of language fall under what in this context is termed *morphological* knowledge.

3. An attributive adjective is placed before the noun in English and
German; the order is in general reversed in French. But an attributive
relative clause will follow the respective noun in German. German is
further characterized by a peculiar splitting of the verb: the auxiliary verb
appears somewhere in the middle and the verb proper at the very end
of a sentence. Familiarity with features of this kind represents *syntactic*
knowledge.

4. Any language associates particular sound patterns with particular
meanings, that is, has a vocabulary (lexicon) consisting of function words
(*in, after, and, not*) and content words (*table, freedom, eat, rich*); in
addition it has a repertoire of idiomatic expressions and figures of speech.
Most languages admit word combinations (*second language acquisition*);
German treats them as single words (*Zweitspracherwerb*). All this is part
of *lexical* knowledge.

This enumeration of domains is by no means exhaustive, but it does
indicate the breadth of the problem facing the learner, who must acquire
a solid body of knowledge in each of these and several other domains,
and yet not study them in isolation. Language knowledge is a functional
whole, composed of varied yet interrelated elements. The functional interdependence of the entire linguistic knowledge poses a problem for the
learner: in what way and to what extent can he effectively single out from
the whole the elements that need to be acquired? To put it differently,
how should he go about assimilating phonological, morphological, syntactic, lexical, and other kinds of knowledge in a synchronized fashion? For
example, the acquisition of certain morphemes requires familiarity with
certain phonological combinations. As long as a learner remains ignorant
of the rules for splitting verbs in German, he cannot hope to place the
negative particle in its correct position (see below, section 6.2.3). Each
successive stage of acquisition requires the maintenance of a delicate
balance among diverse aspects of linguistic knowledge. In other words,
each language variety developed by a particular learner constitutes a unique
system composed of elements of phonological, morphological, syntactic,
and lexical knowledge (to mention only the major domains). With the
transition from one variety to the next, the learner must establish a new
balance until he reaches the end state (ideally, a perfect command of the
target language).

Accordingly, it is not easy to determine the structure of the acquisition
process. At the surface it can be identified by enumerating the newly

acquired forms, thus establishing a certain order of acquisition. However, the real change takes place within the system (the language variety), where a dual balance must be maintained: internally it consists of an interplay of the various forms of linguistic knowledge and externally it is the balance between linguistic and nonlinguistic knowledge. In both cases the balance is relatively unstable; its variations characterize the process of language acquisition.

There is of course the possibility of identifying the order in which the particular forms are acquired by making a longitudinal study of a learner. With luck, fairly similar acquisition sequences might be obtained for a number of learners. In a series of morpheme order studies (Dulay and Burt, 1974; survey in Burt and Dulay, 1980) – one of the most discussed research paradigms in the study of second language acquisition – the exact order was determined in which children and adults acquire eleven important English morphemes (e.g. plural *s*, genitive *s*, *-ing*, copula, etc.). There was considerable agreement across subjects,[2] although not without a number of exceptions, but the fact that these morphemes appear in this order does not tell us why language is acquired as it is. It might be interesting to learn that some trees blossom before others in the spring, but this would not tell us anything about the laws of plant life.

B.   Variability

It is obvious that the structure of the acquisition process varies across learners. The causal factors are many, among them the various propensity components, the biological endowment of the learner, his knowledge, the availability of a specific linguistic input; all these form a specific constellation which can never be exactly the same in any two learners. Notwithstanding this variability, language acquisition is evidently subject to certain regularities: the fact that things are so different all over the world, that a great variety of plants and animals populate our planet, does not deny the existence of natural laws. This is not to say that language acquisition is governed by deterministic laws, as are biological or physical processes. But unless we assume that the learning of a language, like any other process involving human beings, must follow certain regularities, there is no point in systematic investigation, and we should rather 'cultiver notre jardin'.

This statement of the obvious is a warning against two misconceptions: First, that the learner can be manipulated at will in the process of instruction. The acquisition process, in view of its variability, can indeed be influenced by a skilful control of the various factors at work, but to accomplish this it is necessary to take note of the underlying mechanisms, to know the 'laws' governing the process. The second misconception is that second language acquisition is essentially a uniform process with only superficial variations (on this see also Adjémian, 1976; Meisel, Clahsen, and Pienemann, 1981). Our view of this was expressed in answer to the questions: Are first and second language acquisition not the same thing? Are spontaneous and guided second language learning not identical in essence? As noted above, all these forms of language acquisition are subject to the same 'laws', but the determining factors may differ in each case, resulting in a different structure of the process, different tempo of acquisition, and different end state.

2.6 Tempo of acquisition

The three groups of factors discussed under the headings propensity, language processor, and access determine not only the structure of the process but also the tempo of language acquisition. The pressure of communicative needs is likely to accelerate the learner's progress (other things being equal), whereas limited access to linguistic material or limited communication opportunities is likely to slow it down. As to the language processor, it is not easy to say whether or not it can influence the tempo of acquisition independently of the other two factors, but it is plausible that a poor memory is a serious hindrance. Equally plausible is the idea that a person learning his forty-first language will have an easier time than someone struggling with his second one. But these are rather extreme cases.

Propensity and access are therefore more important here; and both tend to vary in the course of language acquisition. The learner's communicative needs can be better satisfied as his proficiency increases; as a result, the influence of this factor diminishes. The Turkish worker in Berlin may enter a new social environment (by moving or by marrying a German woman), and thus the 'social integration' factor would acquire a new impetus. At the same time, the German language would become more available to him. Variations of this kind cannot fail to affect the rate of progress in language acquisition. At some point, there is no more propensity left, at least not enough to drive the process. By then, at the latest, the end state has been reached.

2.7 End state

Ideally, the end state represents a perfect command of the language. The term 'language', should not disguise the fact that any language comprises many variants: dialects, registers, sociolects, and the like. No single speaker can be in command of all these variants and even native speakers differ tremendously in their effective command of the language. Indeed, a second language learner may succeed in outstripping the average native speaker in his mastery of the language, at least in certain domains, such as vocabulary or syntax (no Englishman of the Victorian era could boast the kind of English vocabulary used in his novels by the Polish-born writer Joseph Conrad). As a rule, however, the process of language acquisition ceases at a point long before a true mastery of the language can be claimed: 'fossilization'[3] has set in. Two aspects of such fossilization at a particular level of language proficiency are discussed below: (A) selectivity in fossilization and (B) backsliding into an earlier language variety.

A.   Selectivity in fossilization

Fossilization can affect particular components of language knowledge (in the sense of proficiency) at different points in time: it is selective. The best-known example is the premature termination of progress in acquiring the pronunciation of a second language – long before a satisfactory state is reached – whilst progress in syntax and vocabulary continues. The case of Joseph Conrad mentioned above, who is said to have never acquired an authentic English pronunciation, proves the point. The reasons are numerous; we can name only a few:

> a learner may simply feel it is unnecessary to improve his pronunciation any further, in the light of his communicative needs;
> he may feel the need (without being aware of it) to keep at a distance from his social environment, that is, to preserve at least a part of his previous social identity;
> the language processor itself may have undergone physiological changes with age (in the central nervous system) which prevent the learner from acquiring a native pronunciation of the target language (see the discussion on the critical period in language acquisition in section 1.1.3; and also Seliger, 1978; and Scovel, 1981);
> the learner may no longer notice the difference between his own production and that of his environment, and again this failure may have quite different reasons. Learners are nevertheless capable in principle of mastering the phonology of a foreign language to an extent that prevents native speakers from recognizing them (in blind testing) as non-natives (Neufeld, 1979).

In other words, although highly desirable, there is no simple way of accounting for the selective nature of fossilization.

B.   Backsliding

On occasions a learner may suddenly, in the midst of an exchange, slide back into an earlier stage of acquisition. This may last for only a few sentences, in which the learner ignores the appropriate endings of inflected nouns, verbs, etc. Relatively fluent speakers of a second language often note that fatigue after a prolonged period of conversation results in moments dominated by a sudden rise in the number of errors and a general sense of insecurity in the language. This is probably a sign of the repressed presence of earlier language varieties. The latter do not disappear without trace but rather are overridden by the new varieties, in the manner of a tree's annual rings, the last one being the end state. (This, incidentally, is not specific to SLA, see Arditty and Perdue, 1979.)

2.8 **Summary**

In this chapter an attempt has been made to draw an overall outline of language acquisition. It includes six dimensions, and some of these will be discussed in greater detail in the second part of the book, with particular emphasis on the interactions of the input to and properties of the language processor. The problem of motivation ('propensity') will be treated marginally, but what has so far been neglected for the sake of clarity, namely the interaction of the various factors, will at last receive the attention it deserves in view of its overriding influence upon the structure, tempo, and end state of language acquisition.

3
Some consequences for foreign language instruction

This book is concerned with second language acquisition, not with foreign language teaching (for an excellent survey of the present state of this field, see Els *et al.*, 1984; see also Faerch, Haastrup and Philipson, 1984). It might be useful, however, to see what our general view of language acquisition suggests for the broad field of second language instruction.

The picture of language acquisition which emerges from the preceding chapter is that of a quite complex process which systematically develops under the influence of a set of factors. What changes in the course of this process are parts of the language processor, i.e. the learner's faculty of producing and comprehending utterances in a given context. Exposed to the pressure of driving agents subsumed by the term 'propensity', the language processor is set to work on the novel linguistic material, adjusting its potentialities in the process and invoking all available knowledge for this purpose.

It is perfectly possible to influence, within certain limits, the structure, the tempo, and the termination of the acquisition process. The obvious way to do this consists in trying to control skilfully the interactive influence of the various factors. It is clear that the various factors differ in the degree to which they are amenable to this control. The factor easiest to control is access, from the point of view of the input as well as of opportunity to communicate. It is possible, although not quite as easy, to influence the propensity to acquire the target language. Most difficult to control is the language processor itself. The biological endowment consisting of our hearing, memory, etc., while being not invariant, can be influenced only within very narrow limits. The language processor is preset in a certain manner, leaving no room for manipulation. An attempt may at least be made to understand the way in which it operates, that is, the laws and principles of language processing in the human being. The working of the language processor is subject to gradual changes, but intentional outward intervention can do very little to accelerate these changes. The processor's workings should, however, be taken into account by organizing language instruction in ways that would not run counter to the principles of language processing (for example, when preparing the 'prefabricated' input to the processor).

To ensure effective guidance in language acquisition, three tasks must be solved:

1. The first is to determine the ways in which the human language processor functions in language acquisition. The underlying laws should be more obvious in the case of learners *not* subjected to some particular method of instruction, i.e., those who acquire a language in a manner practised for millennia. In other words, in order to identify the principles of language processing we would do better to start with studying spontaneous language acquisition. The more we learn about these principles, the earlier can we try to work 'hand in hand' with them (rather than against them) by making provisions to increase the access to linguistic input, by appropriately 'prefabricating' the input, and the like.

2. The second task is then to find out how the language processor should be assisted and put under pressure. Though any method of instruction is potentially tuned to these ends, the actual elbow room is simply not available. The most powerful drives, such as 'social integration', are absent in ordinary instruction and cannot be generated artificially. It is equally difficult for a teacher to build anything like 'communicative needs' into the process of language instruction. The unhappy conclusion is that the potentially strongest propensity factors cannot be put to work in guided language acquisition. The talk about 'motivation' in classroom work (e.g. Solmecke, 1983) is usually in reference to such secondary propensity factors as attitude to language and culture or specific communicative needs, like understanding the lyrics of pop songs.

3. The principal concern of second language teaching is to attain a particular end state in the shortest possible time, rather than to exert influence upon the *structure* of the acquisition process. So the third task would be to define this objective (cf. Els and Oud-Glas, 1983). In second language instruction in schools or universities certain descriptive standards are used to measure the learner's performance in terms of the number and gravity of the grammatical errors committed. This is an eminently practical approach to the problem, except that it does not make sense in view of the fact that the ability to understand a language and to produce it in actual communication is not the same as meeting a descriptive standard. As it is, most native speakers of the given language would probably fail on the sort of tests used for measuring language proficiency in schools

and universities. This is because actual language use involves many varieties of knowledge which no one has ever attempted to squeeze into textbooks or grammars (cf. section 2.3.B) and because ordinary language proficiency based on fully internalized knowledge of the language does not imply awareness of the underlying rules of descriptive grammars.

We are still some way from a full clarification of all three objectives. Although psycholinguistic research has provided some important insights into human language processing, it cannot be claimed that the crucial laws of language acquisition have been 'cracked' already. This realization casts doubt on the success of attempts to guide optimally the process of language acquisition in those few areas where it seems possible. As long as we have only vague ideas about how our mind (or brain) uses the available knowledge to build up more knowledge, and how knowledge is extracted from the material supplied from outside, we must rely on practical common sense in our attempts to structure the linguistic input in terms of a suitable acquisition sequence. It may also turn out that the learner is unable to put the material to any use, i.e. that his language processor must first be provided with some other kinds of knowledge.

If all this is essentially correct, then second language instruction appears in both a gloomy and a bright light:

(a)   In a gloomy light, because the objectives stated above are clearly unattainable in the foreseeable future. Anyone who claims that second language instruction must be arranged in a particular way on the evidence available from linguistics or neurophysiology or any other science, displays a fair measure of naivety if not presumption.

(b)   In a bright light, insofar as the three tasks, no matter how difficult, are not utopian. They can be approached step by step, and some progress has already been made. It might prove easier to solve these tasks than to set up an institutional framework for truly efficient second language instruction.

A language teacher or a designer of language courses or materials will be perfectly within his rights to reply that he cannot sit with his arms folded until answers are available. True enough. But the study of the mechanisms and laws of language acquisition is not an all-or-nothing process. Certain mistakes can be avoided by drawing on what we know (or seem to know) even today. One such mistake would be to overlook the inherent dynamics of human language processing and hence also language acquisition.

PART II
From the learner's point of view

In the second part of this book we will attempt to trace the ways in which learners utilize the linguistic input available to them in order to develop their individual language varieties and, in doing so, how they gradually approximate to the target language. Since we are not primarily interested in finding out how this works when the learner is under the influence of a specific teaching method, examples from spontaneous second language acquisition will generally be used. The process in question shows two kinds of regularity:

(a)   Every learner variety, no matter how elementary and inadequate it might be, constitutes a *system in itself* whereby the learner can meet at least some of his communicative needs. The efficiency of the system depends not only on the linguistic repertoire developed by the learner but also on the latter's proficiency in handling the system.

(b)   The transition from one learner variety to the next follows a certain pattern: it is a shift to a different and, as one would hope, more advanced system. Such a transition can take place only as long as the learner is in a position to notice a discrepancy between his particular language variety and the target itself. The scale of the problem grows as successive learner varieties approximate the target language more closely.

Chapter 4 gives an overview of the formidable task faced by the learner and, for purposes of analysis, this will be subdivided into four problems, which are then examined in more detail in chapters 5–8.

4
The learner's four tasks

4.1 The problem of analysis

The input available to the learner consists for the most part of complete, meaningful utterances embedded in a particular situational context. The perceived and processed information is of two kinds:

a complex sequence of acoustic signals which constitute the linguistic information proper, and

a complex of concurrent, chiefly visual signals which will be termed 'parallel information'.

One of the speaker's problems is to segment the stream of acoustic signals into constituent units and to bring the latter into line with the parallel information on concurrent events which constitutes the situational context of the utterance. This is the problem of analysis.

This may be illustrated by the following example. Suppose you are a Japanese visitor and you happen to be in Germany without knowing a single word of German. You are having breakfast in your hotel with a couple of Germans. One of the Germans turns to you and produces a sequence of speech sounds like this:

(1)   axkœnənzi:mi:rma:ldaszaltsraɪçənbɪtəʃœ:n

In this transcription the intonation contour of the utterance has been omitted, and it is assumed that the native speaker happens to have perfect High German pronunciation. We further assume that you have been able to identify all the sounds correctly – a very unlikely thing for an untrained ear (cf. Lambert, 1977; and Rösel, 1980). In normal spelling (1) would be written as, *Ach, können Sie mir mal das Salz reichen, bitte schön?* ('Oh could you please pass me the salt').

An awareness of the parallel information – the speaker's visual search over the table (actually preceding the utterance), the gestures possibly accompanying the acoustic event, the entire breakfast context, and the like – might enable you to grasp the overall meaning of the utterance without understanding it word by word. In a sense, the act of communication could not be any more successful if you were in perfect command of German. In order to learn the language, however, it is necessary to analyse the stream of speech sounds and separate out its constituents. That is, it must be broken up into sound segments, each corresponding to one word. If these segments are identified as [ax – kœnən – zi: – mi:r...], the analysis is successful, but if they are identified as [axkœn – ənzi:mi:r...], it is unsuccessful. This task is far from straightforward, since, contrary to common-sense views, there are scarcely any pauses in spoken language that would provide cues for word boundaries. (Phonetic transcription rather than orthography was used in (1) above in an attempt to make this slightly more suggestive.) Normally, we become aware of this fact only when confronted by a strange language; in the native language our familiarity with the constituent units leads us to perceive pauses where there are none. This can be tested by tuning in to some foreign radio stations and attempting to identify single words.

Suppose you have really succeeded in identifying certain units in the sound stream of the German speaker, and that you have become aware of two sound entities in particular: [zalts] and [das]. Let us further assume that precisely at the time of saying [das zalts] the speaker had pointed to the salt. Why should [zalts] rather than [das] be associated with the salt on the table? Well, this depends crucially on one's knowledge. An English native speaker might find it plausible that the sound sequence [zalts] means 'salt'. For a speaker of Japanese however there is not a trace of a cue like this; what remains is pure guesswork. Nevertheless, some basic knowledge of German – the knowledge that *das* appears mostly in front of nouns – leads to a fairly safe assumption that [zalts] stands for 'salt', even without knowing its meaning.

This illustration of the first problem of the learner severely oversimplifies it and leaves out many complications that inevitably crop up in communication, but it does serve to point out the complexity of what is by no means a merely perceptual problem. The process of understanding speech comprises innumerable cycles of formulating a hypothesis, testing it, and drawing a conclusion – all based on the knowledge available to the learner. The process will be discussed in more detail in chapter 5.

4.2 The problem of synthesis

Suppose a learner has coped with the problem of analysis to some modest extent: his knowledge of the language comprises fifty words: some nouns, some verbs, a few particles, and perhaps the personal pronouns *I* and *you*. (This happens to be the vocabulary of a foreign worker who had lived in West Germany for five years; see Klein, 1981.) In order to produce utterances that go beyond one-word sentences, the learner has to try and put these words together. This we call the learner's synthesis problem: strictly speaking, the problem of synthesis of words. A similar problem exists for sounds, which are characteristic of the given language and have different variants depending on whether a sound appears in initial or in final position, etc.

The problem of synthesis is relevant not only for the learner's own language production; he must also have grasped the respective rules in some measure in order to understand other speakers of the target language, especially when little parallel information is available to assist him in his interpretations. Generally, however, the two do not coincide (i.e., roughly speaking, the rules of syntax needed for language generation and those needed to comprehend the same language samples): the learner may well be able to analyse and grasp in outline utterances in the target language, even in the absence of essential parallel information, and yet be unable to produce them.

4.3   **The embedding problem**

The salt-passing illustration in example (1) has made it clear that effective communication is possible, under certain circumstances, solely on the basis of parallel information. Evidently, this is not the norm, or else language would be completely unnecessary. However, utterances are generally embedded in copious contextual information and whenever a person intends to speak, he is bound to fit his utterance into this information flow. This is the embedding problem of the speaker. For the learner the problem becomes all the harder the less advanced his language variety is. At an elementary level the communicative success of the learner will largely depend on his efficient use of the parallel information and, not least, on a skilful embedding of the few elementary linguistic devices at his disposal in his overall contextual knowledge; the latter will enable him to generate the parallel information (in the form of gestures and the like) that could supplement his deficient utterance. The dependence of language on contextual knowledge diminishes as the learner's language varieties become more advanced, but full independence does not exist, even in the case of the target variety. From the most elementary to the most advanced learner variety, effective communication presupposes a sort of balance of linguistic and contextual information; learning a language amounts to a gradual shift in this balance in favour of the former.

4.4 The matching problem

In order to improve his command of a second language, the learner must continuously compare his current language variety with the target variety. This matching problem tends to become more and more difficult as the discrepancy between the two diminishes. There is likely to come a point at which the learner, though somehow aware of it, is unable to identify the nature of the discrepancy. This is the fundamental reason why language acquisition comes to a halt at a stage where a marked difference between the learner's variety and the target variety remains, despite a considerable propensity on the part of the learner to move on.

The matching problem may be one of the causes of the erroneous predictions made by contrastive grammar (see section 1.5.2). Where the two languages (the learner's native language and the target language) differ distinctly in structure, the problem is relatively easy to solve: the learner can readily discover the discrepancy between his variety and the target. He may not be able to bridge the gap with one stride, but he will be aware of his task. However, structures of some similarity present much more of a problem: the learner may either remain completely unaware of or be unable to identify them with ease and with adequate precision. Eventually, having identified them, he may find himself unable to acquire the weakly contrasting linguistic elements. There are plenty of examples in the field of phonology: learners of English sometimes find it impossible to master the distinction between the vowels in *man* and *men*, just as French learners of German are often unable to produce the first of two quite similar vowels contrasted in the pair *Mitte–Miete*. In other words, to 'know that' is not the same as to 'know how'.

The four problems of the learner have been considered here in isolation for the sake of clarity. In actual fact the learner must cope with them in parallel, trying to follow their incessant interplay. He will find it impossible to make progress in analysis as long as he has not learned enough about how the elements of the language are interrelated and interdependent. Conversely, he cannot cope with the synthesis problem without assimilating the smaller entities of language from which utterances are formed, or without comparing his output with the target. Our dissection of the overall task into four problems is but one approach to try and solve the 'analysis problem' of language acquisition *research*. As the investigation proceeds, this way of cutting up the cake may turn out to be inappropriate, but for the time being the task stands as outlined above, and the four problems may now be dealt with one by one.

5
The problem of analysis

Trying to tackle the problem of analysis the learner may rely, on the one hand, on all of the knowledge, linguistic as well as nonlinguistic, which is currently available to him, and, on the other, on the structural properties of the input. These two components are examined in the first two sections of this chapter. The remaining three sections discuss some findings in language acquisition research which provide revealing insights into the problem of analysis.

5.1 The available knowledge

The knowledge a learner can utilize at any time to process the linguistic input falls into four categories:

(a) General knowledge about the nature of human languages and of verbal communication.
(b) Specific knowledge of the structure of his first language, or possibly of any other language he happens to know (the latter, as a special case, will be largely bypassed in our discussion).
(c) Knowledge of the target language which he has or presumes to have.
(d) All manner of nonlinguistic knowledge.

Before considering these types of knowledge in more detail, a word about the way the term 'knowledge' is used in this book is in order. It includes, firstly, both 'conscious' and 'tacit' knowledge; but it should also include 'uncertain' knowledge, that is, the learner's assumptions, of which he may be certain or uncertain at the time, which may however prove false or incomplete at a later stage. Thus, by 'knowledge' we also mean assumptions of varying degrees of 'stability' in two respects: 'subjective' uncertainty on the learner's part, and 'objective' correctness with respect to the structures of the target language.

A. General linguistic knowledge

All linguists agree that certain features (universals) are common to all languages, but there is less agreement as to what exactly these universals are, and what kind of role they play in language acquisition (cf. section

1.1.2 and, on universals, Greenberg, 1978). It would appear, nevertheless, that general properties of languages such as the following bear on the problem of analysis:

> an utterance can be dissected into words, the latter into syllables, and syllables into phonemes;
>
> phonemes can be divided into consonants and vowels;
>
> syllables tend to have a vocalic kernel, which is flanked by consonants;
>
> vowels and consonants tend to alternate in a syllable (hence, consonant clusters tend to indicate syllable boundaries;[1]
>
> a pause usually occurs at a word boundary (but not all word boundaries are indicated by a pause);
>
> there are words with predominantly grammatical meaning (function words: *in, and, the, if*, etc.) and words with predominantly lexical meaning (content words: *pipe, withdraw, pleasant, twenty*);
>
> function words tend to be shorter (typically one syllable), occur with greater frequency, and usually carry less stress than content words;
>
> the general rule is: one word, one meaning.

Our knowledge of the general properties of language as exemplified here would not suffice to perform an analysis of a sound sequence like the one in the salt-passing illustration in (1), that is, to dissect the sequence into its constituent words as required by the rules of the language. Such knowledge does, however, reduce the number of possible interpretations, for instance by suggesting a tentative segmentation into syllables.

B.   Specific knowledge of a first language

The learner's knowledge of a first language may have positive as well as negative consequences for the problem of analysis (and the other problems as well). For a positive illustration, we might substitute a Dutchman for the Japanese in our example. A Dutchman will find it relatively easy to identify at least two sound clusters, [zalts] and [kœnən], the two words being very similar in Dutch. This will provide further cues, such as where some of the word boundaries are. So he may be able to identify the two syllables after [zalts] as corresponding to a Dutch word that would be used on this occasion. And since in Dutch this kind of utterance would have a very similar structure (*Kunt U me het zout geven, alstublieft?*), he will expect [raɩçən] to correspond to the Dutch *geven*. There would be no trace of this positive influence of the first language in the case of a Japanese or a Chinese learner. These contrasts in first languages also exert their influence at a more abstract level: since both Dutch and German are characterized by inflection, the Dutchman expects the words in German to assume different endings; the Japanese learner might be deprived of this elementary cue and hence face a much bigger problem of analysis.

All these facilitating circumstances may, however, turn into a trap for the Dutchman: false assumptions may lead to an incorrect segmentation of the sound sequence. Other kinds of negative influences are perhaps more frequent. For instance, the learner may look for what are to him self-evident properties of (his native) language in the second-language input. In Chinese, for example, there are words which differ only in tone and a Chinese learner may therefore be tempted to interpret a German sound sequence as representing two different words on account of variations in intonation. Influences of this kind are usually classified as either 'positive' or 'negative transfer' (cf. section 1.5.2), although these terms usually refer to effects on the learner's *production*, as in the case of sentence patterns modelled on the speaker's first language. In this section we have been referring to first-language effects on the *segmentation* of input, where the learner acts as a listener rather than as a speaker.

C.   Available knowledge of the target language

All the available knowledge of the target language can be used by the learner to 'crack' the input under analysis. He may know, for instance, that in German a voiced 's' appears only in initial position, or else, that voiced fricatives and plosives never appear in final position; this could help him at least to determine some syllable boundaries. Familiarity with some words will indicate the boundaries of some other words. The recurrence of certain, rather short, sound clusters suggests that these are function words; having identified *der, die*, and *das* as articles, he may then try to interpret the following sound clusters as nouns, and so on.

In section 5.3 we exemplify how a few familiar elements in a sentence become the props on which the learner leans in his analysis of an utterance. In doing this, he may be completely misguided, of course. A learner of German whose limited knowledge comprises the article *die* ('the', feminine singular and plural of all genders) may be misled when encountering the same syllable [di:] in other configurations (as in *Didaktik*, which he might interpret as *die Taktik*; or as in *Diesel*, which he might take as comprising the article *die* and some unknown noun *Sel*).

D.   Nonlinguistic knowledge

As argued in section 2.4.A, a person exposed to the mere sounds of a strange language, for however long, cannot be expected to learn the language unless he is provided with plenty of parallel (contextual) information. In the salt-passing example the context is the entire breakfast scene. For such a context to be brought into meaningful relation to the speech sound sequence or its constituent elements, the learner must possess a wealth of nonlinguistic knowledge: he must know that the white stuff on the table is salt, that some people are in the habit of eating it on eggs, and so on. He must understand the significance of pointing as a gesture; he must know that an utterance is addressed to him if the speaker looks at him; he must have learned that strangers can be asked to do a favour provided you keep to certain rules of conduct, in particular, use certain figures of speech. (A learner who is ignorant in this respect will find 'nuts' such as *d'you mind* or *won't you* hard to 'crack'.) For the most part this knowledge seems self-evident; it is like the air we breathe: we don't notice it. And yet it is precisely this knowledge which is indispensable for solving the problem of analysis. This only becomes apparent when we meet a person who has a totally different cultural background and therefore does not share most of our cultural and social knowledge (cf. for instance Perdue, 1982, chapter 4).

Making use of all kinds of knowledge in mutual interaction, the learner tries to segment the flow of speech sounds into its constituent elements and to determine how these elements are related to the parallel information. In the following section we look at the structural properties of the input which aid the learner in his task of analysis.

5.2 Structural properties of the input

Among the structural properties of the (linguistic) input such phonological elements as the voiced/unvoiced distinction, the occurrence of consonant clusters, and the like should be mentioned. But since phonological aspects were considered in the preceding section, we will assume that the entire speech sound sequence has been roughly segmented into syllables, with perhaps a measure of uncertainty about some boundaries. Thus the learner is confronted with syllable clusters ready for further processing. At this point the following structural properties of an utterance may be taken to guide the learner in his task:

(a)   The frequency of individual words occurring in the utterance.
(b)   The place held in the utterance.
(c)   Features of intonation.
(d)   The adequacy and plausibility of implied correspondences to the parallel information.

Properties (b) and (c) come under what is often termed 'perceptual salience', i.e. the degree to which they attract attention. There are segments within the utterance which are perceptually more salient than others, and this is where the analysis begins.

A. Frequency of occurrence

It seems likely that the most frequently recurring words stand a better chance of being perceived, recognized, and hence learned prior to the less frequent words – other things being equal. There are however some problems with this idea:

1. The frequency of a word (especially a content word) varies from topic to topic. Foreign workers, for instance, tend to acquire very quickly not only such common words as *work*, *shop*, *girl*, but also relatively infrequent terms such as *tax collector* or *unemployment office*.

2. Many of the most frequent words appear at a very late stage in some learner varieties. For example, foreign workers in Germany often fail to use the article in their utterances (and the article *die* happens to be the most frequent word in German). It is an open question whether such words are really identified only later, or whether they have been successfully analysed but are omitted in production. In other words, the correct identification of a word (problem of analysis) does not imply that the learner has succeeded in using the same word in his own production (problem of synthesis).

3. The learner cannot start by estimating the frequency of words, he can only try to estimate the frequency of (as yet incomprehensible) syllables or syllable combinations. There are many frequently occurring syllables however that cannot be interpreted on their own, such as the inflectional suffix *-ing*. That is, the learner must first realize that this syllable is not a self-contained lexical unit.

4. Function words are as a rule more frequent than content words, yet the former rarely have any counterpart in the parallel information. In the word cluster *das Salz*, the first syllable is by far more frequent overall than the second, but there is not nearly as much parallel information available for matching as in the case of *Salz*; *das* may consequently present a greater problem of analysis than *Salz*.

All this does not mean that frequency of occurrence is of no relevance for analysis, only that its relevance may be smaller than one is inclined to assume.

B.   Position in an utterance

Within any speech sound sequence (which may represent an utterance) there are always some segments which are more readily available to analysis than others. In fact, the sequence must first be processed auditorily and then preserved in memory for at least a few moments. It is reasonable to assume that the processing gives priority to

> the opening segment(s) of an utterance,
> the concluding segment(s),
> the segment(s) immediately preceding and following any identifiable pauses.

Human perception in general is particularly sensitive to distinct alterations in the perceptual domain. Consequently, the change from sound to silence and from silence to sound is perceptually more conspicuous than continuous sound sequences. (Obviously, such changes are not the *only* criterion of salience.) Moreover, research on memory has shown that retention is better for the first and the last than for any other elements in a series of otherwise equivalent stimuli (position effect; cf. also Foppa, 1965, section 3.1).

The value of the 'more salient positions' is bound to be affected by the relative familiarity of the elements appearing in the sequence. To illustrate this we return to (a simplified version of) our salt-passing example. Suppose the question at the breakfast table is put in the following way (the apostrophes indicate the approximate syllable boundaries):

(2)   kœnən'zi:'mi:r'das'zalts'raɪçən

Case A: Suppose the learner has no knowledge of German and therefore starts his analysis by focussing upon the beginning and the end of the utterance:

(3)   kœnənzi:mi:rdaszaltsraɪçən

We would thus expect – other things being equal – the word *reichen* to be identified prior to the word *Salz*.

Case B: Suppose the learner is able to identify *das Salz* on the basis of his incipient knowledge of the language. This might mean that his attention may shift to the adjacent constituents of the utterance:

(4)   kœnənzi:mir (*das Salz*) raɪçən

At this stage the learner is likely to succeed in 'cracking' the clause-final word: *reichen*.

68

Case C: Suppose the learner happens to recognize just one word in the sequence: precisely *reichen*. This would make the preceding word the 'weak spot';

(5)   kœnənzi:mi:rdaszalts (*reichen*)

Note that in all these cases those elements which are already familiar have to be processed as well, but this is done in the ordinary way, that is, as in the case of any other speaker of the language. Such elements are not subject to the kind of analysis we are concerned with here.

Nothing has been said above about the *relative* amenability of parts of the utterance to analysis; it may well be that in, say, Case A the beginning is more amenable than the end. There is possibly no general answer to this question without a consideration of the many other factors responsible for perceptual salience, and hence recognition and retention. We now turn to one group of such factors: the prosody of utterances.

C.   Prosodic properties

The term prosody mainly refers to such features of utterances as loudness, pitch, and duration of segments; other terms used in this context are: intonation, stress, and rhythm (see for example Lehiste, 1970; Kohler, 1977; Wunderli, Benthin, and Karasch, 1978). Roughly speaking, these features set off certain segments of an utterance. Crucial among the prosodic properties of speech is pitch; loudness and duration of segments are secondary in the most widely used European languages (on this, see Isačenko and Schädlich, 1966; Heike, 1969; on the role of prosody in speech perception see Nooteboom, Brokx, and de Rooij, 1978). Words marked by a change in pitch catch our attention. This kind of stress tends to fall on content words rather than function words, and words emphasized by raised pitch are ordinarily more perceptually salient than other words. The concluding part of our salt-passing example could have the following contour (pitch is roughly indicated by the rising and falling line under the utterance):

(6)   ... mi:rdaszaltsraiçən

From the perspective of a person who has no knowledge of the language whatever, the gesture by which the speaker points to the salt while saying [daszalts] may be crucial. The stress put on [zalts] makes it more likely to be associated with the salt than with the unstressed [das]. Though there can be no absolute certainty, stress can serve as an important cue

69

in the listener's unravelling of an utterance. At the same time, stress explains to some extent why content words are usually acquired more easily than function words, even though the latter are much more frequent. Of course, this is not the only reason: content words are certainly more important for communication than function words. This can be clearly seen when one compares the comprehensibility of an utterance where all the function words have been deleted with one where all the content words have been deleted; in the former case the deficient utterance may still be comprehensible, in the latter you cannot make anything of it. But the different communicative importance does not help our learner, if he still has to identify which syllable (sequence) is a function word and which one a content word; we will return to this in the following section.

Languages vary in the extent to which they make use of the various prosodic properties of speech. Tonal languages such as Chinese employ variations in pitch to distinguish the meaning of otherwise identical words. Consequently, Chinese speakers have much less leeway in using pitch for creating prominence or sentence modality than is done in English, German, and other European languages. Native speakers of English who are learning German will therefore find it much easier to utilize prosodic cues compared with native speakers of Chinese. That is not to say that the former may not be misled in this respect, because there are some differences in intonation between English and German; nor that a Chinese speaker could not distinguish stressed from unstressed elements; but it is more difficult for him to do so.

D.   Correspondence to parallel information

The words composing an utterance can be brought into relation to things or events in the environment (the wider context) with varying success. It is fairly easy to interpret the relation between the word 'salt' and the object referred to. Perhaps the greatest difficulties arise in the case of certain particles of the kind used very often in colloquial German: 'Du spinnst *wohl?*' or 'Was willst du *denn?*' (the equivalents in English might be: 'you must be crazy' and '*Why*, what do you want?', but the first of these phrases would have to be preceded by *surely* to match it with *wohl*). These are the two extremes, and there is a fine gradation between them. In general, content words are more likely to have some correspondence to the parallel information than function words, with many exceptions, of course (a function word like *up* in *upstairs* can be readily made explicit by a suitable gesture, whereas content words such as *electron*, *prostate*, or *freedom* cannot.

To avoid misunderstanding, it should be repeated that the problem of analysis cannot be solved solely on the basis of parallel information; even in the case of concrete words the learner has to infer a great deal from his knowledge. Suppose the man at the breakfast table says only one word, [zalts], while pointing at the salt-cellar: the syllable might mean a number of things, as for instance, 'container', 'salt', 'sugar', 'please', 'help (yourself)', 'well', and so on. The knowledge derived from the situation is only one of many cues that can help us in establishing the meaning of a word; in some cases this cue may prove decisive, in others it may be quite useless.

So far, we have briefly reviewed some more important structural properties of the input. In his effort to cope with the problem of analysis the learner has to make these properties interact with his entire available knowledge. How this is accomplished is far from clear. In the following sections we examine three cases (each involving a number of learners) of partially unsuccessful analyses of the input. The first two come from the Heidelberg Research Project for Pidgin German (1977) in which the spontaneous acquisition of German by Spanish and Italian migrant workers was studied; the last one is borrowed from a study by Wong-Fillmore (1976) on the acquisition of English by Spanish children.

5.3   **Example 1: Repetition test for personal pronouns**

There is no easy way of knowing what the learner actually understands of an utterance in the target language: we cannot see inside his head. Consequently, researchers generally fall back on what the learner can produce, trying to draw indirect conclusions about the processes of analysis performed on the input. Understandably, such conclusions are burdened with a measure of uncertainty.

Some evidence of what the learner has perceived and retained in the short term can be gained from making him reproduce utterances. The learner hears a sentence and is expected to repeat it. The obvious implication is that this kind of repetition does not present any production problems, and this may hold for relatively simple sentences.

The results discussed below were obtained in the Heidelberg Research Project for Pidgin German from 24 Spanish and 24 Italian migrant workers at different levels of advancement in the acquisition of German (the language spoken in the country of their temporary residence). The material was described in detail with the aid of a 'variety grammar' (Klein and Dittmar, 1979, Part I). A number of word classes were further analysed, among them personal pronouns. The relevant data come from a first session with all 48 learners and from another session with 18 Spanish learners held two years after the first. It was during the second session that the informants were asked to repeat nine German sentences comprising personal pronouns (for details, see Klein and Rieck, 1982). We are not concerned here with the analysis of the personal pronouns as such but rather with the results of the repetition test. The results for one of the nine sentences are displayed in Table 3. The sentences were all loosely interrelated in content, so that the learners could guess that *ihn* referred to a passport ('passport' in German is a masculine noun, hence *ihn* means 'him'; in our translation this is changed to 'it'). The speakers (SP) are ordered according to their proficiency in German, from lowest to highest. Evidently, SP-35 has a very limited command of German while SP-11 is pretty close to the local vernacular. In Table 3, we ignore some of the speakers' peculiarities in pronunciation since they are irrelevant to our present concern.

We now turn to some striking features of the material.

1. All speakers without exception reproduce the first as well as the last word, which concurs with the notion that both the beginning and the end of an utterance are privileged in processing. Though this is not a piece of conclusive evidence (there may be alternative reasons for the correct reproduction), it supports the idea that there are distinct parts in the utterance which offer themselves for analysis more readily than others.

2. Nearly all the speakers reproduce *zu Hause* ('at home'), though in a number of variants; there are problems in particular with the preposition *zu*, for which the position effect cannot be held responsible. Though *Hause* does not carry the main stress of the sentence, it is stressed considerably more than the adjoining words; in fact, between the words *vielleicht* and *Eltern* it is the most strongly stressed word, giving way only to *Eltern*. Why should it then be reproduced more reliably than the latter? There are at least two possible reasons for this:

(a) It is the first lexical term after a series of unstressed syllables (*hat sie ihn zu*), so it may be more salient than *Eltern*.

(b) *Haus* (meaning both 'house' and 'home') is one of the words foreign workers tend to learn very early, whereas they have little opportunity to hear or speak in German of 'parents'.

3. Not one speaker reproduces the pronoun *ihn* – not even SP-11 who speaks fairly fluent German. This contrasts strongly with the reproduction of the pronoun *sie* (she) by learners at an intermediate or higher level. What is even more striking is that the speaker's native language normally

Table 3. *Results of the repetition task*

Informant	'Vielleicht (Perhaps	hat has	sie she	ihm it	zu Hause at home	bei ihren Eltern with her parents	vergessen' forgotten)
						Model sentence	
					Reproduced version		
SP-35	vielleicht				zu Hause		vergesse
SP-22	vielleicht (1)*			el pasaporte (4)	Hausen (2)		vergesse (3)
SP-25	vielleicht				deine Hause		vergesse
SP-21	vielleicht				en Hause		vergesse
SP-04	vielleicht			Pass	en Hause		vergesse
SP-12	vielleicht			seine Pass	nach Hause	seinen Eltern	vergesse
SP-18	vielleicht				von die Hause	/ . . . ? . . . /	vergesse
SP-30	vielleicht				en zu Hause	von ihren Eltern	vergessen
SP-36	vielleicht				en zu Hause	bei ihren Eltern	vergessen
SP-08	vielleicht	hat	sie		in ihre Haus	bei ihren Eltern	vergessen
SP-15	vielleicht	hat	sie		ihren Haus	bein seine Eltern	vergessen
SP-06	vielleicht	hat	sie		in ihre Haus	bei ihre Eltern	vergessen
SP-24	vielleicht	haben	sie		zu Hausen	bei ihre Eltern	vergessen
SP-19	vielleicht	hat	sie		zu Hausen	bei ihre Eltern	vergessen
SP-29	vielleicht	hat	sie		zu Hause	bei ihre Eltern	vergessen
SP-11	vielleicht	hat	sie		zu Hause	bei ihre Eltern	vergessen

Note: * Numerals in parentheses indicate actual word order

omits 'she' as subject whereas the counterpart of *ihn* ('him', in English) *cannot* be omitted as object. Again we would suggest two possible explanations:

(a)   It may well be that *ihn* is in the least salient position of the whole sentence; it is without any stress and it is distant from both the beginning and the end of the utterance.

(b)   In German, pronouns in nominative are distinctly more frequent than pronouns in accusative, hence the former are generally acquired much earlier (for details see Klein and Rieck, 1982); learners at an intermediate or higher level may be familiar with *sie* but not with *ihn*, no matter what this particular utterance teaches them.

The results of the repetition test are a good illustration of how various factors interact in the process of analysis: an illustration, but not evidence, unless we view them as evidence of how little is known about the interplay of all these factors.

5.4   **Example 2: Translation test for modal verbs**

Another possibility of gathering evidence of how learners analyse utterances as input to the language processor is to have them translate orally from the target language into their native language. The sample sentence is read out slowly, and the learner gives a free translation. This procedure excludes in principle the interfering effect of production problems if we assume that the learners have no difficulty in expressing themselves in their native language (the relevant production being of a simple, colloquial type). It has one disadvantage, however: the learner may be able to *guess* a number of things correctly. But even guesses can tell us something about the ways of processing the input.

The data below were obtained in precisely this way at the same session as the previous set of data. Spanish-speaking learners heard a (tape-recorded) simple story in German consisting of 29 sentences; the original study was mainly concerned with the modal verbs which occurred in the sentences, but this is irrelevant to our problem (on modal verbs, see Dittmar, 1980). Subsequently, the sentences were repeated one by one, each being translated by the learner into Spanish. In our illustration below we quote the translations of three sentences by four learners.

(The story tells of a Spanish worker who is completely exhausted because of his wife's illness; he has to take care of the child, but cannot go on holiday. The clause preceding the one quoted below read: 'In the night the child is crying . . .')

(7)   . . ., *und ich kann nicht schlafen*
         (and I cannot sleep)
SP-22   esta noche no he dormido
         (I didn't sleep tonight)
SP-25   dormir
         (sleep)
SP-21   que hoy no he dormido nada
         (that I didn't sleep tonight at all)
SP-11   no puedo dormir
         (I cannot sleep)

(8)   . . ., *können wir im Juli nicht wegfahren*
         (we cannot go away in July)
SP-22   que en Julio no he trabajado
         (that I didn't *work* in July; in German: nicht *gearbeitet* habe)
SP-25   en Julio
         (in July)
SP-21   que en Julio no me voy de permiso con el coche
         (that I do not go on holiday with the car in July)
SP-11   no podemos en Julio marcharnos
         (we cannot go off in July)

(9)   . . ., *sonst können wir nächstes Jahr nicht nach Spanien zurückgehen*
         (otherwise we cannot go back to Spain next year)
SP-22   en esto año va mi hijo a España y no volvera más
         (this year my son goes to Spain and will not *come back* again; German:
         zurückgehen)
SP-25   me voy a España y no vuelvo mas
         (I go to Spain and don't come back again)
SP-35²   el niño se lo llevan a España a Madrid
         (they bring my child to Spain to Madrid)
SP-11   porque de no ver asi, no podemos el año que viene ir a España
         (because otherwise we will not be able to go back to Spain in the
         coming year)

(10)   *Ja, ja, man kann nicht so, wie man will*
         (Yes, yes, one cannot do as one would want)
SP-22   que no he vuelto a ver a mi hijo
         (that I didn't come back to see my son)
SP-25   si, si, si
         (yes, yes, yes)
SP-21   que mi hijo no le veo
         (that I don't see my son)
SP-11   si, si, si, las cosas no salen como uno quiere
         (yes, yes, things do not go as one would wish)

75

The problem of analysis

The first three learners are beginners (SP-21 being slightly more advanced). In contrast, SP-11 is very advanced, and his excellent translations are quoted here only to show that the task can be managed by an advanced learner.

The translations of the first three learners exemplify two points which deserve attention:

1. Vastly different translations were offered by SP-22 and SP-25, even though the two are at about the same level, at least in speech production. SP-25 seems to have understood very little indeed; he tends to produce isolated words and makes little effort to link them in a meaningful way (his translation of (9) being an exception). In contrast, SP-22 speaks a lot, but his translations are wrong in many places. Having scrutinized all his utterances, we concluded that his understanding of the German sentences was more or less the same as that of SP-25, except that SP-22 was quick in making up a story which sometimes happened to fit. (He is to SP-25 as Holmes is to Dr Watson, except that his interpretation of the small cues is often somewhat less felicitous.) This shows that learners differ very much in their willingness to take risks and jump to conclusions.

2. Strangely enough, several speakers (SP-21, SP-22, SP-25 and SP-35 – the latter having been included for this very reason) refer to *hijo* (son) or *niño* (child) in their translations; the corresponding German sentences contained nothing of this kind, although the child was mentioned once in the sentence preceding (7). The number of these references indicates that they are not accidental; there must be some equivalent in the German text. In the case of (9) it may have been the word (*sonst*) ('otherwise' or 'else'), with which only very advanced learners seem to be familiar. The German for 'son' (*Sohn*), on the other hand, is a fairly common word.[3] Now for native speakers of German the two sound sequences (*Sohn* and *sonst*) differ in the final consonant cluster and in vowel duration: the former has a long closed 'o', the latter a short open one. Spanish does not distinguish between short and long vowels; moreover, it does not have consonant clusters at the end of words, and in learner varieties they tend to be mutilated (cf. Tropf, 1983). Similarly, in sentence (10) two speakers seemed to have discovered *Sohn* in *so* ('thus', 'so'). Our examples have made it clear how a syllable can be misconstrued as a familiar word, resulting in a distorted interpretation of the utterance. They further show that the learner may 'frame' an input initially in terms of the phonetic rules of his native language. Erroneous analyses of the kind recorded in our test could not occur if a sound sequence were perceived in a linguistically unbiased fashion.

Our exemplification is no exceptional case. In the example below, SP-35 seems to interpret *aber* ('but') as *Abend* ('evening', 'at night') and arrives at a bizarre interpretation with which he is not quite happy.

(11)   *Aber ich will das Geld nicht verlieren*
        (But I don't want to lose the money)
        Por la noche, por la noche, la noche la ha perdido
        (at night, at night, night, he lost her)

The two points made above make it clear that we must be very cautious in our assumptions about what the learner actually 'hears' and how he interprets what he has (or seems to have) heard.

5.5   Example 3: Prefabricated patterns

In a paper on the acquisition of English by native speakers of Japanese, Hakuta (1974) notes that his compatriots tend to acquire syntactically complex patterns of speech by perceiving them as an entity. Standard examples are such set phrases as *How are you?, Nice to see you, What a day!*, and the like.

In her study of spontaneous second language acquisition by children whose first language was Spanish and the target language English, Wong-Fillmore (1976) concluded that these 'formulaic expressions' are not only far from rare in early language varieties but in fact make up a substantial portion of the learner's repertoire. Indeed, their skilful use seems to contribute greatly to the communicative success, and hence the social integration of the learner. Such integration is in turn a major precondition for gaining access to the target language. Two points are of special interest in this context.

(a)   The learner may be forced to use entities of the target language before having completed their analysis. In other words, the analysis problem need not necessarily be solved before the synthesis problem is taken up. A synthesis may be attempted after a preliminary analysis, with the prospect of a detailed analysis at a later point. Conventional phrases like the ones quoted above qualify for such treatment in the first instance, especially since they constitute semantic entities resisting analysis; at the same time, they are syntactically rather complex.

(b)   The pressure to analyse utterances in the target language may vary from case to case. Formulaic expressions are (i) comparatively short, (ii) fairly frequent, (iii) semantically 'rounded off', and (iv) mostly isolated from other utterances. They are thus readily identified as entities and used as such. The pressure to analyse them is accordingly rather weak (for a discussion see also Raupach, 1984).

The problem of analysis

The first of the two points above has already brought us to the problem of synthesis and the interaction of analysis and synthesis. But before we turn to the synthesis problem, we must point out that our discussion of the analysis problem has been by no means exhaustive; there are many aspects which have not been discussed. To mention two examples, it should be clear that not all the linguistic elements successfully analysed by the learner are retained and utilized in the construction of the incipient language variety. This utilization will depend on the *communicative value* attributed to the given entity, the learner's judgement in this respect being contingent on a variety of factors. A second important aspect of analysis which we have not dealt with is connected with the finding mentioned above (section 2.4.A) that native speakers tend to adjust their speech production (in speed, choice of words, etc.) to the learner's processing capacity – a phenomenon described as 'foreigner talk'.

6
The problem of synthesis

As we saw in the preceding chapter, the problem of analysis comprises two major components: the knowledge available to the learner and the input on which the analysis is to be performed. In the synthesis problem, there is a counterpart to the first component, but there is no component comparable to the input in analysis, unless it be the speaker's 'communicative intention'. In a sense, this communicative intention is the raw material on which the speaker has to work with all his available knowledge in order to produce an utterance which he considers understandable and appropriate in a given context. But the analogy is obviously rather fuzzy: the speaker cannot learn from his communicative intention in the same way as he can indeed learn from the input with its various structural properties. The essential component is therefore the learner's available knowledge, particularly but not exclusively his knowledge of the target language, acquired through earlier input analyses (we know that such knowledge varies in reliability, from solid facts to vague suppositions or even to false assumptions). Before attempting to synthesize an utterance, the speaker must have at his disposal some elementary entities that can be put together. This is not to say that he must be fairly advanced in his analysis when starting a synthesis: he may try to form some utterances on the basis of a rather limited repertoire, which do not conform at all to the standards of the target language. These early attempts at synthesis are indispensable if the learner is to gain broader access to the target language and thus perform more and more advanced analyses. Finally, synthesis is for the learner a test of his analyses, especially if it turns out to have gone the wrong way, in which case he will feel the need to correct himself; i.e., to perform the synthesis – as well as the analysis – anew.

The problem of synthesis concerns above all the field of syntax, where the learner is faced with the task of aligning words as components of a structure – the utterance; but it is also present in phonology. A learner may have identified the phonemes of the target language, but this does not imply that he is in command of the 'phonotactics' of the language, i.e., the ways in which these phonemes are combined into syllables and words. Nevertheless, in our discussion below we have chosen to concentrate on syntax. (On phonology, see Tropf, 1983, chapter 9.)

As in the analysis problem, the knowledge available to the learner at a given time is of four kinds; (1) general knowledge of language and communication, (2) knowledge of the first language, (3) incipient knowledge of the target language, and (4) nonlinguistic knowledge. Having dealt with these categories individually in section 5.1, we will now focus rather more upon their interaction. With this in mind, let us first see how the four kinds of knowledge are involved in the construction of the learner's elementary utterances. Subsequently, we will try to show how the rules of this 'basic syntax' of basic learner varieties are gradually superseded by the rules of the target variety.

6.1 The syntax of basic learner varieties

This section attempts to outline a few principles that seem to underlie the syntax of basic (i.e. early) learner varieties. These principles must somehow be related to the four major linguistic devices on which the syntax of a language is based:

> word order,
> word classes,
> inflection and the corresponding devices (e.g. particles),
> intonation (although its role in syntax is disputed by some researchers).

Without these four linguistic devices, it is impossible to state the rules according to which utterances of a natural language are organized. Their relative weight, however, may vary from language to language. Chinese for instance does not have the kind of largely unequivocal assignment of lexical units to word classes that we know from classical Greek or in most Western European languages; but even in Chinese there are lexemes that cannot be used at will as verb, noun, preposition, etc., which shows that the language provides for some kind of differentiation in this respect. Similarly, languages differ in the degree to which they follow word order constraints; but there is no language where words can be grouped arbitrarily.

The adult learner is likely to be more or less aware of the existence and perhaps the nature of these devices (in contrast to the child learning a first language): they are part of his general linguistic knowledge. What he does not know, at the outset, is how the devices function in the target language. Nevertheless, his overall knowledge of their existence will help him in acquiring this more specific knowledge. In basic learner varieties, there is typically no inflection. The smallest elements emerging from the learner's initial analyses of the linguistic input turn up in a basic form, as a sort of word stem, without any morphological variation. These elements we will call *morphs*. In this sense, a morph is a word used in a (standard) invariable form[1] where the rules of the target language would often require differentiated forms. English can supply only very few examples: the omission of past-tense endings (*-ed*), plural marking (*-s*), etc.; the phenomenon in question is far more apparent in languages with rich inflectional systems.

Morphs are not easily assigned to word classes. Take for example the morph [doila] in the language variety of a Spanish migrant worker living in Germany: it is used to refer to *deutsch* (adjective 'German'), or to *Deutschland* ('Germany'), or to *Deutscher* (noun 'German'). The morph [abai] refers to *Arbeit* ('job'), *Arbeiter* ('worker'), (*ich*) *arbeite* ('I work'), or *arbeiten* ('to work'). This simplification results from the fact that in the beginning the learner cannot perform a sufficiently precise analysis of the input to identify all the subtleties of the various inflections and word-class assignments obtaining in the target language. Further advancement in this respect, and particularly the gradually accumulating experience in synthesis, will enable the learner to make further distinctions. There is one kind of word class partition which comes very early; this is the distinction between morphs used predominantly as content words and morphs serving predominantly as function words (e.g. [arbai] vs. [niç], for 'not'); but this is far from a characterization of the word-class partition of the target language.

Summing up, we would say that at an early stage of synthesis the learner has a limited repertoire of standard word entities, termed *morphs*, which most often

> show no grammatical variation,
> cannot be unequivocally assigned to a word class,
> are used predominantly as either content or function words (the former being in the majority).

The learner's repertoire of basic entities may include figures of speech and prefabricated phrases (to which we referred in section 5.5), but these are of little relevance for the problem of synthesis because the learner views them as unanalysed entities. Hence we may safely leave them aside.

The problem of synthesis

We will likewise ignore erroneous analyses, as when the learner assimilates forms such as *I'll* or *don't* from the input at his disposal and later uses them as if they were self-contained morphs.

From what has been said so far about morphs as the functional entities of basic learner varieties it follows that assigning such morphs to word classes (N for nouns, V for verbs, A for adjectives) only means that they have *counterparts* in the target language which belong to these classes, from which the morphs actually derive, and which are the ultimate target in the gradual evolution of the morphs. We are thus entitled to state only that a morph like *Arbei* (in lieu of *Arbeit*, for 'job, work, labour') is a noun *by analogy*. This appears to make sense for purposes of comparison, and is perfectly feasible in many cases, but it does not do justice to the properties of learner varieties as such. In order to emphasize this fact, care will be taken to mark the morph classes as N', V', A', etc., on the understanding that the corresponding words of the target language belong to the classes N, V, A, etc.

It should be clear from the discussion so far that to begin with the learner can actually rely on only two of the four syntactic devices mentioned above: word order and intonation, with possibly a semblance of word-class differentiation as a rudimentary third device. Now how does he make use of these devices? What we are trying to show here is that the learner tends to go by 'functional' or 'pragmatic' principles or rules, rather than any 'grammatical' rules as specified in the syntax of a language. An analysis of the data obtained from the Heidelberg Research Project for Pidgin German (1979, chapter 3; see also Klein and Dittmar, 1979), combined with some evidence dispersed in the literature (see, especially, the excellent study by Huebner, 1983), suggests the following tentative list of pragmatic principles that seem to guide the learner in his early attempts at synthesis:

(a)   Put 'given information' before 'new information' (principle of increasing communicative dynamics, cf. Sgall, Hajičová, and Benešová, 1973).

(b)   Put what is *spoken about* before what is to be *said about it* (principle of theme–rheme segmentation).

(c)   Keep elements linked in terms of meaning close together (principle of semantic connectivity).

(d)   Place elements of predominantly functional value consistently before (or consistently behind) the corresponding elements of predominantly lexical value (principle of consistent serialization).[2]

(e)   Place orientational elements (place, time, modality, etc.) at the beginning of an utterance (principle of orientation).

(f)   Mention events in their factual temporal order (principle of natural order, cf. section 7.2 below).

(g)   Indicate sentence modality (interrogative, declarative, requesting) by intonation (principle of sentence modality marking by intonation).

(h)   Mark rhematic information by intonation (principle of rheme marking by intonation).

These 'principles' are guidelines which the learner tends to follow in the early stages of language acquisition, rather than rigid rules. Many of them pertain to the informational aspects of an utterance (a, b, e, h). We have taken care to separate the 'given–new' principle from the 'theme–rheme' one, because although they tend to go together, this is not necessarily so: for instance, anaphoric elements, by definition addressed to 'given' information, may be rhematic ('Either of them will know, but you would be better to ask *her*, not *him*'). On occasions, the principles may contradict each other, and it is up to the speaker to decide which to follow. All in all, the initial construction of utterances by learners can be conveniently described with principles like these. What has been ignored however is the fact that the learner's utterances are highly geared to contextual information – i.e. by the omission of information implied by the context. This 'embedding problem' will be taken up in chapter 7.

A similar, though different formulation of such pragmatic principles was proposed by Givón (1979, see also Givón 1984a for a more comprehensive view). Givón views his principles as applicable not only to learner varieties evolving in second language acquisition but also to pidgins. His central idea is that all utterances (also those in ordinary languages) are structurally determined by either of two modes (or any intermediate form between the two): the pragmatic and the syntactic mode (in Givón 1984b, he changes the term 'pragmatic' to 'pre-syntactic'; but since his view became known under the former label, we will keep it here). For each language, and indeed each communicative situation, a specific balance of the two modes is maintained. Colloquial speech, for instance, is dominated by the pragmatic mode, while carefully planned written language is governed by the syntactic mode. Many rudimentary languages – i.e. basic learner varieties or pidgins – have nothing, or very little, of the latter mode, the construction of an utterance being governed by the pragmatic mode. The typical features of the two modes are listed in Table 4.

The mode features proposed by Givón converge to some extent with the eight principles listed above. Among the differences we note Givón's identification of word classes even in the most basic varieties of language. Which formulation is preferable, is a matter of dispute. But any further discussion would be pointless given our present state of knowledge.

Table 4. *The two poles of the communicative mode*

Pragmatic mode	Syntactic mode
(a) topic-comment structure	subject-predicate structure
(b) loose conjunction	tight subordination
(c) slow rate of delivery (under several intonation contours)	fast rate of delivery (under a single intonational contour)
(d) word-order is governed mostly by one PRAGMATIC principle: old information goes first, new information follows	word-order is used to signal SEMANTIC case-functions (though it may also be used to indicate pragmatic-topicality relations)
(e) roughly one-to-one ratio of verbs-to-nouns in discourse, with the verbs being semantically simple	a larger ratio of nouns-over-verbs in discourse, with the verbs being semantically complex
(f) no use of grammatical morphology	elaborate use of grammatical morphology
(g) prominent intonation-stress marks the focus of new information: topic intonation is less prominent	very much the same, but perhaps not exhibiting as high a functional load, and at least in some languages totally absent

Source: T. Givón, 1979, p. 98.

We will now consider a number of examples from the speech of one learner as investigated by Becker and Klein (1979) and further analysed by Klein (1981) and Dittmar (1982). The learner is a Spanish migrant worker who, at the time of the interview, had been living near Heidelberg in West Germany for about five years. His modest knowledge of German derives solely from his very limited social interactions at work and in his leisure time, and possibly from listening to the radio and watching the television. His learner variety is of a very basic type: among his utterances one in two is without a V', that is, lacks anything that would correspond to a (finite) verb in the target variety. He employs no copulas and never uses auxiliary verbs or modal verbs together with an infinite verb. His active command of the language is based chiefly on nouns; function words occur very rarely; and there is not a trace of inflection.

One would think that not very much can be said with such limited devices. But in fact, SP-22 is a skilful speaker (see the translation test in section 5.4); he knows how to use the little of the target language he has in order to construct fairly complex utterances. Here is a sample from one of his stories:[3]

(12)   Ich Kind – nicht viel moneda Spanien
          (I child – not much moneda Spain)
(13)   Ich nicht komme Deutschland – Spanien immer Bauer arbeite
          (I not come Germany – Spain always farmer work, i.e., before coming
          to Germany I used to work in Spain on a farm)
(14)   Arbeite andre Firma – obrero eventual
          (Work other firm – obrero eventual, i.e. he who works for others
          is a handy man)

(15)   Autonomo – nicht viel Geld
            (Autonomo – not much money, i.e., as an 'independent' you don't
            earn much)

Each of these utterances consists of two parts separated by a short pause
(marked by a dash). The two segments differ in intonation: the first ends
on a high tone, the second has a falling intonation. The first segment
introduces a topic, or serves as background for the rest. In many ways
it corresponds to what is known in the literature as 'topic', 'theme', 'presupposition' (in Chomsky's sense), or just 'background information'. We
have chosen a neutral term: *setting*. In the second segment something
is stated about the topic introduced in this way. For want of a better
term we call that segment *focus*. It corresponds in many ways to what
is known in the literature as 'comment', 'rheme', or 'foreground information', or just 'focus'.

The structure of a rather complex utterance produced within this particular learner variety can be patterned as

(16)   Setting – Pause – Focus

This pattern results largely from an application of principles (a, b and
e) from the list on pp. 82–3. Note that each of the two segments shows
a certain functional latitude. The setting may simply indicate the topic
on which something is going to be stated, or it may specify the place
and time for what follows. Both setting and focus may be compound structures, i.e., may have an internal segmentation, which is illustrated by
the examples in (12–15).

The pattern in (16) can be subject to four modifications:

(a)   The setting may be missing. Such is the case above all when the
            topic or the place and time specification contained in the preceding
            utterance is retained – including the case where it is offered in response
            to a question.
(b)   The setting is a 'string', i.e., an overall setting is made up of a number
            of subsettings.
(c)   The entire pattern is a 'string', i.e., repeated two or more times.
(d)   The entire pattern is modalized.

The first case does not require any illustration. The other three need
a few more samples from the speech production of the same migrant
worker:

(17)   Sechsundzwanzig – Kind komme; sechsunddreißig – zehn Jahre
            (Twenty-six – child come; thirty-six – ten years, i.e. in 1926 I was
            born, in 1936 I was ten)

85

Here we have a string pattern: setting and focus are juxtaposed twice in a sequence. This technique of contrastive stringing is a key device for the construction of complex text. The same technique was used in the following, fairly complex example.

(18)   Heute – vier Schule neu meine Dorf; ich klein Kind – eine Schule vielleicht hundert Kind; heute vielleicht ein Chef o Meister – zwanzig oder fünfundzwanzig Kind; ich Kind – vielleicht hundert Kind
(Today – four school new my village; I little child – one school perhaps hundred child; today perhaps one boss o master – twenty or twenty-five child; I child – perhaps hundred child)

What he wants to say is that there are now four schools in his native village; when he was a young child, there was one school with perhaps one hundred children; today one teacher may have twenty or twenty-five children; when he, the speaker, was a child (one teacher had) perhaps one hundred children.

Basically, this long utterance has two settings set in contrast: 'today' – 'in the past'; each is supplied with a focus. In addition, each setting is developed: 'today' + 'per teacher' – 'in the past' ('+ per teacher'). The contrasting time specification is repeated while the (same) expansion is omitted. This structure could be schematized as in (19).

(19)
Setting	*Focus*
today	four schools . . .
in the past	one school . . .
today + per teacher	twenty children
in the past (+ per teacher)	hundred children

A further internal structuring of the components is possible, as exemplified in the expansion of the third setting compared with the first one. Let us consider another, even more complex utterance, where we find a qualification of the second general pattern:

(20)   Dieses Jahr Winter gut, nicht kalt, nicht Schnee, verstehst (du)[4] – immer fort, Zement fort. Vielleicht Schnee, vielleicht kalt – Zement nicht fort, keine Arbeit
(This year winter good, not cold, not snow, (you) see – always off, cement off. Perhaps snow, perhaps cold – cement not off, no job)

The speaker is employed at a cement works and reflects on the mildness of the winter this year, thanks to which cement is selling well. If there were snow and cold, cement wouldn't be selling and he might lose his job.

Now the first setting consists here of three concatenated subsettings preceded by a time specification: 'this year' + 'winter good' + 'not cold' + 'not snow'. Note that this is not a simple string of statements like 'this year we had a good winter, this year it wasn't cold, there was no snow'; it is an elaborate setting for the subsequent statement. In actual fact, the conversation centred around the unemployment afflicting his workmates and the chances that it might hit the speaker too. In the second pattern the first general statement is juxtaposed with a hypothetical situation. The particle *vielleicht* ('perhaps') frequently used to introduce an utterance can be taken to mean 'Suppose (that) . . .'. That is, the subsequent statement is qualified as a supposition. In fact, the second utterance could also mean: 'Had there been snow and cold, we would have sold no cement and lost our jobs'. The foci are likewise strung together in both cases, but their internal structure is relatively simple.

Finally, one more sample where the components show a much more complex internal structuring is given in (21).

(21)   Ich meine Vater kaputt vier Jahre – meine Oma komme; meine Mutter
         wieder komme heirate – ich zurück Mama
         (I my father gone four years – my grandma come; my mother again
         come marry – I back Mama)

We learn that four years after his father's death, the speaker went to live with his grandmother,[5] but when his mother got married again, he could live with her once again.

The components of the utterance, notably in the first setting, are of such complexity that the apparatus introduced so far to assist our illustration of the problem of synthesis might seem inadequate – as indeed it will be sooner or later, as learner varieties become more and more complex. Rather than developing it any further, we will say a few words on three issues emerging from the last illustration.

1. One might suppose – and such is clearly our first impression – that the components of the utterance are simply 'scrambled' without any rule. Such an interpretation is unsatisfactory on three counts. First, 'scrambled' is but a poor descriptive term for our ignorance of the underlying rules, or our inability to identify these rules in this particular instance. Secondly, it would merely postpone the solution of our problem, which is to interpret the processes of synthesis in language acquisition, by suggesting that the synthesis 'proper' does not start until a later stage in language acquisition. Thirdly, even the utterances considered so far, including (21), clearly

reveal some underlying rules. From our observations it follows that arbitrary reshuffling does not occur: strings like *zurück Mama ich* or *wieder heirate meine Mutter komme* are inconceivable in this learner variety.

2. Looking at the more complex examples, it appears that at some stage of the acquisition of complex structures the segmentation into setting and focus is multiplied not in parallel but vertically: 'stringing' is supplemented by 'embedding'. The second of the two 'sentences' in (21) could be represented by a tree, as shown in the figure:

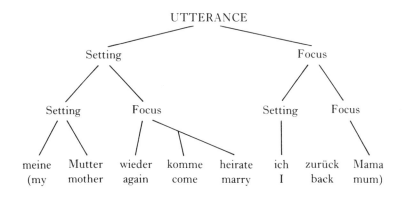

Structures of this sort may be an early stage in the development of a syntax comprising word classes, subject–predicate structures, and the like. The idea is tempting, but it also raises new problems. The intonational segmentation becomes less distinct: the pause tends to disappear, and for many utterances an analysis of this kind is not so easy to perform. Although in the second part of the first sentence in (21) (*meine Oma komme*) the segmentation into setting and focus can be identified by substituting the missing 'I' (the same setting as in the first part), this would not be feasible for the first part itself where 'I' is followed by a complicated time reference (*meine Vater kaputt vier Jahre*). Thus, the whole setting would consist of two subsettings: the topic and a temporal specification which would, however, be expected to precede 'I' (in line with the principle of orientation).

3. Example (21) makes it clear how difficult it is to grasp the earliest steps in the synthesis of language. Considering for example the importance of the position of the finite verb in German as a syntactic feature, it is disconcerting that for all the four main components of (21) it is virtually impossible to discover any regularity with respect to the finite verb and its placing. The first setting (*ich meine Vater...*) and the second focus

(*ich zurück Mama*) have no trace of a finite verb. One could argue, of course, that it is 'there' and somehow deleted at the surface; but what would be the argument to prove that it is in one position rather than another? In the remaining two components *komme* could be viewed as the semblance of a finite verb – although they are not 'tensed' at all. But its position cannot be readily identified. In the first focus it appears in final position (*meine Oma komme*), which would correspond to the position in subordinate clauses. In the other case (*meine Mutter wieder komme heirate*) it is unclear, to begin with, what should count as the 'finite verb' – *komme* or *heirate*; *komme* seems more plausible here, but if we accept this for the moment, the question arises whether *wieder* should count as a major constituent ('Satzglied') or not. In German, in contrast to English or Spanish, for example, the finite verb in declarative main clauses is preceded by one major constituent (cf. section 6.2.1 below). However, in this variety, it is unclear what should count as such. In standard German, *wieder* would count as a major constituent, but to claim that it also does in this learner's language begs the question: it amounts to no more than the claim that this learner variety already *has* the structure of standard German in this respect. Now, depending on whether *wieder* is analysed as a major constituent or not, we also get different positions for the 'finite verb' in this example. Given all this uncertainty, it becomes clear how far we are from a consistent and straightforward account.

We conclude our discussion of the problem of synthesis in early learner varieties on this somewhat pessimistic note, but the discussion has served to underline the reasons for the paucity of our knowledge in this area. In the next section we will try to illustrate with two examples (the development of the finite verb and the development of negation) how within these 'pragmatically' oriented language varieties, there is a gradual approximation to the syntax of the target language.

6.2   **Further advances in synthesis**

The illustrations offered in the preceding section have helped to analyse the ways in which the beginning learner seeks to organize his utterances from the few basic entities he has been able to derive from his analyses of the input, but which he has as yet failed to assign to clearly defined word classes and which he is unable to inflect. It is assumed that at this early stage the learner bases himself on 'pragmatic' principles or regularities which are not language-specific. At this stage the learner cannot apply the specific rules of the syntax of the target language because he simply does not know them.[6] On the other hand, he cannot apply the syntax of his native language because he still lacks the 'bricks' needed to make a construction. Even if he knows from his native language that the finite verb can be put in final position, this is of little help to him (if it *could* be of any help) as long as he has not learned how to express this category in the target language. We elaborate on this problem below.

At a fairly early stage the learner can undertake a rough classification of the lexical units by their semantic properties – specifically by distinguishing those units of predominantly functional use from those used chiefly to express content. This differentiation is a starting point for the construction of word-class systems as they exist in more advanced learner varieties, and of course in the target variety. Nevertheless, purely semantic criteria would not suffice to build up such a system. The learner must first become familiar with the distributional regularities and the morphological criteria which characterize the given word class; he will succeed in this only if he keeps trying to construct utterances, has the chance to test them in his linguistic environment, and seeks to adjust them to environmental requirements.

The two examples discussed below should offer some insights into these processes and highlight the problems which the learner faces. The first illustrates the development of a key device in the syntax of German and many other languages: the finite element of the verb. This has received little attention until now, but it can serve as a good illustration of the issues at stake. The other example is taken from the development of negation, a question investigated in some detail by many researchers and from a number of angles, and it will serve to demonstrate to what extent the development of certain structural features of language use depends on the parallel development of other features.

6.2.1 *Acquisition of finite elements*

The finite element is that part of the verbal complex which marks tense, number, and person; it may be contained in the verb itself (come*s*), or consist of an auxiliary verb (*has* gone), or involve a modal verb (*should* have gone).

Like many other languages, German makes extensive use of finite elements in sentence construction. Firstly, the position of the finite element in the sentence largely marks modality: it is in second position in declaratives, in initial position both in yes/no interrogatives and in imperatives, and in final position in subordinate clauses, whatever their modality, and so on. Secondly, some other elements of the sentence are closely linked to (and hence positioned next to) the finite element; such is the case with

negation. It is an important task for the learner to recognize these regularities and adhere to them in his use of the language. Familiarity with the
relevant rules of his native language cannot assist him in this task. Take
for instance a native speaker of Basque whose target language is German.
Now in Basque the finite element is usually in final position. This knowledge – however misleading it might be – cannot affect his performance
in German as long as he has not advanced in his analysis of German
input to the point where he has learned what the finite elements are in
German. Even if he were misguided enough to follow the pattern of his
native tongue, he would not know what to put in final position. His advantage (or disadvantage, as the case may be) over the first-language learning
child is in this basic knowledge: he knows that there might be something
like a finite element and he knows (or does not know, as the case may
be) where to look for it.

Attempting to isolate the finite element in the flow of speech sounds
is a hard nut for the learner to crack: the finite item goes close together
with the verb, but is not identical with it. In a form like *hat gearbeitet*
('has worked') the finite element – an auxiliary in this case – and the
participle occupy different places. It is the position of the finite element
that should concern the learner. The fact is however that for the learner
the lexical verb itself is more conspicuous, being relatively invariant across
all sentence forms (take for instance *arbeit* as the stem of the verb *arbeiten*).
This contrasts with the rather abstract meaning of the finite element, which
in addition happens to be tied up with a variety of items in the sentence.
See, for examples, the six utterances (22–7).

(22)	Er aß ein Brot (He ate a (piece of) bread)
(23)	Er hat ein Brot gegessen (He has eaten a. . .)
(24)	Er muß ein Brot gegessen haben (He must have eaten a . . .)
(25)	Er aß ein Brot auf (He ate up a . . .)
(26)	Er hat ein Brot aufgegessen (He has eaten up a . . .)
(27)	Weil er ein Brot aufaß (Because he ate up a . . .)

The verb itself carries the same meaning each time: eating. Although
the lexical items vary somewhat in appearance, especially on account of
the strong inflection, they nonetheless offer a fairly solid basis for the
learner's analysis, aided by the parallel (contextual) information. This
is how the morph *esse* is extracted from such varied input. However,
these cues are not available when it comes to identifying the finite elements
in the utterance. In (22–7) the finite element is related in different ways
to the lexical verb. In (22) the case is one of complete merger (*aß*): the
two (fused into one) are in second position. In (23) the two components

are separated (unlike in English), the verb proper appearing in final position; the finite item is an auxiliary. In (24) the finite element is carried by a modal verb which by itself has a lexical meaning; the element that carries the verb meaning is now in penultimate position. In (25) we have a merger of the finite element and *one* part of the verb *aufessen*; the remainder (*auf*) is pushed to the end. In (26) the latter is again in penultimate position and the other part of the verb in final position. In (27) once again the finite element and part of the verb are merged and appear in final position, directly after the other part of the verb. These six utterances are a selection from a much longer list of commonly used constructions, and the learner's formidable task is to isolate from this immensely varied input the finite elements of each verb; only then can he hope to come to grips with what is a pivotal, rather than a marginal, aspect of German syntax. In doing so the learner cannot fall back on any invariant segment of the sound sequence of a corresponding item of parallel information (as is the case with the verb 'essen' and most other concrete words).

What else could the (Basque-speaking) learner rely on to identify the finite elements and their regularities? In his analysis of the input he may try to appeal to his knowledge of his native language, which tells him (a) that there usually is such a thing and (b) that he should look for it at the end of the sentence. The first cue is indeed valuable insofar as it causes him to search the input for the finite elements. The second cue however could only mislead him, as can be seen from the examples above.

Evidently the finite element and its positional properties cannot simply be identified by analysing the input according to first-language knowledge and the general principles outlined in the preceding sections. Rather, the learner must acquire a solid body of knowledge of the grammar of the target language, in particular all that bears on the inflectional properties of words and on word classes. To use our example, he must come to know that *aß, essen, gegessen* are inflectional variants of one and the same verb, that verbs are often linked with auxiliaries such as 'have' or 'be', as well as with modal verbs such as 'must', 'should', 'can', each of these being likewise subject to inflection (at least in German). It is from this kind of knowledge that the learner will eventually extract, through processes of abstraction, the category 'finite element' and derive from the diversity of word positions the regular patterns characteristic of the language. To achieve this, the learner is committed to producing utterances, some of which might coincide with the patterns of the target language. (This latter fact should not induce us to suspect that the learner has already grasped the underlying target language rule or principle, see note 6.)

From what we (think that we!) know about the process, the acquisition of the basic positioning rules in the target language may be subdivided into three main stages:

Stage I: Utterances are composed of non-inflected lexical units which can be roughly assigned to (basically two) word classes in analogy to the corresponding words of the target language. These *morphs* (as we have called them) may already show some categorical differentiation through meaning. In their construction, the learner follows what seem to be purely 'pragmatic' principles, as outlined in section 6.1. The relevant examples are (12–21) in the same section.

Stage II: Utterances are gradually developed to include lexical units that show traces of inflection and assignment to word classes in rough correspondence to the classification of the target language. There is no consistency in this: exceptions and overgeneralizations are quite common. The learner is particularly vulnerable at this stage to the interference of his first language, since he is now able to construct utterances according to the rules of some particular syntax, but still lacks the rules of the target language. Some of his utterances may be perfectly correct while many others may not. The following speech production of an Italian migrant who had been living in Germany for five years illustrates this point (the spelling attempts to catch the flavour of his pronunciation):

(28)   Also wenn isch hiä gekommt sin, ha (für) misch wa's zu schwea, deusch lerne, zu schwea. In Amerika isch wa zwei Jahr, in Amerika, isch zwei Jah' in Amerik', isch hab noch mea English ge'ead wi'ia fünf Jahr.
(It seems quite superfluous to render an equivalent English version.)

Example (28) shows that a learner at this stage is capable of placing the finite element in its correct position, but not consistently. He seems to know the relevant rules and at the same time does not observe them on many occasions.

Stage III: The learner has grasped the rules of finite elements and succeeds in building utterances that conform to the standard of the target language.

The three stages are meant merely to convey an idea of a development process in which a gradual transition from one stage to the next is taking place, with considerable overlap and a rich inner structuring of each stage, particularly Stage II.

At this point it might be useful to sum up the two key problems.

The problem of synthesis

1. A verb form has two components: a finite component and the lexical component. As long as the learner uses solely the infinitive form of a verb, only the latter comes into play. In developing, for example, positioning rules for basic learner varieties, we must bear this in mind. With an utterance like, *Ich Espanje komme* ('I Spain come') the beginning learner expresses the lexical meaning of the verb through an infinitive form. And since in German a verb takes second position only when consisting of the two, finite and lexical, components, the learner can *not* be said to depart from the target variety here.

2. The use of an inflected form, as for instance *kam* ('came', past tense, singular), does not imply that the learner has fully grasped the positioning rules of the finite element, let alone that he is aware of the dual role of such a form (as a merger of the finite element and the element expressing lexical meaning). He may occasionally place this form in the correct position of the finite element (second in the main clause) while on other occasions pushing it back to final position, which is the usual position of the infinitive verb. The latter is characteristic of the second stage; the third stage demands a careful distinction of the two cases.

Despite its obvious importance, the development of the finite element in language acquisition has attracted little attention from researchers (but see Felix, 1978, for some detailed observations). In the next section we consider another aspect of syntax acquisition, the development of negation, which, in contrast, counts among the most thoroughly studied questions of second language research. The amount of attention we have devoted to the finite element reflects the fact that in the target languages most often mentioned in this book, the development of negation goes hand in hand with the acquisition of the finite/infinitive distinction and the concomitant position rules. As an overture to our discussion of negation development in early language varieties, we will sum up the basic rules governing the use of both the finite element and the infinitive in German and in English – the two languages most thoroughly investigated from this angle.

For the sake of brevity, a few symbols will be used: F for finite element; V(erb), Aux(iliary), and Mod(al) for the respective 'infinite' component. For example, *kommen, gekommen, come* (also as past participle) are V; *kam, kämest, came* (with tense and person or number) are F-V; *haben, gehabt, have, had* are Aux; *hast, hatte, has, have,* and *had* (with 1st person, 2nd person, etc.) are F-Aux; *müssen, gemußt* (infinitively, not in English), are Mod; *muß, müßte, must* and *should* (with tense, etc.) are F-Mod. Several infinite elements can 'queue', as in: *gelesen haben müssen* ('must have read'). Such a string shall be designated INF; the order in German is: detachable particle – V – Aux$_1$ – Aux$_2$ – Mod, e.g. (*hätte*) *aus-geschaltet worden sein müssen* ('should have been turned off').

With slight modifications, the same holds for English. *Must, should* and similar forms are mergers of finite and 'infinite' elements. In the case of INF, the order is reversed: (*should*) *have been turned off*.

The basic rules which a learner will eventually have to grasp can be summarized (in slightly simplified form) as follows:

I German

(i)   F is movable; in subordinate clauses it comes in final position, in declarative main clauses in second, otherwise (in yes/no interrogatives, imperatives, etc.) in first position.

(ii)   INF is always in final position.

(iii)   The extreme right element of INF, if merged with F, then takes position with F.

II English

(i)   F is movable: in second position in subordinate clauses and in declarative main clauses, otherwise in initial position.

(ii)   INF is always in third position.

(iii)   The segment of INF merged with F follows the latter, excepting V (which does not take initial position in any clause but the non-negated imperative). F is expressed through some form of *do*, when not adjacent to V in those clauses where only F and V are present.

The crucial thing in these rules is that F is movable while INF is not, except when merged with F.

6.2.2   *Acquisition of negation*

Negation is a vast subject. For present purposes we shall only consider three forms which are important in German as well as in English.

1. Denials in response to questions, assertions, or requests effected through one-word sentences (*Nein* or *No*). The fact that such a denial can be followed by a positive statement (*Did Frank do it? – No, Otto did*) bears no relation to negation. Termed 'anaphoric' by Bloom (1970), these negations have been studied in first language acquisition and – to a lesser extent – in second language learning (Felix, 1978; Wode, 1981). Apparently they present no major problem in acquisition.

2. Clause negations used to deny, roughly speaking, the appropriateness of a predicate for a certain object. In addition to the basic negation elements

nicht or *not*, there are those with adverbial meaning: *nie* or *never, nirgends* or *nowhere*, and the like.

3. Constituent-related negations referring to just one constituent of the sentence: *Nicht Hans war hier* ('It was not Hans who was here'), *Ich habe keine zwei Stunden gewartet* (literally: 'I have waited for not two hours', meaning: for less than two hours). At least one variant of this negation type is very important for language acquisition, specifically in vocabulary: from two words of opposite meaning the learner acquires only one and uses it with negation to express the opposite (*good – not good*, in place of *bad*).

So much for a rough outline; for details the reader is referred to any grammar book (a sound up-to-date treatment of theoretical problems is offered by Jacobs, 1982). As far as second language research goes, investigators have tended to focus on clause negation, giving marginal attention to the other types. In sections 6.2.2.1–4 we present the order of negation acquisition as found in four studies, two for English, one for German, and one for Swedish – the latter in view of its exceptional significance. A few other investigations are mentioned in passing.

6.2.2.1 Cancino, Rosansky and Schumann

These authors began their investigation of spontaneous English learning by six Spanish speakers (two children, two adolescents, two adults) in 1973. Every two weeks the learners were tested for about one hour, over a period of ten months. Their speech was tape-recorded and later transcribed. The data include:

> spontaneous speech (conversation with the experimenter),
> experimental elicitations (e.g. imitation or negation of a model utterance),
> pre-planned interactions, e.g. attending parties, sports events, and similar natural situations.

The learners had been in the United States for less than three months when the project began (for further details see Cazden, Cancino, Rosansky, and Schumann, 1975; and Schumann, 1978a). The investigators focussed upon auxiliary verbs and their concomitants: interrogatives and negation. The acquisition of negation was found to proceed in four stages, with gradual transition from one to the next. The following illustrations and comments are quoted from Cancino, Rosansky, and Schumann (1978, pp. 210–11). (In our stage designations below we introduce letters to mark the respective authors; thus I–(C) means: stage I according to Cancino *et al.*)

I–(C): *no V*

1. The subjects began negating by using *no V* constructions

Marta:	I no can see.
	Carolina no go to play.
Cheo:	You no walk on this.
	You no tell your mother.
Juan:	Today I no do that.
	No, I no use television.
Jorge:	They no have water.
	But no is mine is my brother. (= It's not mine; it's my brother's.)
Alberto:	I no understand.
	No like coffee (subject deletion).

This form is found in the early speech of English speaking children. It is also very similar to the way the negative is formed in Spanish (e.g. *(yo) no entiendo*; *(yo) no tengo agua*).

II–(C): *don't V*

2. At the same time or shortly after the *no V* constructions appear, the subjects began to negate using *don't V* constructions. Examples of *don't V* utterances are:

Marta:	I don't hear.
	He don't like it.
Cheo:	I don't understand.
	I don't see nothing mop.
Juan:	I don't look the clock at this time.
	Don't have any monies (subject deletion).
Jorge:	My brother and I don't have more class.
	That don't say anything.
Alberto:	I don't can explain.
	I don't have a woman.

Many of these utterances are all right, but upon closer scrutiny of the evidence the learner is found to be ignorant as yet of what *don't* involves (verb form plus negation); instead, the sound cluster is perceived as another negation particle, a variant of *no*. In the samples above this can be seen in forms such as *That don't say anything* or *I don't can explain*. These 'particles' are put in front of the infinitive verb form.

III–(C): *Aux-neg*

3. Next the subjects used the *Aux-neg* constructions in which the negative is placed after the auxiliary. In general the first auxiliaries to be negated in this way were *is* and *can*.

Marta:	Somebody is not coming in.
	You can't tell her.
Cheo:	It's not danger.
	He can't see.
Juan:	I haven't seen all of it.
	It wasn't so big.
Jorge:	No, he's not skinny.
	But we couldn't do anything.
Alberto:	∅

At this stage the learner already uses contracted forms – for negation (*-n't*) as well as for other words (*-'s*). Yet one of the informants, Alberto, failed to reach this stage altogether. The reasons for this early halt in his learning the language are discussed in Schumann (1978a) as an illustration of his pidginization theory (see section 1.5.5 above).

IV–(C): Analysed *don't*

4. Finally, they learned the analysed forms of *don't* (*do not, doesn't, does not, didn't, did not*):

Marta:	It doesn't spin.
	One night I didn't have the light.
Cheo:	I didn't even know.
	Because you didn't bring.
Juan:	We didn't have a study period.
	It doesn't make any difference.
Jorge:	She didn't believe me.
	He doesn't laugh like us.
Alberto:	∅
Dolores:	My father didn't let me.
	It doesn't matter.

With the fourth stage the learner has reached the target variety. However, it should be noted that any such dismembering of a continuous process into distinct stages amounts to a distortion of reality; what really happens is a gradual shift in the share of particular constructions. (The precise frequencies are quoted by Cancino *et al.*, 1978, pp. 212–17.)

The investigation served as a point of departure for several follow-up studies. In one of these, the most comprehensive to date, Stauble (1981) analysed the speech samples of four Spanish and six Japanese speakers learning English. Her findings essentially concur with those quoted above,

but Stauble offers an overview intended to depict the development of negation. The successive learner varieties are found to fall into three groups
which she terms *basilang, mesolang,* and *acrolang.* Each can be further
subdivided. The list below features a Spanish–English negation continuum
(Stauble, 1981, p. 26). The corresponding continuum for Japanese English
(p. 44) is more or less the same, apart from a greater persistence of *no*
in the former (in the latter we find more *not* and *never*; the explanation
might be that in Spanish the principal negation is precisely *no*).

BASILANG
Features: Pre-verbal negation
1. NO + VERB constructions
2. NO + PHRASE constructions
3. Some overt variation

↓

From BASILANG to MESOLANG
Features: Pre-verbal and post-verbal negation

LOWER MESOLANG	MID MESOLANG
1. Dominant use of unanalysed *don't-* /*doesn't*	1. Decline of NO + VERB construc- tions
2. Some COP/AUX + negator con- structions	2. Expansion of COP/AUX + negator constructions
3. NO/NOT + PHRASE construc- tions in variation	3. NOT + PHRASE domination

↓

From MESOLANG to ACROLANG
Features: Loss of pre-verbal negation and establishment of English post-verbal
negation rule

UPPER MESOLANG	ACROLANG
1. Present/past tense distinction among the negative forms	Establishment of COP/AUX paradigm which is governed by the English post- verbal negation rule
2. Elimination of non-standard nega- tive forms	
3. Restructuring of the unanalysed negative forms	
4. Standard use of DO auxiliary as car- rier of tense and negation	

We are struck by the finding that speakers of Spanish do not differ
essentially from speakers of Japanese, particularly where the development
of positioning rules is concerned, even though clause negation takes on
quite different forms in the two languages: in Spanish it precedes the
finite element, in Japanese it takes final position after the verb.

6.2.2.2 Wode

Within the framework of his large-scale 'Kiel Project' devoted to different modes of language acquisition, Wode undertook to trace the spontaneous second language learning in his children during a six-month stay in the United States. At the beginning of this period the four children (speaking German) were aged from four years, eleven months to eight years, eleven months (Wode, 1981, p. 83). Wode took great care to tape-record systematically the speech of his children (totalling 120 hours), to make detailed notes (some 3,000 pages), and to conduct various experiments, such as occasional translation, casual inquiring about constructions, etc. (The general objectives, the background to the project, and the data collection and evaluation procedures are described in Part C of Wode 1981.) The investigation covered negation, interrogatives, verb inflection, and phonology; negation was studied most extensively (Part D, and also Part G). Wode's five acquisition stages are summarized below (the sometimes substantial differences between the children have had to be ignored).

I-(W): Anaphoric negation *no*

The children's earliest negations consist of denials of preceding occurrences, in much the same way as effected in German by *nein*. Borrowing from Bloom (1970), Wode calls them 'anaphoric'. This *no* can be followed by a positive rectification of the preceding utterance, but initially the correction is expressed in the first language (*No, du mogelst ja*, p. 103). In actual fact, a positive continuation like this has little bearing on negation itself, so the question (raised by Wode) whether there are two substages within Stage I may be left open.

II-(W): External non-anaphoric negation *neg X*

The negated constituent is X: first N, V, or Adj, later also VP; *neg* is effected as *no* and always appears in initial position. A few examples:

> neg Adj: no cold   neg N: no bread
> neg V: no sleep   neg VP: no catch it

Note that the entire utterance consists of two or at most three words. The delayed appearance of *neg VP* is connected with the gradual progress in utterance complexity rather than with negation as such. Both Cancino *et al.* (1978) and Stauble (1981) would interpret it as *no V*. Incidentally, instances of this construction have been recorded prior to the anaphoric *no* (Wode, 1981, p. 98).

III-(W): Internal *be*-negation

The first negations inside clauses occur in connection with forms of *to be*; they appear mostly in (presumably unanalysed) set phrases such as *That's no good*. It is at this stage that *not* is used in place of *no*.

IV-(W): Internal full verb negation *no/not* and imperative *don't*

Full verb negation appears consistently in succession to internal negation in copula clauses. Wode distinguishes five main types; each is illustrated with one example:

Subj V neg X	John go not to the school
Subj neg VP	Me no close the window
Subj Aux neg (VP)	He cannot hit the ball
Imper-V (Pron) neg (X)	Hit it not over the fence
Imper-*don't* VP	Don't broke

The negation can be effected through either *no* or *not*; its position in relation to the verb varies. Wode assumes that the form *don't* is treated as an unanalysed entity.

V-(W): Suppletive *don't/didn't* and sentence-internal *don't/didn't*

The former description refers to reiterations like *No, you don't*, the latter to correct *do* insertions perfectly, as in *I didn't see*. There are signs, however, that these forms function in an unanalysed manner, because utterances like *Do you don't know (that)* or *I don't can't* were recorded even at the very end of the observation period. The children appear to converge upon one single rule by placing the negation before the verb, whether it is Aux, Mod, or V, trying out different negations: *no, not, don't,* or *didn't*.

It would seem therefore that during the six months of their stay in an English-speaking environment the four children had not reached the stage denoted as IV-(C), in which the *do* construction has been analysed and is used as in the target language. There is occasional evidence, however, of a transition to that stage; Wode even writes of a 'post-stage V' (pp. 107–8). Wode's stages II to V would thus correspond to stages I-(C) to III-(C), and to the development from basilang to mid mesolang, in Stauble's terminology. At the same time, one realizes how arbitrary the distinction of stages can be.

6.2.2.3   Felix

Felix conducted his investigation as part of the same Kiel Project, as a complement to Wode's study. He traced the spontaneous acquisition of German by four English-speaking children over periods of five, ten, and (for two subjects) eight months. One of them had just arrived in Germany, while two had lived for three months and one for nine months in a German environment when the study began. Their ages at the start varied from 3;4 (= three years, four months) to 7;6. Each child was seen twice or three times a week for periods long enough to allow the tape-recording of at least one hour of spontaneous speech in social interaction. The principal analyses were performed on word order, interrogatives, and negation. The brief survey of negation development below is based on Felix (1978, chapter 15) and Felix (1982, pp. 20–33), from which all the quotations and examples come.

Felix distinguishes three stages, leaving room for some finer distinctions as well.

I-(F): Holophrastic negation

This term refers to a response with *nein* ('no'). The response occurs not only when some statement or request is to be contradicted but also in order to communicate lack of understanding.

II-(F): Clause-external negation *neg + X*

Like Wode, Felix distinguishes between anaphoric and non-anaphoric negation; in the former case X is merely a positive correction, in the latter X is denied. In both cases this is done with *nein*. In the following examples 'I' stands for interviewer, 'L' for learner (Felix, 1978, p. 241).

(29)   I: Das ist ja kaputt (That's broken)
         L: Nein kaputt (No broken)
         I: So, wir gehen jetzt nach Hause (Well, now we go home)
         L: Nein Hause (No home)
(30)   I: Soll ich helfen? (May I help?)
         L: Nein helfen (No help)
(31)   I: Komm, wir spielen ein bißchen mit Sambo (Come, let's play a little with Sambo (the cat))
         L: Nein Sambo (No Sambo)

From time to time the negation is placed at the end:

(32)   I: Darf ich alle essen?
         L: Du nein, ich ja

Contradicting Wode, Felix maintains that 'non-anaphoric' negation tends to precede, or run in parallel with, anaphoric negation.

III-(F): Clause-internal negation ($X + neg + Y$)

Felix's characterizations of this stage are not entirely uniform. In Felix (1982, p. 76), he says: 'Up to this moment the negation morpheme appears invariably at the beginning of the clause. The subsequent developmental stages are characterized by an embedding, from this point onwards, of the negation morpheme in the clause. Thus the structure $neg + X$ is replaced by the structure $X + neg + Y$.' Two of his examples are:

(33)   Ich nein essen
(34)   Ich nein schlafen

This structure is somewhat contradictory in relation to the previously mentioned structures. In Felix (1978, p. 346) he states (our translation): 'It is very important that the appearance of this structure coincides approximately with the non-anaphoric *nein* in initial or final position. Over a period of about six weeks both structure types were used by David. This chronological coincidence suggests the conclusion that the case with those two structures is presumably not one of two successive acquisition stages.' Felix continues to argue very convincingly that $neg + X$ (or $X + neg$) is but a borderline case of $X + neg + Y$, namely one where either the subject or the VP is missing; all three cases occur simultaneously. He then says: 'From these chronological and structural relations ensues the need to describe clause-internal and clause-external negation with *nein* in a common framework, rather than . . . as two successive acquisition stages which differ in their structural complexity.' One wonders rather why Felix has abandoned this plausible analysis in favour of two successive stages (given here as II (F) and III (F)) – possibly because such a sequence is evidenced in Wode's data, and that these are taken into consideration by Felix.

A fairly distinct step is made next with the transition from *nein* to *nicht* ('not'), which turns up in initial position in a number of phonetic variants. At the same time, a significant differentiation in the position of neg can be observed: it appears after the auxiliary verb, modal verb, or copula, but before the full verb. A few examples are given in (35–6).

(35)   Das ist nicht Kindergarten (This is not kindergarten)
        Das ist nicht kaputt (This is not broken)
        I: Spring mal runter (Just hop down)
        L: Ich kann nicht (I cannot)
        I: Komm wir spielen weiter (Let's go on playing)
        L: Nein, ich will nicht mehr (No, I don't want any more)

103

(36)   Nein, du nicht kommt (No, you not comes)
         Ich nicht essen mehr (I not eat any more – infinitive)
         Julie nicht spielt mit (Julie doesn't play with us – order of neg and
             V reversed)
         I: Die Puppe muß im Schrank bleiben (The doll has to stay in the
             wardrobe)
         L: Die nicht bleib hier (She doesn't stay here – order reversed)

With the next step neg begins to follow full verbs as well, but there are occasional overgeneralizations of the rule which recede gradually. It is amazing how long this transition takes: over long periods, *nicht* may appear before as well as after the full verb. It is not that the learner grasps the rule all of a sudden; the right structures are acquired as if by a gradual change in emphasis.

Before we proceed to evaluate the studies discussed so far, we might take a look at a fourth one, devoted to the acquisition of Swedish, for a change.

6.2.2.4   Hyltenstam

We have chosen Hyltenstam's work from among the many other studies of negation acquisition because it is complementary, in terms of procedure, to the studies hitherto quoted: it is not longitudinal but cross-sectional. Hyltenstam (1977, 1978) tested 160 learners of Swedish (speakers of 35 different languages) twice, at an interval of five weeks. The four 'typical patterns' that emerged from the material can be roughly interpreted as developmental stages.[7] The critical factor is the position of *inte* ('not') in main and subordinate clauses with and without modal verb. The position of neg in Swedish corresponds to that of *nicht* in German, except that in the subordinate clause the modal verb comes before the full verb, and *inte* is placed in front of the modal verb.

I-(H): Pre-V

Learners in this category place *inte*, irrespective of clause type, in pre-verbal position; this results in two correct and two incorrect structures:

(37)   *Han inte kommer (He doesn't come – reversed order)
         Att han inte kommer (That he doesn't come)
         Han kan inte komma (He cannot come)
         *Att han kan inte komma (That he cannot come – reversed order)

II-(H): Post-V, post-Mod

In a clause with a full verb, the learner places neg after the verb; in the case of a modal and a full verb, he places neg after the modal and hence before the full verb. The rule is observed irrespective of clause type. Again, two correct and two incorrect structures result:

(38)   Han kommer inte
            *Att han kommer inte
            Han kan inte komma
            *Att han kan inte komma

III-(H): Post-V with full verb in main clause, otherwise pre-V

At this stage the learner distinguishes not only between modal and full verb but also between main and subordinate clause:

(39)   Han kommer inte
            Att han inte kommer
            Han kan inte komma
            *Att han kan inte komma

IV-(H): Target-like

In the main clause *inte* comes after, in the subordinate clause before, the verb element:

(40)   Han kommer inte
            Han kan inte kommer
            Att han inte kommer
            Att han inte kan kommer

As pointed out before, learners are by no means consistent: within each type varying frequencies of occurrence for the particular positions have been recorded. Hyltenstam attempts to account for these variations by applying Labov's variable rules (Labov, 1972). Individual transitions are interpreted by him as simplifications or overgeneralizations.

A rather different analysis of these data has been proposed by Jordens (1980), who ascribes a particular significance to the distinction between the finite and non-finite full verb, as discussed in section 6.2.1 of this book. We will now try to find a common principle for *all* the forms of negation acquisition described above. The point of departure will be our discussion in section 6.2.1.

6.2.2.5   Development of negation: Conclusions

By way of introduction, let us briefly recall the rules for F and INF outlined at the end of section 6.2.1 for the two target languages (German and English). The crucial elements were: the sharp distinction between F and INF (the finite and the 'infinitive' elements); the fixation of INF in its position and the variable position of F in different clauses; and that in an INF + F merger, the position of F is decisive. The difference between German and English is primarily that in English F and INF virtually never merge. Swedish is essentially like German, except that – as far as is relevant here – in subordinate clauses F is placed before rather than after INF (the same as in Dutch, incidentally).

The following simple rule can be formulated for clause-internal negation in English, German, and Swedish:

(41)   Neg comes before INF

As neg we may have *not, nicht,* or *inte*. Now there are three cases in which this rule does not hold:

1. If F and INF have merged such that there is no independent remnant of the latter, the position of neg is in doubt. We might say that neg takes the position it *would* occupy if there were an INF. The following examples illustrate the point:

pronoun	F	neg	INF (position)
er	hat	nicht	angerufen
er	rief	nicht	an
er	ist	nicht	gekommen
er	kam	nicht	(shifted)

The same is true with the F position in subordinate clauses and interrogatives. We may try to account for all this by stating: *neg comes before the INF position.*

2. Not every sentence has an INF, that is, an infinitive verb possibly with other infinitive elements. In place of INF there may be a predicative noun or adjective in association with forms such as *sein* ('to be'), *werden* ('to become'), or *bleiben* ('to remain'), etc.:

> Er ist doof (he is dull)
> Er bleibt hier (he remains here)
> Er wurde König von Frankreich (he became King of France)

3. There may be cases, in German at least, when there is also an adverbial and, occasionally, even an object between neg and INF. For example,

in contrast to

> Er hat das Buch nicht gelesen (He has not read the book)

we would say,

> Er hat das Buch nicht auf den Tisch gelegt (He has not put the book
> on the table)
> Er hat nicht Klavier gespielt (He has not played the piano)

It is difficult to imagine a common denominator for these cases. We might assume that the element between neg and INF is in particularly 'close association' with the latter. Indeed, 'Klavier' ('the piano') in the last example is a sort of detachable verb complement (as in *radfahren* or *car-driving*), but this does not apply to all instances. Neither these nor several other problems can be solved here, but they are as much of a problem to writers of descriptive grammars of German as they are to second language researchers.

Nevertheless, for a vast majority of cases the following rule seems to hold:

(42)   Insert neg before the INF position

Note that the internal order of INF as well as the position of F show variations in the three languages.

The learner has mastered negation in the target language (with a few exceptions) if he is in command of rule (42). But how does he get that far? By and large along a perfectly straight path.

Step 1: As long as the learner has only infinitive forms at his disposal, he cannot fail.

Step 2: By the time he has discovered the finite element with its various positions, the learner first of all faces difficulties where INF is completely merged with F. He may be in doubt whether to place neg before INF (and hence before F-INF), as thitherto, or before the INF position. He has little if any difficulty in those cases where the finite element is a modal or auxiliary verb, since there is an INF element left (except where it is omitted on the basis of context ellipsis). After a time, however, he is bound to realize the role of the INF position and the irrelevance of the shift in lexical content to the F position.

Those two steps provide a rough outline of the entire development of clause-internal negation. Clearly they do not say anything about the various

107

'special' negations, or about the form of the negation terms (*no, not, none,* etc.), but the latter would not be difficult to describe.

At this point it should be evident why we chose to place so much emphasis upon discussing the acquisition of the finite element in the first place. The mastering of clause-internal negation is essentially a mere epiphenomenon of the acquisition of the finite element and its positioning rules relative to those of the infinitive element.

Before concluding this issue, we ought to go back for a moment to the structuring of utterances in basic learner varieties, as discussed in section 6.1. It was argued that in the absence of the principal syntactic structuring devices (such as word classes and inflection) the learner tends to construct his utterances according to 'pragmatic' principles. Similar principles operate also in the target language, but only in interaction with the rules of the relevant syntax. In basic learner varieties an utterance comprises a *setting*, which sets a theme and possibly specifies time and place, and a *focus* as the statement proper (predication). When the latter has to be negàted, the (beginning) learner puts the negation before the focus. The setting can be omitted, as is often the case in non-negated statements as well, i.e. Felix (1978) got it right! This purely pragmatic structuring of the most simple utterances has its counterpart in the target language: the focus comes at the end, unless the speaker resorts to intonational devices. At least in English there is such a correspondence: neg is followed by what it is meant to deny, i.e., the focus. A disturbing factor is the finding that not *all* the elements appearing after neg must belong to the focus. In German the matter becomes more complicated insofar as part of the focus may precede neg. The language has created possibilities that cannot be accommodated in terms of what we see as the standard 'pragmatic' order.

6.3 **Conclusions**

1. While being some way from fully understanding the principles which guide the learner in constructing utterances, we have been able to form certain ideas about this process.

2. The more the learner knows, the more likely he is to make errors. In other words: the simple utterances a learner succeeds in constructing on the basis of his early analyses of the input cannot possibly follow the rules of the target language for lack of the necessary (syntactic) devices. The beginning learner tends to rely on certain general principles that have little to do with any specific language, his first language, for example. Thus we are led to the paradox that, to a certain extent at least, the learner

is more apt to make errors due to his first-language knowledge the more he knows about the second language.

3. It may be that no particular benefits ensue from exploring the development of easily accessible structures (for instance, negation) as long as there is no conclusive evidence as to how the given structures function in the target language, and also in the respective first languages. From our analysis it would appear that the development of clause-internal negation is but a corollary of general developmental tendencies. This conclusion in no way detracts from the value of the many thorough investigations of negation, some of which have been discussed in this chapter. What it does show, however, is the present limited extent of our knowledge of the structure of utterances in fully developed languages.

4. The final point to be made is this: our highly inadequate knowledge of the structure and function of utterances in fully developed languages is also a major obstacle to the synthesis problem, a matter which will become apparent as we investigate the embedding problem in the next chapter.

7
The embedding problem

A native speaker of the target language is apt to perceive as ungrammatical,[1] if not ludicrous, many of the utterances produced by a beginning learner; at the same time, he may have no difficulty in grasping the gist of what the learner is trying to convey. In actual fact, such 'defective' utterances are quite often more to the point than the corresponding circumlocutions of many an educated native. Imagine a migrant worker saying the following in a bakery:

(43)   Me bread

Any native hearer (barring the odd linguist), will notice the apparent ungrammaticality of the utterance, and yet perceive it as perfectly meaningful, interpreting it as a request for a loaf of bread. On the first point (ungrammaticality), the hearer is wrong; the utterance is grammatically correct if uttered in a suitable context – as we will try to show further below. On the second point, the hearer is right because he takes note of the situational context of the utterance.

Take the second point to begin with: why should a *hearer* interpret the meaning of (43) as a request for bread, rather than as 'I am the bread' or 'I've eaten bread'? Three factors have to be considered:

(a)   The speaker is perceived to be in a baker's (awareness of the current situation).
(b)   A baker's is a place where, among other things, bread is for sale (knowledge of the world).
(c)   The preceding events as well as the preceding utterances may provide important cues (the same wording could be encountered in the course of a narrative).

Here, our interpretation of (43) is based not only on the actual wording of the utterance (what is explicitly expressed in it) but also takes place in the broader context, or against the wider background, of all manner of 'concomitant knowledge'. Indeed, without the concomitant knowledge of the hearer, utterance (43) could not be interpreted, or would be misinterpreted.

The crucial role of concomitant knowledge is by no means a specific feature of learner varieties; it is equally essential for fully-fledged languages. In other words, a certain amount of nonlinguistic knowledge is indispensable for the meaningful interpretation of utterances, and it is precisely this which gives us the correct interpretation of (43).

Nevertheless, (43) still sounds totally ungrammatical. Now, imagine an assistant in a bakery who says,

(44)   Here's your apple-pie, Madam. Now what would *you* like, Sir?

In this situation it would be perfectly alright for the next customer to say *Me bread*. Also, anyone could say (43) as the second part of a double request: *He wants cake, me bread*. In other words: utterance (43) may be perfectly grammatical if it has been preceded by events (especially utterances) that justify it. Our initial discomfort at seeing (43) was not because of its ungrammaticality, but because it was wrongly matched with our concomitant knowledge.

We have dwelt on this illustration in order to highlight the pitfalls of the unfortunate practice of analysing learners' utterances out of context and therefore separated from the concomitant knowledge which we assume to be available to both speaker and hearer. Any utterance, whether belonging to a learner variety or to the target language, is embedded in the speaker's and hearer's informational set-up, composed of current perception, recollections of preceding events and utterances, and knowledge of the world. Indeed, the set-up may be so extensive that the information contained in the utterance itself is largely or even totally superfluous. (Remember the salt-passing scene of chapter 3.) These are extreme cases; normally, it is the balanced interplay of linguistic and nonlinguistic information that enables us to make out what is actually meant.

The essential role of concomitant knowledge for the hearer has its counterpart for the speaker. Constructing his utterance, he must also make up his mind what would 'go along' with the utterance in the way of contextual information and what the hearer's concomitant knowledge might be in that situation – hence, what he, the speaker, need not make explicit. This is the first part of the speaker's *embedding problem*. The other is the use of the necessary linguistic devices, which may or may not be specific to the given language. The three major devices to be considered are deixis, anaphora and ellipsis; word order and intonation are also very important.

Any attempt at communication by language requires that the learner, as every speaker, copes with the embedding problem; if he is concerned with learning a language he will in time have to acquire the specific devices developed by that language.

In section 2.3.B it was noted that balance between contextual information and the uttered information gradually shifts during the acquisition process in favour of the latter. A growing linguistic repertoire makes the learner less and less dependent on the contextual information that must be available to the hearer. Of course, we cannot totally dispense with contextual information, but by mastering the language we can acquire more freedom from context-dependency.

Little is known as yet about this particular aspect of language acquisition, partly because we still do not know enough about the interaction of contextual information and linguistic information in ordinary language use. In the next section we will consider some general aspects of the problem, in order to enlarge subsequently (in section 7.2) on one subdomain of deixis that has been studied quite extensively in recent years, namely, the expression of temporality.

7.1   **Some devices of context-dependency**

Let us refer to the information conveyed by the wording of the utterance itself as *utterance information*; in order to extract this information from the utterance, the rules of the language must be known. All other information available to speaker and hearer in a given situation is *contextual information*, or concomitant knowledge. This is of course a clear simplification, because, firstly, the speaker's concomitant knowledge cannot be identical with the hearer's (or there would be nothing to communicate), and secondly, it is not true that the total knowledge of both partners is relevant to the task of constructing the utterance, on the one hand, and grasping its meaning, on the other. For the sake of precision we ought to speak of the *relevant* contextual information (or concomitant knowledge) of the speaker and the *relevant* contextual information of the hearer. For simplicity's sake, however, we will gloss over these in principle indispensable distinctions.[2] What must be stressed at this point, however, is that the concomitant knowledge of the two is in constant flux. Each successive utterance, each new element of perception, and each resultant inference serves to modify our knowledge. The utterance information conveyed by utterance A becomes a new part of the contextual information (or concomitant knowledge) available for processing utterance B. This dynamic is a critical factor in some important manifestations of

113

contextuality such as ellipsis and topicalization (discussed in further detail below).

For practical purposes, we distinguish three types of concomitant knowledge: world knowledge, situational knowledge, and preceding information.

A.   Knowledge of the world

As the term implies, this type of knowledge comprises all that we have accumulated in our long-term memory about the physical, social, and other aspects of the world around us. As mentioned before, this knowledge is limited by a measure of uncertainty: rather than knowing this or that, we believe we know this or that. Among the many presuppositions included in our knowledge of the world, there are also those pertaining to other people: we expect them to behave meaningfully and we assume that they intend to express specific things by the particular forms they use. It is in reference to such presuppositions that the failure to perceive an utterance as meaningful causes us immediately to look for alternative, perhaps less obvious interpretations – until the utterance becomes meaningful (cf. Lewis, 1979). World knowledge has a cultural specificity and, in addition, an individual specificity. That is to say, some elements of this knowledge vary from culture to culture and, within the given culture, from individual to individual. These cultural differences are the source of serious problems for the spontaneous learner; numerous misunderstandings and communicative conflicts originate from a lack of discrimination (cf. Heidelberg Research Project, 1979, chapter 3; Becker and Perdue, 1982; Perdue, 1982).

Let us illustrate this point with three cases of communication by language.

(a) In most cultures there exist specific means for expressing social relations between speaker and hearer, for example in the many different ways in which people address each other: by first name, *Mr* plus name, title plus name; most languages have special pronouns to mark greater or lesser intimacy (German: *du/Sie*; French: *tu/vous*; etc.) (cf. Ervin-Tripp, 1969). In Japanese, in particular, there is an extremely intricate system of forms of address. A person who has not learned them (and the underlying system of social relations) is bound to get into trouble when trying to communicate.

(b) In some cultures a woman would never address a male stranger in the street. Even if she merely wanted to ask her way, her act would inevitably be interpreted as conveying some ulterior motive.

(c) The rules for saying *please*, *thank you*, *sorry*, and the like differ from culture to culture. Punjabi speakers in England, for example, tend to find the natives two-faced and hypocritical on account of their constant use of thanks and apologies, while they themselves appear rude and arrogant to the natives (cf. Perdue, 1982, chapter 4).

The three exemplifications above derive from a relatively narrow segment of world knowledge, namely, the field of social behaviour involving the use of language. But it is precisely in this domain that the powerful influence of world knowledge upon the learner's use of language for purposes of communication becomes apparent (more on this subject in Gumperz and Roberts 1978; cf. also Barkowski, Harnisch, and Kumm, 1980).

Although our knowledge of the world is in constant flux, it is relatively stable compared with the other categories of concomitant knowledge. Evidently, the former is well rooted in our long-term memory, whereas the latter are of a transient character. How our knowledge of the world is stored in memory and how it is retrieved for purposes of communication by language is extensively discussed in the literature (e.g. Kintsch, 1977; Lindsay and Norman, 1977, chapters 8–11), and it will not be discussed in detail here.

B.   Situational knowledge

This term refers to all the information speakers derive from their perception of the current situation; only the acoustic waves received by our hearing are in fact excluded – these carry the utterance information. The main source of our situational knowledge is normally our vision. Visual perception permits, for example,

> a meaningful use and interpretation of gestures (a communicative device of crucial importance in early language varieties);
> a continuous tracking of the hearer's facial expression and other signs of comprehension (cf. Scherer and Wallbott, 1979);
> an interpretation of deictic terms (*here/there*, *now/then*) with reference to the space, time, and similar coordinates of the speaker.

Compared with vision, other channels through which the current situation is perceived are of minor importance. The role of olfaction, to give but one more example, will be crucial in interpreting the meaning of *it* in the utterance, *Can you smell it?*

We have little reason to suspect that speakers of particular languages differ in their perceptual capacities; they are apt to differ, however, in the relevance attributed to particular aspects of the situation, and hence

115

the ways in which they associate their perception with the utterance information. This question will be taken up in our discussion of deixis (section 7.1.1).

In contrast to world knowledge, situational knowledge normally need not be retrieved from memory, simply because it is obtained simultaneously with the utterance. Even if the hearer has to consider what happened a moment ago, these perceptions are available instantaneously, as they are stored in short-term memory.

    C.   Preceding information

        What is meant here is the information obtained from preceding utterances, in other words, the preceding linguistic context of the current utterance. The importance of such preceding information was pointed out in connection with examples (43) and (44). Many of the most basic linguistic devices take advantage of this principle of falling back on what has been said before:

> anaphora, i.e., the use of personal pronouns (*he*, *she*, *it*, *they*) and such terms as *therefore*, *then*, *also*,
> ellipsis, i.e., the rule-bound omission of some elements in the sentence;

to quote but a few of the more important ones. More about these further below (cf. also Halliday and Hasan, 1976).

Within the entire range of concomitant knowledge, preceding information is the area in which the structural properties of a language most forcefully come into play. As it happens, this part of the embedding problem in early learner varieties has been largely neglected in research so far. The fact is that anaphoric personal pronouns[3] which refer to information given in preceding utterances enter the learner's repertoire at a much later stage than deictic pronouns like *I* and *you*, whose meaning ensues from the situation (cf. Klein, 1981; Klein and Rieck, 1982). This is not so, however, with all anaphoric terms; thus, *dann* ('then') is used relatively early to express temporality (see section 7.2).

Preceding information is subject to continuous change; it is kept in short-term memory for a time and can be transferred to long-term memory. Its relevance for what is being said diminishes with time, and so does its role in the embedding problem.

In discussing the three types of concomitant knowledge separately we have neglected the fact that they interact in any utterance situation. We perceive a situation and its components (one of them being the utterance) in that we interpret all of them in the light of our knowledge of the world;

the preceding information results from an interpretation of the preceding utterance(s) in the framework of all the concomitant knowledge available at the time.

We have repeatedly mentioned various structural properties of languages in relation to which our concomitant knowledge comes into play. In the following sections we will briefly discuss five of these: deixis, anaphora, ellipsis, word order, and intonation.

7.1.1 *Deixis*

Deictic terms are those lexical units that point, but do not fully specify, elements of a particular situation. In most languages, at least four kinds of deictic terms can be identified:

(a)   Personal deixis, or words like *I* (the person who is just speaking), *you* (the person who is just addressed), *we* (the person who is just speaking and at least one other person), etc.

(b)   Local deixis, or words like *here* (space containing the speaker),[4] *there* (space not containing the speaker), etc.

(c)   Temporal deixis, or words like *yesterday* (the day preceding the day of the utterance), *just* (a time shortly preceding the time of the utterance), etc. Tense, a grammatical category often expressed by verb inflection, is a very important means of conveying temporal deixis (more on this in section 7.2).

(d)   Object deixis, or words like *this*, as long as they are accompanied by a suitable gesture (pointing to the referent).

Deixis seems to function, in principle, in the same way in all languages (cf. Bühler, 1934, Part II; Fillmore, 1971; Wunderlich, 1971; Jarvella and Klein, 1982; Rauh, 1982). In order to identify the referent of a deictic utterance, the hearer must know:

The 'origo', i.e., 'I – here – now' of the speaker, as defined by the utterance situation;

the lexical meaning of the deictic word, as it is given in dictionaries (e.g. the sound pattern [hi:r] in German means 'space containing the speaker')

where to draw the boundary: while knowing that *here* means the place around the speaker, the hearer must consult his knowledge of the world to establish the extent of this place (compare *There is a draught here* with *Inflation has reached 7 per cent here*).[5]

We may safely assume that, unlike a first language learner, a second language learner is capable of understanding the basic principles of deixis, which are more or less the same in his native language. Difficulties may arise where the two languages differ in the segmentation of the various deictic domains (for example, by linking specific temporal or spatial notions with particular terms).

This will be illustrated with a well-known difference between English and German in local deixis. In English there are basically two local deictic terms: *here* and *there* (other English terms, such as *over there, yonder, left, right,* etc., may be disregarded in this context). The German *hier* and *dort* have the same meaning (*hier* = space containing the speaker, *dort* = space not containing the speaker), but there is a third term, *da*, which in most cases means 'there' as well. However, in some cases it does not. The meaning of *da* cannot be easily explained and continues to be the subject of controversy (cf. Ullmer–Ehrich, 1982). The fact is, nevertheless, that in English the 'deictic space' is sliced into two, and in German into three domains. An English-speaking learner of German will encounter tremendous problems in analysis, should he attempt to solve the embedding problem within this treacherously similar system of deictic space. The similarity of the two systems may lead him into a trap if he assumes, for instance, that *da* and *dort* mean 'there', or that *da* means 'there' if it is close and *dort* means 'there' if it is far away. He may, nonetheless, have arrived in this way at a solution to the embedding problem which so closely resembles the German one that he may never have any difficulties in communication.[6] No such compromise is possible in the case of two languages with markedly different systems of deixis, which is not at all infrequent (cf. Denny, 1978; Weissenborn and Klein, 1982).

7.1.2 *Anaphora*

As a syntactic device of cross reference, anaphora serves as a link with information contained in preceding clauses or utterances, or expands on such information. Some of the more important types are:

(a)   Third person personal pronouns (*he, she, it, they, him, them,* etc.) and possessive pronouns (*his, her, its, their*).

(b)   Some adverbs and particles, e.g. *above, before* (but not in reference to a *situationally* given point in time), *subsequently, then, below,* etc; *thus, so, hence,* etc; *also, likewise, in contrast,* etc.

(c)   Demonstratives like *this, that* and the definite article (*the*).

Many of these terms can also be used deictically (for pointing out elements of the situation), and there are cases where both situational knowledge and preceding knowledge converge upon one and the same term.

In any fully-fledged language, anaphora is the principal device for ensuring continuity and coherence in spoken language. Little has been done so far to investigate its development in learner varieties (the only major exception being Huebner, 1983), although this applies less to personal pronouns, which have been studied by a few authors (e.g. Felix and Simmet, 1982, with further references). Still, the emphasis seems to rest on pronouns as tied up with verb inflection and the marking of 'person', rather than on their anaphoric function. (In much the same way, the deictic and anaphoric role of pronouns is neglected in second language teaching.) One of the rare attempts to investigate pronouns as anaphoric and deictic devices (Klein, 1981; Klein and Rieck, 1982) suggests that in early learner varieties the role of anaphora is negligible, that is, the beginning learner avoids using pronouns in reference to preceding information. As to the order of acquisition of personal pronouns in general, the following observations were made by Klein and Rieck (1982, p. 69):

(i)   The deictic system of referring to speaker (*I*) and hearer (*you*) is acquired very early, but first without distinction between singular and plural (*I* may also mean *we*). The nominative case is used earlier than the derivative forms (*mir*, *mich*, or dative and accusative). Other early deictic acquisitions are *da* (the rather vague 'there', used also as 'here') and *jetzt* ('now').

(ii)   In early learner varieties the anaphoric pronouns are represented by just one form: *das* ('this'), and even fairly advanced learners tend to lag behind the target variety in this respect for quite a long time.

(iii) The missing anaphoric pronouns are usually replaced by repetition of the earlier mentioned nouns (names). Not infrequently there is a complete omission, i.e. ellipsis (see section 7.1.3).

At this point let us recall the results of the speech repetition task given in section 5.3 (Table 3): Asked to repeat the German sentence approximately equivalent to 'Perhaps she has left it at home with her parents', none of the eighteen speakers succeeded in reproducing *ihn* (in reference to a passport, i.e. 'it') and only one in two reproduce *sie* ('her'). These results dovetail neatly with the findings above.

It is not at all clear why learners tend to neglect anaphora as an important syntactic device for so long, relying instead – contrary to the norms of the target language – on two other devices, namely repetition and ellipsis. The matter is taken up in the following section.

7.1.3   *Ellipsis*

Both deixis and anaphora make use of specific words to indicate the point in the utterance where contextual information and utterance information join forces to supply the meaning. In an ellipsis the missing contextual information is not even indicated by lexical means; what is indicated by the structure of the utterance itself is the place at which the contextual information ought to be inserted by the hearer. The notion of ellipsis also comprises the rules for such complementing of missing information. Take for instance the elliptic utterance in (45).

(45)   Rainer Maria

A speaker who knows these two first names will complement this utterance either with ... *has married* ..., if the question was *Who has married whom?*, or with *Rilke's Christian name was* ..., if the question was *What was Rilke's Christian name?*.

The respective concomitant knowledge need not be supplied by the preceding utterance(s), it may just as well derive from our knowledge of the world (as in the case of weather forecasts) or situational information (as when you order: *Another two!*). Alternatively, the missing elements can be supplied in the subsequent (con)text, mostly in the form of a coordination: *He walked into and she walked out of the building* (the hearer inserts *the building* after *into*). The interaction of contextual and utterance information is also evident in the use of pronouns in anticipation of a subsequent noun, which is so common in English: *Ever since he became deaf, Beethoven fell behind the orchestra when conducting it*.

An ellipsis cannot be applied arbitrarily, in the hope that the hearer will complement the missing element from his concomitant knowledge, or guess it from the context. The deletion of lexical elements must follow certain rules: the answer to the second question cannot be *His Rainer Maria*. The rules tell us where the complement must be inserted, or where something can be left out. In spite of a fairly comprehensive literature on the subject, chiefly with a transformational-grammar orientation (see, eg., Sag, 1979; Kuno, 1982), the rules of ellipsis have not been explored in any depth; more has been done to analyse the use of ellipses involving reference to concomitant knowledge previously supplied in the same text (or discourse). Examples of the latter use are questions and answers, as in (46), assertions with supplements or corrections, as in (47), and coordinations, as in (48).

(46)   Who has married whom? – Rainer Maria
(47)   John has married Inge – No, Rainer Maria
(48)   John has married Inge and Rainer Maria (i.e. Rainer has married Maria)

As the purest embodiment of the embedding problem, ellipsis is of special importance for the investigation of learner varieties on at least three counts:

1. Learners tend to overuse ellipsis as a syntactic device, considerably stretching the possibilities offered by the target language (this holds particularly for beginners). A pertinent example is the by now well-known request, *Me bread*, uttered in a bakery. While perfectly in order when uttered in response to a specific question (*What would you like to have?*), this construction is also used in the absence of the relevant contextual presuppositions. It should be noted that, even so, communication *is* possible, in view of the overriding importance of the concomitant world and situational knowledge. In other words, the learner can afford to violate the ellipsis rules of the language.

2. A problem arises whenever the learner is forced, by his limited lexical repertoire, to omit elements in his utterance although he may know himself that they cannot be assumed to exist in the concomitant knowledge of the hearer. Though elllipses of this kind have nothing in common with the embedding problem, that is, with the appropriate language-specific adaptation of the utterance information into the total information flow, they are indistinguishable, on formal grounds, from proper ellipsis. This alone often creates problems for investigators of learner varieties.

3. The availability of some element in the hearer's concomitant knowledge is indeed a necessary, but not a sufficient condition for leaving this element unexpressed. It must be clear, too, *which element* of the concomitant knowledge is to be added at which phase in the utterance. Situational knowledge normally makes clear who is speaking. Hence, that information is part of the hearer's concomitant knowledge. But obviously, this fact does not yet allow the speaker to omit the personal pronoun *I*; after all, he might choose to talk about someone or something else. We stress this point in order to make clear that 'given' information – that is, elements of concomitant knowledge – and 'topic' information must not be confused. What the speaker might do, however, is to follow a principle such as this one:

> Any element introduced in a particular function (e.g. as subject) in a preceding utterance retains this function until a suitable cancellation has taken place.

Strictly speaking, the above principle can be viewed as a general ellipsis rule; whereas it may not obtain in either German or English, it does have certain parallels in these languages.[7]

This principle amounts to a shortcut to the solution of the embedding problem. This shortcut implies that a whole string of utterances must be put in line with the initial one, where the crucial element is explicitly

121

mentioned; all subsequent utterances are then strung together in parallel to the opening utterance. As we have seen in section 6.1, this is how learner texts are often structured: after introducing an element in the first segment (the setting), the speaker goes on referring to it implicitly in each successive focus, until a new setting is offered. This device makes anaphoric elements largely superfluous, especially those that contribute no new information, such as *he*, *she*, *it* (as opposed to such elements as *then*, which indicates a reaching back to a preceding utterance with the intention of supplementing it with new information).

The price paid for employing this technique is a more or less rigid word order, dealt with in the following section.

7.1.4   *Word order and intonation*

In any fully-fledged language the order in which words appear in an utterance is conditioned by a number of factors, one of which is the distribution of given and new information. The rule that the OLD comes first, to be followed by the NEW, was stated most explicitly in Behaghel (1923). The idea was subsequently developed by other investigators, notably those from the Prague School, who claimed that there is a rising gradient of 'communicative dynamics' in a sentence, that is, that the informational value of subsequent segments tends to increase in the course of a sentence (cf. Sgall, Hajičová, and Benešová, 1973). This kind of information distribution causes anaphoric and deictic elements to occur chiefly at the beginning of a sentence.

A variety of departures from what appears to be the normative information distribution are feasible. Consider the following four sentence pairs:[8]

(49)	What has Peter done?	(Peter has) smoked
(50)	Who has smoked?	Peter (has smoked)
(51)	Who has done what?	Peter (has) smoked
(52)	What has happened?	Peter has smoked

Each of the four questions supplies somewhat different preceding information as a point of departure for the answer. In consequence, the information distribution in the answers to (49) and (50) is exactly reversed: in (49) only *smoked* is new, while *Peter has* is given (in German, 'Peter has' can be deleted); this information distribution may be considered normal. In (50), *Peter* is new and *has smoked* is given. In the answer to (51), however, the only presupposition is that someone has done something: both *Peter* and *smoked* are new, nothing but their relation, stated by *has*, is given; here only *has* can be deleted (in German, at least). Finally, in (52) practically nothing is given. Thus we can see that the same word string can imply radically different information distributions. Now, the difference is clearly marked by different intonation patterns in each case. Simplifying greatly, the general rule is that the new element is stressed by dramatic pitch changes.

The interplay of word order, intonation, and information distribution creates the possibility of reversing the order of the constituent elements in the first two answers (in German: *Geraucht has Peter*). In the case of such a topicalization (of the infinitive part of the verb), a change in intonation is inevitable. What remains unaffected is the position of the finite element *has* as a sort of pivot. No such reversal is possible with the last two answers.

The implications of such observations for the embedding problem are these: users of language enjoy a certain freedom in the arrangement of utterance constituents (word order), provided they undertake appropriate shifts in intonation. If the learner is to make use of this freedom without infringing the rules of the language, he must have internalized some basic syntactic rules. For German, he must know how to keep the finite element in place, at the risk of the hearer being unable to identify the topicalized constituent. He must further know how to mark the case of nouns, or else the hearer may confuse subject and object. Thus it becomes clear that the embedding problem has some direct implications for the solution of the synthesis problem. Only sufficient syntactic and lexical means will allow the learner to endow his utterance, and the information it carries, with a certain weight in the totality of the information processed by the hearer.

Concluding our cursory discussion of various grammatical means for the integration of utterance and concomitant information,[9] we must again point out the paucity of evidence that could be brought to bear on our key problem of language acquisition. In the next section, the question of temporality will give us the opportunity to elaborate on the interactions of concomitant knowledge and utterance information, and to explore how the gradual shift in the balance maintained between the two sources of information enables the learner to reduce his dependence on the former.

7.2   How learners express temporality

In English and German, as in many languages, each complete utterance must contain some time reference, that is, whatever is expressed by the utterance must be brought (directly or indirectly) into relation to the time of speaking. The main time marking device is the finite verb. It will therefore be legitimate to say that the marking of time is a fundamental characteristic of utterances (in German, French, English, etc.). In the acquisition of German and many other languages the beginning learner is rarely aware of the rules governing the use of the finite element; in general, he has little or no verb inflection. This alone makes it worth while exploring to what extent, if at all, the learner marks time and how he approaches the target variety in this respect. In section 7.2.1 we discuss, in general, time marking as part of the embedding problem, in order to examine in some detail a piece of text from an early learner variety in section 7.2.2.

7.2.1   *Temporality*

The term 'temporality' in its wider sense refers to all manner of temporal marking of events, actions, states, etc. (in brief, events). The following distinctions are observed in many languages, including English, German, and French:

1. *Time reference* (temporality in its narrow sense) serves to mark the temporal relation of the event to which the given utterance refers, to a stated or implied point of reference. This point of reference must always be anchored in either the situational or world knowledge of the speaker and hearer. It is part of the situational knowledge if the time of speaking is also the time of reference; it is customary to term it the (deictic) 'origo'. Alternatively, the primary point of reference may be an event with temporal designation in the world knowledge of the two parties (e.g. Christ's nativity); we might then speak of 'calendar origo'. The time relations of an origo and the stated event may be *before*, *after*, *contained in*, and the like.

2. *Aspect* refers to the particular time perspective adopted by the speaker in his reference to the event in question: e.g. is the event 'completed' (perfect) or not? In some languages this category is even more important than time reference as effected by tense alone (e.g. in the Slavic languages); in French it is part of the tense system (perfect/imperfect); in German, its role is debatable. Being of secondary importance for the problem of embedding, it can be bypassed in this context.

3. *Action type* ('Aktionsart') refers to immanent temporal properties of the event, as implied by the lexical meaning of the respective expression (usually of the verb): punctuality (at one point in time), duration (over a period of time), inchoativity (about to begin), etc. In German, action type if often marked by prefixes: *blühen* ('blossom'), *aufblühen* ('begin

124

to blossom, flourish'), *verblühen* ('finish blossoming, fall off the trees') etc. Like aspect, action type has little bearing on the embedding problem.

We will therefore restrict our discussion to temporality in the narrow sense of the term. Giving a time reference to an utterance is evidently an embedding problem. Time must be marked in relation to the hearer's knowledge and the situational context, from which the time of the event can be inferred. Four kinds of factors are involved in time marking:

(a)   A common time conception shared by speaker and hearer.
(b)   Common primary points of reference, such as the deictic or the calendar origo.
(c)   Means for marking temporal spans or relations, such as adverbials or verb tense.
(d)   Certain discourse rules based on the speaker's and hearer's common knowledge, notably on the knowledge of the properties of events, etc.

In the following, factors (a–c) are discussed briefly, factor (d) in some detail.

Different cultures seem to have developed specific conceptions of time. In Western European culture, time is conceived as flowing uniformly in one direction and being amenable to segmentation, or slicing into arbitrary segments or intervals. Any event can be located at a certain point on, or over a certain span of, the time dimension. This approach enables us to define a temporal relation between any two events, or between an event and a specific time span or point in time.

A point of temporal reference can be provided by any event, if it is included in the hearer's and speaker's common knowledge of the world or the situation. A particularly suitable point is the time of the utterance itself, to which the hearer is ordinarily witness. This is why all currently known languages make use of this 'deictic origo' by means of a number of deictic terms (see also section 7.1.1). And yet the time of the utterance is in constant motion. Furthermore, this device fails in the case of written communication: the time of writing cannot be the same as the time of reading the written text, so that the reader may not have any clue as to the former. In such cases there exists the possibility of choosing as a point of temporal reference an event considered as epoch-making in the given culture and hence safely anchored in the world knowledge of its members. In our culture such an event functioning as 'calendar origo' is Christ's nativity; it might also be some revolution. This possibility is widely though not universally used. A further possibility would be to state a reference time explicitly in a preceding utterance. This kind of 'specific origo' (*when I was a child* or *right after the deluge*) is thus a component part of the preceding information, just as the deictic origo belongs to the situational knowledge, and the calendar origo to the world knowledge of speaker and hearer alike. In actual fact, specific origo is a derivative case insofar as the term implies some reference to the deictic or the calendar origo.

Once the speaker can be reasonably sure that a given time concept and a given origo exist in the hearer's concomitant knowledge, he may try to tie up the event in question with that knowledge. To accomplish this, he will need the language-specific terms denoting time intervals (e.g. 'seconds', 'moments', 'days', 'epochs', 'eternities') and temporal relations (e.g. 'A before B', 'A contained in B', 'A simultaneous with B', where A and B are time intervals). To denote the latter, each language has a rich repertoire of simple as well as complex terms. The two major devices serving this purpose are the following:

(i)   Adverbials, specifically simple adverbs (*yesterday*, *before*, *now*, etc.), prepositional phrases (*at sunset*, *over dinner*, *round the clock*, etc.), or related expressions (*last summer*), and subordinate clauses (*when the time was ripe*, *before falling asleep*, etc.). Many of these adverbials tie up with a deictic origo (*tomorrow*, *three years ago*) or with an earlier named reference time (*thereafter*, *three years earlier*).

(ii)   Tense marking as effected by suffixes, prefixes, root modifications, or auxiliary verbs: tense is a singularly deictic category in that it takes reference (primarily) from the deictic origo.

Adverbs and tense marking interact in a highly complicated fashion, varying from language to language, just as the repertoires of lexical terms do. What we are concerned with here are the principles involved (for a detailed discussion see Wunderlich, 1970; Bäuerle, 1977; Rohrer, 1980; Grewendorf, 1982).

If these were the only devices to mark temporality, beginning learners could not hope to make themselves understood in this respect. The Spanish migrant whose fossilized learner variety was described in section 6.1 has, for example, no inflection whatever at his disposal, and hence cannot mark tense in this way; moreover, he uses only very few adverbials. Despite this, he is a skilled story-teller (cf. Heidelberg Research Project, 1979, chapter 3). He is greatly helped by discourse rules, which do exist in the target language but are used to a much lesser extent. The question deserves more attention, since it is a good illustration of how learners try to express temporality in the target language.

The notion of discourse rules can be explained most conveniently with some examples. Sentences (53–4) describe the same event in different ways.

(53)   Hans got tired and he fell asleep
(54)   Hans fell asleep and he got tired

The temporal sequence of the two events is of course different in the two sentences. Consequently, (54) sounds strange, since our knowledge of the world prevents us from imagining someone falling asleep first and getting tired next. Incidentally, this has nothing to do with any causal relation between the two events. In our world knowledge, the two events *are* causally related in that falling asleep is often a consequence of getting tired, but the same effect of strangeness is produced by sentence (55) where no causal relation is involved.

(55)   Hans fell asleep and he turned the light off

These and similar observations can be summed up in a discourse rule, the principle of natural order (PNO):

> PNO: Unless marked otherwise, the sequence of events mentioned in an utterance corresponds to their real sequence.

This kind of principle has been proposed, in one form or another, by a number of writers (cf. Clark, 1970; Labov, 1972). Even the Ancient Greeks were familiar with it, when they referred to its violation as the rhetorical figure of 'hysteron proteron' (the earlier as the subsequent). In the form quoted above, PNO is surely inadequate. Consider the sentences in (56).

(56)   Hans fell asleep. Maria got tired

There is nothing in them to indicate that the event mentioned later had actually occurred later, or earlier, or simultaneously with the event mentioned first. It is simply open. The same might hold for examples (57–8), even though they are more likely to be interpreted in terms of PNO.

(57)   Hans fell asleep and Maria got tired
(58)   Hans fell asleep. He got tired

Evidently, whether the principle is effective or not may depend on such factors as the grammatical structure of the examples: are these two self-contained clauses or are they two coordinate clauses? Does the subject change or not? The principle seems fully applicable to a coordinate sentence with the same subject if the subject is deleted by ellipsis in the second part of the sentence, hence (59) is much more strange than (58).

(59)   Hans fell asleep and got tired

The decisive point seems to be whether the two events are conceived as *components of a single larger event* or not. Such a 'frame event' is considered to have a temporal structure with which the hearer is supposed to be familiar. He is thus expected to fit the two events into the temporal structure of the frame event.

Two factors may be involved in our assessment of whether any set of clauses concurs with PNO or not:

(i)   The temporal structure of the frame event.
(ii)   The cohesion of the grammatical link between two successive clauses
           or sentences, coordinate clauses being more intimately linked than
           two asyndetically stringed main clauses (as in (56) or (58)); change
           of subject reduces this cohesion while anaphoric elements, and even
           more so ellipsis, serve to enhance cohesion (cf. Halliday and Hasan,
           1976).

As some of the above examples imply, the frame event need not be explicitly mentioned; it may merely ensue from a number of component events. At the same time, by explicitly providing a temporal frame of reference, the speaker can predetermine the temporal relations between the subsequently specified component events. A sufficiently 'dense' temporal network will make the subsequent specifications of temporal relations unnecessary. We will illustrate this with three examples where a framework is offered first, and then three different events are fitted into it. Thus there is in each of them a string of four events (counting the frame event as the first): *a, b, c, d*. All events are marked as timed prior to the time of speaking; otherwise, there are no temporal markings.

(60)   They played a string trio. Wolfgang played the violin, Norbert played
            the cello, and Christiane played the viola d'amore
(61)   They listened to a string trio. Jorge got tired, yawned, and fell asleep.
(62)   They all suffered misfortunes. Mary married a butcher, Angelika emi-
            grated to Sweden, and Frank died a young man

For (60), nobody would assume that events *b, c*, and *d* followed each other, i.e., PNO would not apply here. From our world knowledge we infer, as far as playing a string trio goes, that the three events are temporally interrelated, being simultaneous rather than successive. In (61) the frame event imposes much less constraint upon the three remaining events, leaving open their sequence at first. But the strong cohesion in the second sentence causes us to line up the three events *b*, *c*, and *d* as specimens of Jorge's behaviour temporally embedded in *a*, and hence makes us apply PNO to them. That is to say, the explicitly stated framework *a* is filled by three sequential events *b* + *c* + *d* whose temporal relationships are governed by PNO. Finally, in (62) the frame event *a*, which is extremely general here, is filled by the three events *b*, *c*, *d*, but since the framework itself does not impose any order on these events, and since there is only a weak cohesion among them, they do not combine into a temporal structure that would underlie PNO. The temporal sequence of the three events remains an open question.

A reformulation of the PNO discourse rule would have to account for the degree of cohesion within a sequence of clauses as indicative of their internal temporal structure. Having illustrated this with our examples, we cannot go into the details, but the principle should be evident. In any fully-fledged language, such discourse rules, no matter how specific, are only one among many other devices which enable a speaker to mark explicitly every possible temporal relationship. The more limited the grammatical devices, the greater the weight of discourse rules which impose sequential constraints on a string of utterances. The learner variety explored in the next section shows compellingly how a limited linguistic repertoire forces the learner to rely on discourse rules when trying to express temporal relations.

Obviously, we have had to bypass many factors which make the picture far more complicated. There are, for instance, generic events with no immediate temporal implications (*Neanderthal man feared the rigours of the weather*), timeless events (*The soul is immortal*), and fictitious events (*Sherlock Holmes fell in love with Dr Watson*). Unlike singular events which can, in principle, be brought into relation to the time of the utterance, the latter are very difficult to accommodate in such a temporal framework. Furthermore, the expression of temporality varies with discourse type (cf. Weinrich, 1964): narratives are different from route directions, etc. We will touch upon this issue in the next section.

7.2.2 *Temporality in a basic learner variety*

We turn now to a lengthy story told in a basic learner variety. An Italian woman who has acquired a very limited command of German during her two years in the country is telling two native speakers of German how her husband was involved in an industrial accident and what kind of problems she encounters in Germany.[10] Before presenting the story itself, we must give a brief account of the learner's repertoire. The following observations are based on an excerpt from the conversation mentioned above, which amounted to about 1,100 words.

(i)   a. The text contains no auxiliaries and no copulas.

b. There is no inflection whatever; although we do find certain phonetic variants among the 15 different 'verbs' (cf. section 6.1) used in the text (e.g., *sag, sage, sagen*), this variation had no grammatical function.

c. There is one modal verb: *wollen* (e.g. *ich wollen arbeiten*); again, it is not inflected (note that, in Standard German, the appropriate form would be *will*).

d. The learner does use – somewhat in opposition to what was stated under (i)b. – two isolated participles, *gestorb* and *gearbei* (leaving out the endings), but their function cannot be ascertained.

In short, there is practically no trace of the complicated tense system of the target language.

(ii)   a. Two context-dependent adverbs are regularly used: *dann* ('then') and *jetzt* ('now'); *morgen* ('tomorrow') and *einmal* ('once', but employed in the sense of *einst*, or 'once upon a time' – in English the two meanings go together but not in German) occur sporadically.

b. There are many adverbials which serve to denote a time span; they usually take the form Q + N, where Q is one, two, three ..., and N is week, month, year, and the like.

c. Prepositional adverbials are absent, with two exceptions: *bei Arbeit* (which should be *bei der Arbeit*, or 'at work') and *auf Arbeit* (again, the article is missing, though the meaning is not at all clear); their function is taken over by numerous NPs (noun phrases), like *ses Uhr* (which should be *sechs Uhr* for 'six o'clock'), *diese Monat* (which should be *in diesem Monat* for 'this month'), *Februar* (which should be *im Februar*), and also when the year is given.

d. The only temporal conjunction, *wann* ('when') is used in all contexts both in its own place as well as in place of *wenn* (unlike English, German distinguishes between *wann* = 'at what time' and *wenn* = 'if').

e. Contrary to the rules of the target language, the learner frequently uses the adjective *fertig* ('finished, ready') to indicate the conclusion of an event or action. It is usually preposed, i.e., *ich fertig arbeit sage Chefin* (approximately: 'I stopped working, said boss') or *fertig Arbeitsamt bezahle* (probably: 'when the unemployment office stopped paying'). When the event is implied by context, *fertig* appears, in the same function, without a verb: *wann fertig, doktor sage* ('When the hospital treatment was finished, the doctor said...').

In 7.2.1 we spelled out the factors which contribute to a successful expression of temporality and are therefore indispensable for solving the embedding problem. These are: a common time conception (supplied by world knowledge), a common origo (strictly speaking, two: a deictic origo deriving from situational knowledge and a calendar origo deriving from world knowledge), a repertoire of linguistic means and devices, and certain discourse rules. Our Italian speaker assumes, quite rightly, that the first two factors do operate in the case of her German interlocutors. Her repertoire, on the other hand, is very limited, and she has no choice but to lean heavily on discourse rules. Let us now see how she goes about solving a relatively difficult linguistic task which demands considerable proficiency in temporal marking.

The text cited in (63) was originally transcribed in phonetic notation, but since we are not concerned here with the phonetic aspects of the speech production, it was re-written in the ordinary alphabet with a spelling that tries to capture some peculiarities of this language use (e.g. *nix* for *nichts*). For easy identification, the text is segmented, each segment preceded by a letter. Square brackets are used for questions put by the two German partners, the dash indicates short breaks, and my own interpretations and comments are put in parentheses. The excerpt in (63) was preceded in the interview by talking about the speaker's problems in Germany. An approximate translation is given for each segment.

(63) a. Andre Problem, Problem, wann mein Mann Unfall, ooh
         Other problem, problem, when my husband accident, oh
         [Question: how did it happen]
      b. Ein Jahr, däs Oktober, ja
         One year, that October, yes
      c. Auf Arbeit
         On work
         [Request to describe the accident]
      d. Mein Mann Unfall?
         My husband accident?
         [Yes]
      e. Arbeit
         Work (job)
      f. Bei Arbeit, arbeite oben, un dann kaputt
         At work, work above an then kaput
      g. Vielleicht – andere Kollegen sage, vielleicht – gestorb
         Perhaps – other workmates says, perhaps – died

131

h. Und dann telefonier Klinik, Klinik Heidelberg, Ambulanz
And then telephoning clinic, clinic Heidelberg, ambulance

i. Und dann fort in Klinik
and then away in clinic

j. Ich nix sage Arbeit
I nothing say work (I wasn't told of it at work)

k. Mein Cousin (1 sec. unidentifiable) da in Fabrik
My cousin. . .there in factory

l. Und dann sage
And then say

m. Dein Mann – Unfall
Your husband – accident

n. Ich fertig arbeit
I ready work

o. Sage Chefin
Tell boss (female)

p. Ich wollen mit hin Heidelberg, Krankenhaus
I want along over Heidelberg, hospital

q. Da mein Mann
There my husband

r. Ja, gut, Chefin sagen
Yes, okay, boss say

s. Ich fort in Krankenhaus
I away in hospital

t. Un dann wieder dort mein Mann
An then again there my husband

u. Ich sagen
I say

v. Vielleicht – gestorb
Perhaps – dead

w. Drei Tage nix spreche, nix gucke, nix esse, nix drinke, wo?
Three days no speak, no look, no eat, no drink, where? (what's going on?)

x. Ich weiß net
I don't know

The story continues for a while (with a happy end), but this much suffices for our purposes.

Narratives of this kind[11] are subjective descriptions of real and often highly complex events which occurred in a particular place at a particular time. In addition, they reflect the speaker's feelings and thoughts. Temporality is involved in such narratives in three ways:

1. The whole event must be embedded in the discourse context, which entails in particular its timing with respect to the utterance time (temporal 'anchoring').

2. The global event has a complex internal structure: it comprises a number of episodes which are mutually related in the temporal and other dimension (episode *a* may precede *b*, or be coincident with *b*, or be contained in *b*, etc.). This internal temporal segmentation must be expressed in one way or another. It is up to the speaker to segment the whole event into its constituent episodes and to select those to be referred to explicitly. In every case, the story must have its temporal 'timbering', and the decision to recount an episode implies placing the latter in this temporal framework.

3. At any place in the narrative the speaker is free to insert information which, while not belonging to the event itself, has to be incorporated into the 'timbering'. It might be background information (*oh, that's my brother-in-law*), evaluations (*how stupid of me!*), judgements of other people, and the like. All this information is the 'plasterwork' of the narrative.

These three functions of temporality must be carefully distinguished. Take a sequence of two clauses, *a* and *b*; the first describes an episode, and the second may describe a subsequent episode. But *b* might also be a commentary on *a* and thus stand outside the flow of time (compare, *He broke a leg; they called in a doctor*, with *He broke a leg; easily done at a building site*).

Now back to our story. Its 'anchoring' is of a simple kind. Having introduced the overall event 'accident' in (a), and having thus set the framework for what is to follow, the speaker answers the question about how this had happened by timing the event: initially by 'one year, that October', with which the event is timed in relation to the utterance time ('one year'), although the kind of relation is not made explicit; the following specification ('that October') leaves us guessing if it was last October or October last year, but the partners to the conversation must know what she had in mind. Nonetheless, the temporal framework has been provided: October last year. An additional specification follows: 'on work', which is not context-dependent and offers what Labov (1972) called an 'orientation', without relating to the utterance time. After another specific time reference ('work'), in response to a question, the narrator begins to recount the successive episodes in (f). This utterance consists of three segments, the first of which provides a sort of 'brackets' for the other two. This structure could be presented as *A*, *B*, then *C*, where *B* is in *A*, *C* in *A*, and *C* after *B*. The framework designated by *A* is first of all filled with a string explicitly marked by 'then'. The stringing continues in (g), where we have two parallel utterances, each modalized by 'perhaps' (their structure follows the 'principle of orientation' – see section 6.1). Other such cases (cf. Heidelberg Research Project, 1979, chapter 3) have made it clear that 'perhaps' tends to be employed to mark the subsequent statement as contingent, hypothetical, or even counterfactual. Aided by the context, we may thus speculate that the narrator tried to say the following: 'Thereupon apparently/possibly the other workers said: "Maybe he is dead-/might die/is going to die"'. The first segment (D) evidently continues the temporal stringing, being a sequence to B. Less evident is the timing of E ('perhaps – died', which is the same as C). The participle *gestorb(en)* would suggest that C occurred before D (the latter, incidentally, also being an utterance time, although a derived one: the time of the workmates' utterance). On the other hand, the telephone call to the clinic (and not to the mortuary, for example) and then the transfer to the clinic (i) seem to invalidate this interpretation. The other two alternatives are: he might die, or he is going to die. In relation to the derived utterance time, this would be an anticipated event. The two facts – that this is 'quoted speech' and in addition modalized – make it very difficult to time the event in relation to the speaker's utterance time. The introduction of 'quoted speech' cancels the primary temporal reference and replaces it with a derived point of reference, a 'secondary origo'. This consists of the utterance situation described by the narrator; it is in this situation that the quoted speech is anchored. The technique of 'repeated anchoring' is a typical feature of the narration of foreign workers.

Utterances (h) and (i) continue the temporal stringing with explicit markings for F and G, respectively. The original temporal framework set in A ('at work') has been definitely abandoned by the time we arrive at G, but in order to determine this point, we may look for support in our world knowledge: A was originally provided merely to time B, and C was timed in relation to B, D was timed in relation to C, and so on. The temporal relation of C to A is thus specified indirectly. We could try to depict the episodes and their temporal interrelations in a schematic way, employing two symbols: $\frac{A}{\ulcorner B \urcorner}$, meaning A provides the temporal framework for B, and $A \rightarrow B$, meaning A precedes B.

$$(64) \qquad \frac{A}{\ulcorner B \urcorner} \longrightarrow C \longrightarrow D \underset{\searrow E}{\overset{\nearrow F \longrightarrow G}{}}$$

There is no telling if C (or anything else) falls into the framework set up with A. Otherwise, E and F (or G), both following D, lack a mutual reference. This temporal structure could be presented linearly as in (65).

$$(65) \qquad A, B, \text{ then } C, \text{ perhaps } D, E, \text{ then } F, \text{ then } G$$

Three techniques were involved in our derivation of (65) from (64):

134

framing (on the basis of sequence and world knowledge),
chaining (on the basis of sequence and marking by 'then'),
quoted speech, i.e., repeated anchoring.

Utterance (j) opens a series of statements in which the speaker herself
enters the scene. Phrased concisely (j) conveys the idea that she had not
got the message at work; *ich* ('I') tends to be used in place of *mir* and
mich (cf. Klein and Rieck, 1982). As we try to time this event (or non-
event), we realize that, in principle, singular events are explicitly timed
in relation to the utterance time and to other singular events of the same
narrative in that each of them occupies a certain time span. The time
span in which the speaker had not received word of the accident must
obviously fall between the time of the accident and the time when she
was actually told of the event. The exact length of this time interval is
not specified.

The narrative continues with (k), part of which is unintelligible unfortunately. It would appear that in the meantime the speaker's cousin had
arrived in the factory, but we cannot tell if *da* ('there, then, so') is to
be understood temporally or spatially. In any case, this event occurred
after all the others recounted up to this point: the chaining is continued
in (k) and also, explicitly ('and then say'), in (l). The utterance in (l)
introduces a derived utterance time once again; the subsequent utterance
('your husband – accident') is timed by (l). The 'principle of natural
order' does not apply to utterance (m): the recounted event is clearly
timed prior to the event mentioned in (k), since it is the accident itself.
That is to say, the insertion of derivative utterance time together with
quoted speech overcomes the constraints imposed by PNO. Leaving aside
temporality, it is clear that the technique of secondary anchoring also con-
tributes in some other ways to finding a solution to the embedding problem.
It enables the narrator to refer to other persons by employing 'I' in place
of 'he' and 'she'; by using an earlier acquired deictic pronoun as a substitute
for anaphoric elements, the learner succeeds in broadening the applications
of her very limited linguistic repertoire (cf. section 7.1.2).

However, only (m) is quoted speech; with (n) the narrator resumes
the account of her own moves. Temporally, (n) links up with (l) by span-
ning (m). As mentioned before, *fertig* ('finished, ready') is commonly
used to mark the conclusion of an action; hence, (n) could be paraphrased
as 'I stopped working'. In view of the closeness of the 'I' in (n), the
personal pronoun is omitted in (o), where the narrator introduces direct
speech once again. The latter continues in (p) and (q); the temporal relation

between the derived utterance time and the quotes in (p) and (q) is simultaneity. (r) follows on from (o), but with a change in speaker. The quoted speech is extremely terse, amounting to a timeless comment ('yes, okay').

The chaining continues with (s), (t), and (u), the third introducing direct speech once again. Both (u) and (v) are parallel to (g), where some workmates were quoted as saying 'perhaps...died'. The word *sagen* in (u) should not be taken literally; it might mean 'I thought' (he could die), but this does not affect the principle ('quoted speech' encompasses 'quoted talking to oneself').

Utterance (w) describes a situation: 'for three days (he) didn't speak, didn't look (was unconscious), didn't eat, didn't drink'. The time span covered in (w) obviously cannot be placed *after* the final non-embedded event (t,u) because (v) is direct speech. The narrator does not suggest that her husband had lost consciousness after she had 'said' (thought) he might die. Rather, the time span covered in (w) begins with the accident itself, or shortly thereafter. Anyway, (w) clearly departs from PNO; in fact, it provides a new temporal framework which encompasses many of the preceding developments. The duration of the time span (though not its starting point) is explicitly named with the initial adverbial. The last utterance, (x), falls within this framework.[12]

From our analysis of the narration it follows that the speaker employs four techniques to construct the temporal scaffolding of her story:

(i) *Framing*: a time span is stated explicitly, and this encompasses the time span of the next-mentioned event.

(ii) *Chaining*: the time of the mentioned event becomes the reference time for the next-mentioned event, as effected by simple serialization in keeping with PNO and, additionally, by 'and then'.

(iii) *Repeated anchoring*: a derivative utterance time is introduced by a *verbum dicendi*, and the quoted speech is referred to that time by deictic means.

(iv) *Reset*: examples are found in (j) and (w); they involve the assumption of a new perspective, as for instance by introducing a protagonist, a new place, or an explicit timing, as in (w). The temporal reference of the first event mentioned in a reset to earlier-mentioned events can be inferred only from world knowledge.

These procedures or techniques are also employed in more advanced learner varieties as well as in the target language, although the degree of the speaker's dependence on them varies. A speaker who has at his disposal adverbials such as 'before', 'at the same time', etc., as well as some tense marking devices, is free to depart from the sequence implied by the four procedures without jeopardizing communication. The speaker whose narration is given in (63) obviously cannot do so.

7.3   **Conclusion**

We will conclude this chapter on embedding with two remarks. First, our ideas about the ways in which the embedding problem is solved by learners are still very unsatisfactory. This chapter was therefore not intended as a comprehensive review of available research evidence, but rather as an essay on the importance of this problem for the development and functions of learner varieties.

Secondly, a major reason for this unsatisfactory state of the art is the paucity of evidence on the interplay of concomitant knowledge and utterance information in the use of any fully-fledged language as well as in learner varieties. A similar point was made at the end of the previous chapter and it also holds for the following one on the matching problem. Let us also add that the analysis of this interplay in early learner varieties, where it emerges particularly clearly, may be of help to those interested in the same problems in fully-fledged languages.

8
The matching problem

The learner's constant objective in language acquisition is to reduce the gap between his language performance and that of native speakers of the target language. The progress towards this goal is not necessarily even-paced or direct. The learner may make false assumptions and will find it very difficult to get rid of them; he may even slide back in his proficiency. Apart from these irregularities, language acquisition in principle proceeds from one learner variety to the next in gradual approximation of the target variety – until this process comes to a halt. With luck, the remaining discrepancy may be negligible and hence scarcely noticeable.[1] In general, however, most learners end up with a language variety which contrasts strongly with the target variety. Of course, not all learners may be aware of this: some are unable to tell the difference and harbour illusions as to their language proficiency. Others will be generally aware of their imperfections but unable to pinpoint them with the precision needed for subsequent amelioration. Progress in language acquisition requires the learner to match continuously his own language performance against the standards of the target language speakers. This matching task confronts the learner at all stages of the process: at the beginning the discrepancy is striking and cannot go unnoticed; the smaller it becomes, towards the end of the process, the greater the matching problem.

This chapter deals with certain aspects of the matching problem. Although not very much empirical evidence is currently available on this matter, it is possible to offer some mostly theoretical considerations. In section 8.1 some of the obstacles to an investigation of the matching problem are outlined. In section 8.2 we discuss the various matching procedures: self-monitoring, feedback from other speakers, etc. In 8.3, the central section of this chapter, we try to establish what exactly is matched with what, and we come to the conclusion that at any point in time the learner can focus on only a limited number of aspects of his defective language performance. Finally, the concluding section is devoted to one of the few comprehensive studies of self-correction in second language learning available so far.

8.1 **General issues**
8.1.1 *Objective and subjective discrepancy*

A discussion of the discrepancy between a given learner variety, on the one hand, and the target variety, on the other, is a gross simplification. There may be, and indeed are, discrepancies in all domains of language: phonology, syntax, vocabulary, discourse proficiency, etc.[2] Large variations across these domains are typically found in individual learners: a learner may be fairly advanced in vocabulary while showing elementary gaps in syntax, another may have an excellent pronunciation and yet be unable to engage in a conversation. All these differences must be accounted for in order to determine the scale of the matching problem.

Even so, discrepancy (in a particular domain) is not the same as *perception* of that discrepancy. We would not do justice to the matching problem if we were to restrict our investigation to the structural differences between a given learner variety and the target variety. What really matters is the learner's subjective evaluation of the discrepancy. Amongst a group of learners showing the same objective discrepancy (in a particular domain), we will encounter any number of different subjective evaluations, or 'subjective discrepancies'.[3]

The inability to notice this discrepancy is one of the reasons why some learners come to a halt at a certain point in the acquisition process while others continue to advance well beyond the same point. The former may be unable to estimate the discrepancy, or underrate it considerably, the latter may even overrate it: their subjective evaluations vary greatly, whereas at a given time there is objectively no difference between them.

This does not mean, of course, that objective discrepancy is unimportant. First of all, it forms the basis for subjective estimates, and secondly, it is the objective discrepancy which the learner must seek to reduce. In fact, awareness of an actual discrepancy is a precondition for gradually overcoming it. However, awareness alone will not suffice: the learner may have a very precise and correct idea of his deficiencies in, say, pronunciation, and yet be quite unable to reach the standards of his social environment.

8.1.2 *Variations in the target language*

A natural language is in actual fact composed of a number of varieties: dialects, sociolects, medium-specific forms (written language

139

as opposed to spoken language), and so on. Many speakers of the language can avail themselves of more than one such variety ('register'), applying each in the appropriate situation or milieu. To distinguish between objective and subjective discrepancy in general is therefore an oversimplification of the issue, in particular when this is done in reference to the 'standard of the target language' (less so when in reference to the standard of a particular target variety, e.g. the language spoken by the industrial workers of a region). Generally speaking, there is no one particular target variety but rather a whole range of them; both the subjective and objective discrepancy may vary from one variety to the next. This is often obscured by the tendency to ascribe weight (or in fact a monopoly) to one of the many varieties of a language, namely the 'standard language' (in the case of English one often speaks of 'Queen's English' or 'BBC English'). Alternatively, the standard may be a certain brand of colloquial language coloured by some dialect, as spoken in the social environment of the learner. All these complications must be borne in mind whenever the term 'discrepancy in relation to the target variety' is used in the following discussion.

8.1.3 *Conscious and subconscious perception of discrepancy*

The most difficult question within the matching problem is perhaps the extent to which the learner has to be *consciously* aware of the existing discrepancy. Although we cannot discuss here exactly where the dividing line ought to be drawn between conscious and subconscious processes, it seems that human beings consciously or unconsciously strive to reduce the gap between their current condition and some 'goal' condition (standard). This striving presupposes that the difference be noticed in some way, but it need not be registered consciously. Much of our behaviour is controlled in a completely automatic fashion: the ability to stand or walk upright involves an incessant 'equilibration' by our sense of balance, and this is effected subconsciously; the ability to season our *coq au vin* correctly involves a similar but conscious matching of the current state with the ideal state; the ability to negotiate our car smoothly through a stream of traffic is based on a continuous interplay of conscious and subconscious control processes (and notice that this interplay changes if we are driving an unfamiliar car). In the use of language, there is a similar interaction of conscious and subconscious processes. Different modes of language acquisition show vast differences in this respect, chiefly on account of the way in which the input is made available (in everyday communication or in a 'prefabricated' form). In addition, inherent differences in 'accessibility to conscious introspection' exist between the basic language skills: it is incomparably more difficult to become consciously aware of discrepancies in intonation than in lexical usage. Finally, there are individual variations among learners (outgoing vs. introverted personalities). All formal second language instruction relies heavily on the conscious tracking of discrepancies, whereas in spontaneous language acquisition the role of *unconscious* registering of various signs of discrepancy carries equal if not greater weight. The matter does not appear to have received much systematic attention among investigators (however, see the references in note 5).

8.1.4 *Metalinguistic reflection*

In striving to cope with the matching problem the learner must try to compare his own output with that of others, and in doing so he somehow steps outside of himself to attain a perspective on his own language performance. The latter is thus enriched by a metalinguistic component. Metalinguistic language use pervades many of our activities (this book itself being a case in point), but ordinarily this self-reflection does not demand a major share of our attention. Although natural languages do indeed have a 'metalinguistic vocabulary' comprising such terms as 'speech sound', 'word', 'sentence', which allows us to talk about language, the same applies to other possible subjects of conversation, the weather, for example. Now, some writers have tended recently to regard as metalinguistic every single reference to language phenomena; this is like calling any reference to the weather 'metameteorological'. Nevertheless, metalinguistic language use, taken in a somewhat narrow sense, does indeed play a role in language acquisition. Jakobson (1960) says that language is used metalinguistically as long as the speaker's attention is directed at the 'code' itself. This allows him to construct utterances which do not conform to rules of the given language and to compare these systematically with grammatical sentences in the same language. One might enquire, for instance, *Is there a word like 'strung' in English?* or else, *Is 'He don't want to go' a grammatical sentence?* Such metalinguistic use of language is of direct relevance to language acquisition. The manner of presentation of the language material in some varieties of second language instruction – where the learner is offered carefully phrased statements about the language and its rules – is also, for the most part, metalinguistic. In short, the role of metalinguistic reflection in language acquisition is not inconsiderable.[4]

Some writers have tried to differentiate different phenomena within the notion 'metalinguistic'. For example, Culioli (1976) distinguishes between 'métalinguistique' in a narrow sense as denoting what the learner is conscious of, and 'épilinguistique' in reference to language phenomena of which the learner is not consciously aware but an awareness of which is reflected in his language performance. Moreover, he distinguishes between 'activité métalinguistique' (any behaviour focussed upon language, including absolute reflection on language and man's capacity for language) and 'discours métalinguistique' (metalinguistic use of language). Culioli's work has inspired a number of studies of the role of metalinguistics in language acquisition.[5]

The very vagueness of the notion 'metalinguistic reflection' makes it difficult to evaluate its place in language acquisition. It is advisable therefore to turn to particular instances of such reflection and consider how useful they are for the language learner when he wants to compare his language use with that of others.

8.2 Types of (self-)control

The learner can match his language performance against the standard of the target variety in a number of ways. These might be defined in terms of 'on-line-ness', meaning their relevance for current speech performance. The learner may try to check on what he is just about to produce in the way of communicative behaviour, in order to make sure that his output conforms to whatever he might regard as the norm. Alternatively, he might merely reflect (to himself or aloud) on how much and in what ways his speech differs from the standard. A sharp dividing line between the two cases cannot easily be drawn, as some reflection is always taking place while we speak. For our purposes, it is practical to distinguish three types of (self-)control:

(a) *Monitoring*, or virtually simultaneous control over our speech, which enables us to modify ongoing speech production.
(b) *Feedback*, or slightly delayed control resulting, in many cases, in more or less successful self-correction.
(c) *Reflection*, or overall control over our language performance, not coincident with speech production.

These three types are effected by the learner himself, although in many cases his self-control is promoted or even induced by other speakers (notably in feedback control).

Other differences to be noted are in the object of the matching procedure: you may compare an utterance with an alternative one, or your own utterance with that made by a native speaker in similar circumstances, or one abstract rule with another. We will first discuss the three types of control and subsequently the possible objects of control.

8.2.1   Monitoring

Any speaking involves an automatic monitoring of the speech output and also a concurrent check on the effect produced in the hearer(s). In much the same way the hearer tries not only to comprehend what he hears but (inadvertently) keeps a watch on the 'standard-conformity' of the perceived speech. In a way, our speech-production and comprehension monitor is always in action (cf. Marshall and Morton, 1978). In everyday communication we are not particularly aware that such a control agency is continuously in operation: the process of communication tends to occupy our attention. But the effects of our self-control can be easily traced in the following phenomena:

1. Self-control is evidently behind such self-corrections as 'He was standing next to, er ... behind the ...', 'A red, well, pink scarf was ...', or 'I met him in Paris, or rather in London'. These self-corrections may be due to a concern for correctness in substance, or else in grammatical form, the latter being the less frequent case. The tendency to undertake such self-repair is evidence enough of the underlying self-control (cf. Cutler, 1981; Levelt, 1983).

2. It is not unusual to correct others, but since the hearer may not know what the speaker is trying to communicate – after all, this is what the utterance is for – he can correct only those utterances which are clearly out of line with the rules of grammar and, on the basis of his concomitant knowledge, those the speaker should have phrased differently in order to say what he had in mind. All this is more or less virgin territory for the investigator.

3. We find ourselves able to bring our utterances in line with the changing requirements of the situation, as evidenced by the fact that we succeed in avoiding certain words that were just about to be pronounced, by substituting paraphrases for what (as we suddenly realize) might turn out to be offensive to the hearer, by varying the volume of our voice or the speed of speaking – all in order to streamline communication. Failures to adjust our speech to the situation may be caused by outward obstacles to monitoring: a speaker with headphones tends to raise his voice beyond the volume appropriate to the circumstances because he does not hear his own voice in the usual way.

Apart from the last example, all these cases can be taken to show that in producing an utterance the speaker matches the incipient product against some 'paragon' stored in memory; this on-line matching enables him to effect modifications in his final output, or else, to modify his understanding of the utterance he hears. In production as much as in comprehension we match the linguistic output/input against our internal standards.

The first procedure is of immense importance to the language learner (Fathman, 1980). It enables him to inspect what he is just about to say, in the light of his (limited) knowledge of the rules of the language, and to undertake suitable modifications or self-corrections (more on this in section 8.4). The second procedure is likewise of importance in second language learning, but in a different way: rather than the learner, it is the hearer who assists the learner. The third possibility is probably less important for the acquisition process.

8.2.2   Feedback

The control discussed above applies to ongoing language processing. The learner may however also benefit from feedback 'after the fact', that is, after his utterance has been completed. Feedback of this kind occurs when the speaker is offered by the *hearer*:

> explicit information signalling lack of understanding (*What?*),
> information implicit in utterances signalling incomplete or misunderstanding,
> explicit corrections.

Only in the last case does the speaker have access to the model needed to solve the matching problem. Of course, the model may be helpful and grammatically correct but may miss the point which the learner intended to make.

Corrections by others are felt to be important props for the learner. Currently, however, there are only a few systematic studies of either the scale of such corrections or their true significance for the learner (Gaskill, 1980; Day *et al.*, 1984).[6] Everyday experience tells us that native speakers vary greatly in their readiness to correct defective utterances explicitly. But even if it were found that corrections by others are ubiquitous (which they are not), this does not predicate anything about their effectiveness in the long run. Becker and Klein (1979) analysed a conversation involving an immigrant worker and three Germans, in search of discourse organization devices; corrections by others were also examined. These were found to have a very short-lived effect: the learner does take note of the corrected form, but, a few sentences later, he is back to his defective form. In this particular case the reason may have been the advanced fossilization of the learner's variety. But we simply do not know how effective such corrections are with other learners, or how different their effect could be in the particular domains (e.g. phonology vs. vocabulary). It may be, too, that there are gross individual differences among the learners in this respect.

8.2.3   *Reflection*

Our language performance is also subject to a control which is distanced from or outside the process of communication itself. Thus one deliberates (alone or with others) on the different senses of a word, or how a word should be pronounced, or how a certain construction should be formed – without immediate application in communication. A linguist professionally engaged in similar issues is likely to overestimate the importance of reflection in ordinary language use. There is likewise no reason to assume that reflection on language plays a significant role in *spontaneous* language acquisition: a Punjabi migrant worker who acquires his English in the course of social interaction with the environment is not likely to sit back and reflect on the peculiarities of the English language, or try to find out the designation for a particular linguistic form. However, such temporally removed control (or 'remote control') looms large in guided language acquisition, in particular when the method of instruction does not provide for real or simulated communication, putting the emphasis instead on vocabulary learning, grammatical exercises, or just pattern drill. The effectiveness and implementation of 'remote control' is an established theme in language teaching research. Some of the relevant problems were pointed out in sections 8.1.3 and 8.1.4 (see also section 1.5.4).

8.3   **Critical rules or: What is being matched against what?**

To advance his command of the target language, the learner must incessantly match his actual performance against some standard, possibly the language variety spoken in his social environment. As soon as he is no longer able to detect any discrepancy between the two, his learning of the language is at an end. In order to go beyond this rather general formulation, the following three questions must be answered:

1. What are the two things to be matched? No matter which of the aforementioned control procedures is employed by the learner, he cannot compare his entire language performance with that of his environment all at once. What he does in actual fact is compare one or some of his utterances with the 'corresponding' utterances as produced by native speakers, or else, certain features of his speech production with some 'corresponding' features of the target variety. Very well, but:

2. Why does the learner select for comparison in a given situation this rather than any other feature of his production? The simple case of explicit corrections by a native speaker will illustrate this dilemma. Suppose the learner utters a sentence which violates the rules of the target variety on a number of counts. The native speaker to whom he addresses the utterance repeats the sentence in a correct form. In this case, although the range of potential matches is reduced to the structural features of the two competing utterances, they are still numerous, and it is open whether the learner then focusses on one of them, or whether he checks them all. Clearly, if there are a great number of features on which the two differ, the learner may not be able to pay attention to them all. He has to decide in a given situation which of the structural features are the most critical and, as such, deserve to be processed first. The others must be ignored, if only because there is not enough capacity to deal with them. This selection may be guided by one more criterion: the structural features of the target utterance must be identified correctly before the match can be undertaken with any success. And so:

3. What kind of access does the learner have to the object of matching? The utterances he produces, including all their grammatical and lexical features, are available to the speaker in a way the corresponding utterances of his partner are not (if they were, he would no longer need to learn). The latter must first be analysed for their structure, and in this the learner must essentially draw on his imperfect ideas about the structure of the target variety, the same ideas that falsely guided him into forming the defective utterances.

These questions will be examined in some detail in the following sections. We start by returning to certain issues raised in section 1.3.1 (learning task vs. communication task) and continue by exemplifying the relevant problems in section 8.3.5.

8.3.1 *Communication task vs. learning task*

Spontaneous language acquisition in the course of communication requires the learner to deal with two tasks at the same time (cf. section 1.3.1 above):

> he must learn the language by which he intends to communicate,
> he must communicate by means of the language he intends to learn.

There is a touch of paradox in this formulation; but this is only due to the fact that using the term 'the language' ignores the many intermediate stages of the learning process at which communication, though reduced, is already possible. Both tasks are closely connected, and in general, they support each other: the more you communicate, the better your access to the input and the richer the feedback, hence the better your chances of learning. The more you learn, the better your chances of successful communication. But in some respects, communication and learning are at variance. Unless we assume prestabilized harmony, communication is based on a set of stable rules which the learner, as speaker and listener, can follow. As a learner, however, he must not consider the rules he is following at the time to be stable: he must be prepared to control, to revise and even to drop them. He has to tailor his raincoat in the rain, or, less metaphorically: for communication, the learner must constantly operate with the rules he has developed at a given point in time; but at the same time, he must consider these rules to be preliminary hypotheses which are subject to revision. If he prematurely takes them to be confirmed, then his acquisition process freezes at that level with respect to these rules. Fossilized learner varieties of this sort indeed offer some advantages for communication: although their expressive power is obviously limited, they are stable and easy to handle.

This distinction between the communicative task and the learning task which the learner has to solve simultaneously seems straightforward, even trivial. But it has several important implications, to which we turn now. The first concerns degrees of communication.

8.3.2 *Degrees of communication and 'test rules'*

Learning only proceeds as long as the 'learner' considers his rules as hypotheses, as 'test rules'. Their degree of subjective confirmation varies. At a given point in time he may take some of them to be very stable and, at that point in time, beyond discussion; about others, he may feel very uncertain. At any point in time t_i, the learner has developed an organized set of assumptions about grammatical and lexical regularities of the target language, or, as I shall briefly say, a test grammar G_{ti}. Each rule of this grammar (including lexicon) is associated with a subjective though possibly unconscious 'confirmation index' ranging from 0 to 1, where 0 means 'clearly false and to be revised' and 1 means 'clearly correct and hence stable', 0.5 being maximal insecurity. Note that this subjective confirmation index changes over time, depending on various factors. We will come back to this point, but let us consider first the relation of degree of confirmation to the application of the rules in communication. This relation is not straightforward. In simple cases, the learner will be able

147

to base his communication on rules of degree 1, but this need not be so. Depending on what he wants or needs to communicate, he is often in a position to apply rules he is very uncertain about or which he even considers false – a case familiar to any speaker of a second language. Grégoire (1937) has already noted that children, too, occasionally use forms they know to be incorrect and which they reject when used by adults. The fact that communicative pressure often forces the learner to rely on uncertain rules is even more apparent when we consider comprehension as well as production. All target-language-specific rules, unless explicitly introduced by teaching, must somehow be derived from the input accessible to the learner. When he *first* interprets a feature of the input as being based on some target-language-specific rule, he cannot already have this rule, and even less can he be sure that this rule is correct. *After* this first instance, he may include this rule in his test grammar, even with index 1. On the other hand, a learner may have within his test grammar a number of rules with relatively high degrees of confirmation which he nevertheless does not use for communication – because he does not need them for his specific communicative purpose, because they are too complicated, or because their application would force him to apply other rules he does not yet master. Thus, for example, the subordinate conjunction *nachdem* in German usually requires the pluperfect. A learner may know perfectly well the meaning of *nachdem* and the fact that it goes with a specific verb form; but, if there is no specific communicative pressure, he may never use *nachdem*, simply because he does not know the pluperfect forms. However, if there is sufficient communicative pressure, he may choose to use this word and to combine it with a verb form he knows to be inappropriate in this context.

Any uncertain rule within a test grammar may have competing rules which are also uncertain, that is, a learner may entertain various alternative hypotheses at a given point in the acquisition process.[7] In this case, again, it is open which one among these alternatives he chooses for communication. He may continue to use a rule which is already quite doubtful for him rather than a more promising candidate, simply because he is used to it and it has proved to be efficient enough for his communicative purpose. Thus, a learner who already 'knows' inflected forms – at least to some extent and with some degree of certainty – may nevertheless go on using uninflected forms for some time, or occasionally return to them.

To sum up: the appearance of a rule in the learner's communication, even when frequent and consistent, does not imply that this is a highly confirmed rule for that learner at that time. The non-appearance of a rule does not exclude the possibility that the learner 'has' this rule – even with a high degree of subjective confirmation.

8.3.3   *Criticalness*

The confirmation indices change over time, that is, the rules are subject to processes of confirmation and disconfirmation. This does not mean, however, that all the rules of a given test grammar are actually tested at the same time. Rather than fighting simultaneously on all fronts, the learner may consider only some rules to be *critical* – that is, to be an object of confirmation or disconfirmation at a given time. There may be various causes which render a rule critical: it may be a first, very insecure hypothesis; it may concern a very frequent phenomenon; it may be the result of an explicit correction – although explicit correction need not have this consequence. Independent from what is operative *in concreto*, we may say here that all elements of G_{ti} are associated not only with a confirmation index, but also with an index '± critical'. The relation between '± critical' and degree of confirmation is again far from straightforward. It seems plausible to assume that there is a preference for testing weakly confirmed rules over rules which, in the learner's eyes, are stable. But it may also be that a stable or relatively well confirmed rule, due to one of the reasons mentioned above, suddenly becomes suspicious and, as a consequence, leads the learner to look for confirmation or disconfirmation. Or else, a weakly confirmed rule may be unimportant for the learner's communicative needs, and is therefore low on the testing priority.

The most important factor which renders a rule critical is communicative failure: a rule which leads to misunderstanding or to non-understanding obviously calls for revision, independent of whether it is well confirmed or not – on condition, of course, that this rule is indeed correctly identified as the source of the communication failure (we will come back to this point below).

To sum up: some of the test rules entertained by a learner at a given point during his acquisition process are also critical at that time, that is, the object of confirmation and disconfirmation; there is a multitude of factors which contribute to making a rule critical; and there is only a loose connection between being critical and the degree of confirmation.

Before turning to some consequences of what has been said so far, we will briefly mention a point which might lead to misunderstandings. A learner need not be consciously aware of the fact that a rule is critical for him, although, of course, this is not excluded. Most steps in language processing are subliminal, and there is no reason to assume that this is different for control processes. Similar considerations hold for the subjective degree of confirmation. Uncertainty and certainty with respect to some rule are relative to the individual learner; but this does not imply that he is aware of his subjective evaluation.

8.3.4 *Some implications*
A.   Sensitivity to explicit correction

Very often, a learner is simply not accessible to attempts to correct him. This has been observed both for first and for second language acquisition. The following case is reported by Braine (1971, pp. 160–1):

Over a period of a few weeks I repeatedly but fruitlessly tried to persuade her [his two-and-a-half year old daughter] to substitute *other* + N for *other one* + N. With different nouns on different occasions, the interchanges went somewhat as follows: 'Want other one spoon, Daddy' – 'You mean, you want THE OTHER SPOON' – 'Yes. I want other one spoon, please Daddy' – 'Can you say "the other spoon"?' – 'Other ... one spoon' – 'Say "other"' – 'Other' – '"Spoon"' – 'Spoon' – 'Other ... spoon' – 'Other ... spoon. Now give me other one spoon?'

The same phenomenon is well-known from second language acquisition, perhaps best documented by the often fruitless attempts of teachers to change 'typical faults' of their students. This resistance to correction may simply be due to the fact that, at that time, the rule in question is not critical for the learner. It may – but need not – be, however, that persistent attempts to correct him may indeed *render* a rule critical; but as already noted, this may depend on a lot of factors.

B.   Backsliding (cf. section 2.7.B)

Sometimes, a learner already knows the (objectively) correct rule of the target language and uses it. But at the same time, he uses previous forms or totally slides back to a previous stage of his acquisition process. One possible explanation for this phenomenon is that the rules in question are critical at that time: the learner tries them and is waiting for confirmation or disconfirmation; but he is clever enough not to give up the older rules, just in case, and only when the new rules are sufficiently confirmed (in his eyes), does he stick exclusively to them. One should not throw away the old shoes until one is sure that the new ones fit.

C.   Fossilization (cf. section 2.7.A)

As mentioned on various occasions in Part I, there is a striking difference between first and second language acquisition in that the former normally leads to full mastery of the language to be learned, whereas the latter typically ends at a stage still far from perfection. This is often imputed to biological factors, for example to the existence of a 'critical period' ending roughly at puberty, after which acquisition cannot continue as before (cf. section 1.1.3). Now this argument is somewhat weakened by the fact that adults *can* indeed learn a second language to perfection if they try hard enough. What has been said above about critical rules offers three additional explanations:

(i)   It may be that fossilized learners know that their rules are deviant; but they still use them for communication, and they satisfy their communicative needs. As noted earlier, fossilized varieties are perhaps reduced in expressive power, but they are easy to handle. So why keep the rules open for revision?

(ii)   It may be that adults have different standards of confirmation. Roughly speaking, we are less self-critical and quicker to suppose that we have already discovered the truth.

(iii)   The ways in which rules become critical may be different for adults and children, that is, for adult learners a rule may not even reach the stage where it would become the object of control procedures (no matter how the standards of confirmation would be then).

All three explanations relate to differences in personal psychology between adults and children (and actually among learners in general). They do not rule out biological explanations, but they offer a simple and natural alternative.

D.   No negative evidence

There is a much-debated 'logical' problem of acquisition, which has to do with the necessary amount of 'negative evidence'. Most of the discussion concerns first language acquisition, but the problem holds for second language acquisition in much the same way. According to a classical study by Gold (1967; see also Levelt, 1974), only finite-state languages are learnable 'in the limit' (i.e. after a finite number of steps), if no negative evidence is given (that is, if only strings of the language to be learned are presented, but no information is given that certain strings do not belong to it). With negative evidence, all primitive recursive languages – i.e. virtually all languages – are learnable in the limit. It is not fully clear where natural languages rank in this hierarchy, but it is agreed that they are above finite-state (and probably below primitive recursive) languages. Hence, negative input is required if they are to be learned. Now most researchers agree that in fact the learner gets no, or only extremely limited, negative input. This leads to a logical problem of language acquisition, one solution being the assumption that a great deal of the grammar is innate. (For a careful discussion of the whole argument, which is grossly oversimplified here, see Pinker, 1979, where different solutions are also considered.) A closely related but not identical problem – in a sense, the empirical counterpart of Gold's theoretical problem – is the (alleged) fact that during the acquisition process some false, but still possible and even highly plausible rules (especially overgeneralizations) do not occur, or, if they do, soon disappear without being corrected (that is, without negative input); for a discussion, see Braine (1971) and Bowerman (1983).

Suppose now the learner has a hypothetical rule r in his test grammar, and, in addition, this rule is critical at a given point in time. It does not matter where this hypothesis comes from – it may be the result of a preliminary input analysis, it may be taken over from his first language (in the case of SLA), he may even have dreamt it. Suppose now that, if r does not show up n times in the next n utterances of the learner's social environment – where 'next' means 'after r became critical' – then it gets confirmation index 0 and becomes uncritical again. Such a verification strategy is quite common in our daily quest for the truth, and it solves the logical problem of negative evidence (though not the empirical problems, of course): it has the same effect that negative evidence would have.

The control technique as described here is totally oversimplified, of course. It may be that r indeed often shows up in the input, but the learner simply does not recognize it. It may also be the other way around, that is, he may misinterpret some utterances as being based on that rule although, in reality, they are not. It is also plausible that confirmation techniques are different for different kinds of rules, for lexical rules as opposed to morphological rules, for example. Finally, confirmation surely does not depend exclusively on frequency of occurrence; there may never be an occasion where the rule in question could be used, and that is why it does not appear; the learner has to check for this, as well. He may also base his judgement on who is speaking – on whether it is an 'authoritative' person or not. However, all of these complications do not affect the general idea.

According to what has been said in section 8.3.3, a critical rule can, but need not be used for communicative purposes, that is, r could be checked for without ever showing up in the learner's production. This may be a simple explanation for the fact that learners often do not make the mistakes one would expect them to make: they may indeed consider this possible way of producing an utterance and unconsciously ponder for some time over the corresponding (false) rules; but they do not base their actual production on them; so the fact that they do indeed deal with this possibility simply does not become apparent. There is an important methodological consequence for acquisition studies. Most assumptions about when a learner 'has' a certain rule and hence about the order of acquisition are based on observations about when the learner displays this rule more or less consistently in his communication. Although this does seem to be the best way to study the process of acquisition, the discussion in the previous two sections casts a shadow of doubt on this conclusion.

All that has been said so far on the modes of self-control and on critical rules is somewhat abstract. In the next section, we will try to make these considerations rather more concrete, and thus step out of the fog of theory into the swamp of empirical facts.

8.3.5 *An example*

Take, for instance, a migrant worker in Germany engaged in a conversation about his family with a native speaker of German. The learner has just revealed that he got married not long ago but has no children as yet. He would now like to convey something that could be said in the target variety (i.e., Standard German) in these words:

(66)   Mein Bruder hat sechs Kinder
         (My brother has six children)

What he actually says is a product of his learner variety:

(67)   Meine Brudä ses Kind 'abe
         (roughly: Me broder sis child 'av)

His utterance differs from (66) in several structural features, in other words, it is constructed according to rules which depart from those of the target language on several points. The differences fall into various domains, for example:

> phonology: *Brudä, ses, 'abe*
> morphology: *meine, Kind, 'abe*
> syntax: final position of the finite verb *'abe*

Now, there are at least three factors which may be responsible for an utterance displaying a particular set of structural properties:

(i)   The speaker's communicative intention.
         In our example, the speaker wishes to state that his brother has six children.
(ii)   The speaker's assumption as to what might be available to the hearer in terms of concomitant knowledge (in brief: the *context*).

Had, for example, the speaker mentioned his brother before, he might now have used the personal pronoun 'he'.

(iii)   The *rules* of the learner's variety.

Remember that these 'rules' may be very tentative assumptions. They cover all domains of language use, i.e. phonology, syntax, vocabulary (here 'rule' is meant once again to include all sorts of devices, including knowledge of words).

It goes without saying that the three factors (or groups of factors) interact in a highly complex way in language production. There is no need to go into these complications at this point; it will be enough to bear in mind that in formulating an utterance the speaker is constrained by these three factors: intention, context, and rules. The matching problem basically applies to only one of them – the rules available to the learner: he is supposed to scrutinize some of his rules and possibly adjust them in the light of new evidence on the functioning of the language. Nevertheless, the other two factors are important here, since control processes involve all three factors, in production as well as in comprehension. As a speaker, the learner keeps track of how the utterance he has just formed corresponds to his intention, how well it fits the situational context, and whether it conforms to the rules of his language variety. As a hearer, he must keep track of the other speaker's utterance, matching what he thinks he hears with the other's presumed communicative intention, with the presumed context (strictly speaking, the presumed image of the context), and the rule he presumes the other speaker to have followed.

In order to solve the matching problem, the learner must relate his own interpretation of how the three factors affect the form of an utterance to the effect they have on his own utterance. This seems comparatively simple when the learner is in a position to contrast immediately two utterances like (66) and (67), also assuming that both intention and context are the same. He may then concentrate upon matching the structural properties of his utterance, ensuing from the rules of his learner variety, against his interpretation of the structural features of the other utterance. With luck, he will attribute a certain property of the other utterance to precisely the rule which is in fact responsible for it; but this need not be so. The facts of language acquisition through everyday communication are harder than that. Ordinarily, the learner does not know the other's communicative intention nor his precise context image and has to infer them mainly from the utterance itself.

We will consider several possible ways in which a native speaker might react to the learner's utterance in example (67). Let us assume that the native speaker correctly understood what was meant by (67), as anybody would, and has noticed at least some of its departures from the standard. He might then respond in a variety of ways:

(68)   Hat
        (Has)
(69)   Du meinst: er hat sechs Kinder
        (You mean: he has six children)
(70)   Du meinst er hat sechs Kinder?
        (You mean he has six children?)
(71)   Dein Bruder hat sechs Kinder
        (Your brother has six children)
(72)   Was? Sechs Kinder hat dein Bruder!
        (What? Your brother has six children!)
(73)   Mein Bruder hat zwei Kinder
        (My brother has two children)

This exemplification could be continued at will, but responses (68-73) will suffice.

Utterance (68) is an explicit correction of just one departure from the rules of the target language; it is a metalinguistic, not a communicative utterance (although its intention is to communicate an error). Obviously, the native speaker is correcting the distorted form of the finite verb (*'abe*). It is up to the learner to identify it as such: the task is not as trivial as it appears to native speakers (the latter fact is itself an interesting topic). After all, the learner simply does not know that *hat* is what he ought to have said. He may nevertheless process (68) as a correction, provided his use of *'abe* was based on a critical rule (a rule in a critical state, so to speak), and he is even more likely to do so if he has in reserve another critical rule, waiting to be confirmed, the rule that third person singular of the verb *haben* ('to have') is *hat* ('has'); in fact, he may have heard *hat* being used many times in precisely this function. Suppose now that the learner is indeed convinced that *'abe* should be replaced by *hat*. Unfortunately, he is faced here by the next problem. The wrongly used finite form of *haben* shows three departures from the standard: in phonology, in morphology, and in syntax (its position is wrong); what is more, the first two are difficult to keep apart in this case. But since the curt correction does not suggest an error in syntax, the learner has to (and can only) decide whether he is to correct the word in its ending or in its pronunciation (missing *h*), or in both. To sum up: even an explicit correction like (68) leaves it up to the learner to find out what he has to submit to revision.

Now (68) is a minimal and therefore possibly not particularly helpful correction. But the problem becomes even more acute as we turn to the next example. Utterance (69) is likewise an explicit correction, provided the learner has correctly interpreted the overture (*Du meinst*, or 'you mean'), which is by no means obvious, considering that the utterance is identical with (70) in every aspect except intonation. Utterance (70) is a reassurance of the kind commonly used among native speakers; it is not necessarily meant as a correction and it is thus perfectly possible for the learner to interpret (69) in the same sense, and to respond with *Ja, ses Kind 'abe* ('Yes, sis child 'ave'). Alternatively, he might interpret (70) as a correction, thus committing the opposite mistake. In any case, all kinds of misunderstandings may crop up in the process of communication. But suppose for a moment that the learner has correctly interpreted (69) as an explicit correction. Indeed, it is a comprehensive correction in two senses: it does not leave out any of the learner's departures from the standard and it comprises so much that the learner is not likely to cope with all that is involved. But it should first be noted that (69) has one element changed compared with (67) on account of the new context: *er* ('he') has replaced *mein Bruder* ('my brother') as subject since the brother is now part of the context and because the other speaker would have to use a different pronoun when referring to the same brother: 'your' in place of 'my'. Even if the learner has recognized 'he has six children' as a correction of (67), his problem is that the differences between the two are due in part to factor (iii) (different sets of rules underlying two utterances) and in one respect to factor (ii) (different context). In order to make use of the correction, the learner must keep the two things apart. The simplicity of the present example makes the matter obvious: 'he' and 'my brother' are so different that the pronoun cannot be taken as a grammatical correction. Should the correction run *dein Bruder ...*, as in (71), the learner might interpret it as either a morphological or a phonological correction of *meine Brudä*, if not as a syntactic one. It may be assumed that this is not so here, i.e., that our learner's knowledge of possessive pronouns is incomplete, since he uses *meine* in place of *mein*: at the same time, it must be 'uncritical' insofar as he is in command of the stems *mein-* and *dein-*. In other words, a correction like (71) can become a correction for *meine Brudä* only if the learner has firmly established *some* rules (about possessive pronouns, in this case) while keeping *other* rules in a state of 'criticalness' (inflection, in this case). Otherwise, he could count only on chance or good fortune.

Another problem with (69) and (70) is that several differences are pointed out at one time. Unlike (68), the two corrections are nonspecific, and it is left to the learner to find out what the hot spots are. To do this, he must first identify the differences as such. The respective tasks differ in magnitude, and we consider them in greater detail by taking the missing [h] to be the phonological, the missing *-er* (in *Kinder*) the morphological, and the misplaced finite verb the syntactic difference. This provides an opportunity to discuss the specific matching problems in three different linguistic domains.

   A.   Phonological matching
        Our example juxtaposes the learner's [aːbə] and the standard [hat]. The two sound clusters differ to such an extent that it would be difficult to find anything they have in common. But let us assume that the learner is capable of grasping the latter as a correction of his form (again, this is by no means obvious, in particular as the position in the sentence is different). But the real problem lies in the fact that the learner's [aːbə] shows a morphological as well as a phonological departure from the standard:

> the wrong inflection is used (*habe* for *haben*, in place of the correct *haben*) – a frequent error in early learner varieties (cf. section 6.2.1);
> the initial [h] is left out, which is again an inveterate habit of Italian-, Spanish-, and French-speaking learners of German.

Now, the learner may have perceived a difference and promptly corrected himself by replacing [aːbə] by ... [at]. That is to say, he has cancelled his morphological deviation but retained the phonological one. Forms like *'at* are frequently encountered among learners who also pronounce *heute* (today) as *'eute* or *Haus* (house) as *'aus*. At this point we are interested in a correction of the phonological deviation in a form that would persist after the learner has solved the morphological problem.

   How is it that otherwise advanced learners consistently disregard what is a frequent sound in a German-speaking environment? Three possible reasons come to mind: (a) the learners cannot hear the sound (perception), (b) they are unable to articulate it (production), and (c) the two factors have a cumulative effect.

   First of all it is clear that the reason is not physiological. Certainly, physiological handicaps may have an effect on second language learning, for example in the case of defective hearing or a hare lip; these and more temporary indispositions (as after a couple of beers) are apt to affect the more difficult sounds first (the question whether some sounds are intrinsically more difficult to pronounce than others is not considered here, but speakers of European languages obviously find clicks and certain laryngals very difficult to pronounce). However, no one would claim that Frenchmen are innately incapable of aspiration (i.e. delicate breathing), although they may find it difficult to pronounce this aspirated German [h]. The crux of the problem must therefore lie not in physiological reasons but in processing. As argued in chapter 5, the hearer must start by analysing the input, and the stream of speech sounds in particular. He cannot accomplish everything at once. The relative accessibility of input elements depends on their characteristics on the one hand and on the hearer's knowledge on the other. It will depend on this knowledge whether the hearer sets out to look for [p], [s] or [u]; in our case he will *not* set out to look for [h]. In other words, the learner's initial knowledge employed to sound out the input is not of the kind that would make the [h] a critical phonological feature. It is at this stage of language acquisition that a deliberate focussing of the learner's attention (by others, for example) upon this property of the input might help him to extract the respective sound segments from [haus], [hat], and [hi:r]. Without this, [h] is not accessible to analysis. But the learner's knowledge is in constant flux during the course of language acquisition: hitherto critical rules cease to be critical, and more and more new properties of the input, even the less conspicuous ones, are analysed. It is at this stage that the learner might become sensitive to corrections like (68) or (70). The latter may prose problems insofar as the learner might not be able to focus his attention upon so many features at the same time.

Suppose now the learner has discovered the [h] in the input, perceives it as a critical feature, and attempts to employ it in his own output. For a while (at least) he may find it difficult to produce the sound, which would result in a discrepancy between his perception and his production. While less plausible in the case of [h] – as we noticed, this sound is easy to produce – the prospect is quite real for some other sounds. The discrepancy is likely to crop up in the case of sounds which do not exist in the native language and are (possibly for no other reason) perceptually salient but difficult to imitate. Being subject to analysis relatively early, these elements will not turn up in production for quite some time, if ever. Let us repeat: the accessibility of input to analysis depends not only on the hearer's initial knowledge; rather, it is the result of an interplay between this knowledge and the properties of the sound stream themselves. Of any two sounds that do not exist in the learner's first language, one may be processed very early, on account of its peculiarity (a click could not pass unnoticed!) while another might wait for an indefinite time. To illustrate with an example: a speaker of English who has set out to learn German may notice the [y] in *Glück* possibly earlier than the [ç] in *reichen*, and the latter earlier than the glottal plosive [ʔ] which often initiates words which seem to start with a vowel; but this order has little to do with the eventual order of acquisition for production.

Turning to our learner again, we could argue that [h] would not present difficulties in production. However, it may be that the learner is complacent about his own production, being convinced that he pronounces the sound as people in his social environment do. This is when perception and production (or monitoring of that production) are at odds.[8] Some striking cases have been reported in the literature on first language acquisition. Grégoire (1937) examined a child who employed the same sound sequence [kɔs] for *cochon* ('pig') as for *garçon* ('boy'), while keeping the two words apart when they were uttered by others (this was evidently not a pure production problem involving awareness of the distinction). Better known is the following dialogue recorded by Slobin (1971, p. 65):

Recently, a three year old child told me that her name was Litha. I answered, 'Litha?' 'No, *Litha*.' 'Oh, Lisa'. 'Yes, Litha.'

As far as I can see, no similar evidence exists in the literature on second language acquisition. But the phenomenon could not have escaped the attention of anyone who has ever conducted second language classes.

At first sight, these confusions may seem odd, but in actual fact one should wonder why they are not more frequent. It has to be borne in mind that the acoustic wave is produced as a realization of an abstract sensorimotor schema. The actual outcome (the objective acoustic shape of a sound) will vary with the position of the sound in the sound sequence, the speed of speaking, or even with such trivial (in)dispositions of the speaker as a sore throat or a runny nose. Contrary to a view still popular among linguists, these variations affect not only marginal features; very important distinctive features (e.g. [± voiced]) are sometimes simply missing, or are produced so feebly that they remain below the perception threshold (see the remarkable discussion in Winkler, 1980). It is a well-known general property of our perception that we reconstruct the missing elements of an image, in hearing as much as in vision (on the perception of speech sounds see Fant and Tatham, 1975; on the role of perception in first language acquisition see Barton, 1978). Owing to this characteristic of human perception, we often need to hear no more than a blurred sound fragment to realize which sound is involved. In more extreme cases, people can 'hear' (or 'see') things that don't exist (see, for example, Clark and Clark, 1977). And to return to our example: in German, an [h] in initial position is sometimes either totally absent or scarcely audible.

Of course, the job of the learner is greatly facilitated when he is offered speech samples produced with special care and hence unnatural precision; such is often the case in second language instruction. But when it comes to understanding everyday language, the problems re-emerge (Henrichson, 1984). Moreover, hearing carefully articulated speech does not necessarily lead to carefully articulated production. In spontaneous learning the hearer is confronted with vastly differing articulations of the speech sounds and he has to put up with it. He has to try to build up his sensorimotor schema through a process of 'averaging' across the entire range of available individual articulations. This task involves the formation of certain expectations as to where the limits of the articulatory variations or the given schema should be set. On occasion, he may be widely off the mark, as when he assumes that his own defective articulation is still admissible, although it is not. On the other hand, he may make the limits far too narrow, rejecting as exemplars of the given sound some articulations that are well within the norm.

B.   Morphological matching

When speaking of six children, our learner employs the singular *Kind* and his partner corrects him with *Kinder* ('children'). We assume for a change that the learner has noticed the phonological difference – which, as we have just seen, is not at all self-evident. We further assume that he is already aware of the fact that in German, nouns are normally marked for plural (in contrast to spoken French, for example), and that such marking is obligatory after numerals. What he is still missing, apparently, is the rule 'The plural of *Kind* is *Kinder*', and this is where (70) comes in.

There may be several reasons for the use of *Kind* in place of *Kinder*. There is a general tendency among beginning learners to avoid inflection, even though the idea of having inflection may be familiar to the learner from his native language. Although sensitive to the problem, the learner has not yet reached a point of such 'finesse' in his input analysis. He is still busy identifying particular morphs (cf. section 6.2). Our learner may be at this stage, or he may be somewhat more advanced: he does mark plural in principle (which, in the case of German, is a realistic assumption even for early learning varieties), but he happens to think that *Kind* belongs to those nouns which take no plural ending (like *Henkel*). So,

160

he has plural marking, but gets it wrong in this special case. A number of other possibilities could be discussed, but these two suffice to illustrate the following point; the learner's sensitivity to morphological corrections depends on his advancement in learning the language. In the first of the two possibilities, the rule 'The plural of *Kind* is *Kinder*' is not yet critical. The learner either ignores the correction or acquires the morph *Kinder*, in analogy to *Henkel* ('brother', singular). The latter would mean that a repetition of the utterance in its corrected version (*Kinder*), or even the incorporation of *Kinder* in the learner variety, has not really brought him any closer to the target variety on this point. On the contrary, by accepting the correction in this sense the learner is taking the wrong track. If, however, the learner is at the more advanced stage described above, the rule is critical for him and he is in a position to make good use of the correction.

Our example pertains to a relatively simple instance of the matching problem, as simple as the underlying semantic category of number. The problems of inflection in the case of both tense and aspect are incomparably more involved (cf. section 7.2). These two categories are conceptualized in quite varied ways in different languages: there are languages with and without aspect, with two-, three-, and multi-level tense systems, with combinations of tense and aspect, and so on. The learner's task is not only to extract from the input the morphological forms, but also to infer from this material the underlying conceptual system – which may differ radically from that of his native language. In addition, in some languages the categories of tense and aspect are marked by inflection as well as by other devices (cf. section 7.2). Here the matching problem becomes even more difficult because the learner's task will be to examine critically and revise if necessary several things at a time: his semantic categories formed on the basis of the native language, the available forms, and the correspondences between form and meaning. To go into these complications would take us beyond the limits of the present discussion.

C. Syntactic matching

In utterance (67) the learner has put the verb in final position; in correction (69) and (70) the verb is in second position. We assume the learner realizes the correspondence of [a:bə] and [hat]; otherwise the correction would go over the learner's head. We further assume that the learner knows the concept of finiteness and is prepared to apply it in his utterance, i.e., that he did not use *'abe* as a morph (cf. section 6.2). The rule to be learned from the correction would thus be: 'The finite verb

takes second position' ($=$V2). We immediately disregard several complications, as for instance, what 'second position' actually means, what peculiar
features are displayed by ellipsis, or the fact that V2 applies only to main
clauses. Now, in view of the distinction between (67) and (70), the learner
should find it easy to acquire V2 by simply adopting the verb position
proposed in (70). The matter is not quite as simple, however, as is clear
from an inspection of (72): *Was? Sechs Kinder hat dein Bruder!*. While
stating the same thing as (67), utterance (72) has transposed subject and
object, thus changing the thematic structure of the sentence. Should the
learner be concerned with word order at this time of his acquisition process,
he might feel tempted to change from the subject – object – verb order
of (67) to the suggested order, object – verb – subject. We know that
(72) was not really meant as a correction; but the learner may not be
aware of this; after all, he is used to learning from utterances not explicitly
meant as corrections. What the learner ought to realize is that the position
discrepancy between (67) and (70) is due to factor (iii) (rules), while
the position discrepancy between (67) and (72) is due to both this factor
and factor (ii) (context assessment). The former points to the position
of the verb, the latter to the position of subject and object. Unless the
learner is aware of this, the correction is of little help to him. But suppose
the native speaker has failed to grasp the meaning of (67) and, rather
than attempting any correction, he seeks to assure himself by (74).

(74)   Hat dein Bruder sechs Kinder?
         (Has your brother six children?)

We are confronted here with a different intention: the same thought is
phrased as a question rather than as a statement. This involves a change
in the position of the verb, but it is not the position to be used for a
rectification of (67). Of course, there is no such danger as long as the
learner has recognized the speaker's intention; but it is precisely the position of the finite element that indicates this intention. Intonation could
also be an important cue here, but in contrast to a popular belief this
kind of question is usually put without a rise in intonation.

The need to identify the underlying causes of such differences arises
not only in the case of syntactic departures from the norm. Utterance
(73) is a case in point. Although not intended as a correction, it nevertheless
contains all the cues needed for the rectification of the defective utterance.
In fact, it is easier to use it for this purpose than either (70) or (71),
insofar as 'my brother' is repeated literally. There is only one difference
– the numeral 'six' is replaced by the numeral 'two'; thus, if the learner

is inclined to interpret utterance (73) as an attempt to correct him, he has a unique chance to discover what should be corrected. But he would be totally wrong, of course. Now, in this special case, it should not be difficult for the learner to realize that there is no phonological or morphological defect in his 'six', numerals being acquired by 'spontaneous' learners at an early stage (albeit in a slightly deviant form). The lesson of this case however is that a correction can only benefit the learner if it is adjusted to his actual knowledge.

What has been argued in this section refers to a variety of hypothetical, but realistic and quite frequent cases and the resulting problems. Our examples illustrate basically just one mode of control, namely feedback. We conclude this chapter with an account of a comprehensive study devoted to another type, namely self-corrections.

8.4 Self-corrections

In the last section we considered the possibilities and obstacles that arise when the learner tries to check his own utterances by matching them with corresponding utterances of target language speakers, with a view to correcting himself, even if not immediately. The situation we now have in mind involves immediate self-correction. As pointed out in section 8.2, utterances are being scrutinized by the speaker while they are being formulated and uttered. Such self-monitoring of speech is abundantly reflected in hesitations, repetitions, and self-corrections.[9] The latter can be taken as a relatively clear indication of the speaker's preoccupation, in other words, whether he is focussing attention on lexemes, or on such features as tense or number, or word orders, and the like. In the investigation reported below, Carroll, Dietrich and Storch (1982)[10] scrutinized a corpus of speech for all corrections of inflected words, that is, verbs, adjectives, pronouns, nouns, and the like, but not adverbs, particles, prepositions, etc. The self-corrections pertained to such categories as number, gender and case for nouns, pronouns and adjectives; tense, mood, person, etc. for verbs; and the phonetic shape of the word as well. The speakers were eight participants in an intensive German course at the University of Heidelberg: four Americans (C, P, D, S) and four Japanese (F, Yo, Yu, K). The investigators conducted informal conversations with these learners over a period of three months. These conversations covered different topics, were tape-recorded, transcribed phonetically (complete with slips of the tongue and self-corrections), and analysed. The learners were aged between twenty-five and thirty-five and had lived in Heidelberg for some time (the Americans for as long as eighteen months), so they had acquired some German through everyday intercourse of varying intensity. The latter circumstance is of no concern to us, nor are the results of various language proficiency tests to which they had been submitted.

The corpus of speech obtained from the eight speakers totals 150,000 words, among them 832 cases of correction of inflected words, which were spread very unevenly across the speakers and the various word classes. From the many tables contained in the study I have put together in Table 5 the data of particular interest to us. Apart from the figures for all inflected words, four word classes are represented separately: verbs (in finite form), nouns, articles (three genders with inflections!), and personal pronouns. Within each class, the first line shows the percentage of the given class in relation to all inflected words in the corpus, the second gives the percentage of errors, the third line gives the percentage of errors which were self-corrected, and in the fourth there is an index number showing the speaker's concentration in his self-corrections on the given word class (the average percentage of words corrected in the entire corpus given the index 1). For example, index 2 tells us that words in this class were corrected twice as often as the average for all words. The first four symbols stand for the Americans, the last four for the Japanese: in each case, the first two are women. In one case (Yo) the data base was so small that the results for personal pronouns were ignored in the calculation of the overall figures (last row). The numbers for the four word classes do not add up to 100% because there were also inflected words of other classes in the corpus.

The first thing to be noted is the varying percentage of inflected words among all the words in the corpus across the eight learners (ranging from 26% for P to 64% for K). This variation is not easy to explain. The non-inflected words are *and, but, not, perhaps, yet, rather* and other such words that serve to organize discourse and have no referential meaning. It may well be that the differential use of these elements reflects the specific focussing of speakers on some grammatical forms rather than others. Since formal language instruction places considerable emphasis on grammatical correctness, notably on inflection, compared with marginal attention **paid** to particles and the like, this focussing may reflect individual differences in the impact of explicit teaching, when compared with the impact of spontaneous acquisition.

There are similar variations in the percentage of errors in inflected words across learners; this varies from 14% for P to about one-third for Yo and K. In itself, this variation is of no particular interest, simply reflecting the learners' differential advancement in just one domain: morphological

164

Table 5. *Inflected-word self-correction propensities in eight learners of German*

	Learners								
	C	P	D	S	F	Yo	Yu	K	Mean
Inflected words (IW)									
IW as % of all words	52	26	46	55	59	33	58	64	49
% of IW with errors	24	14	25	23	19	34	19	33	24
% of errors corrected	12	19	4	2	18	26	9	14	9
Finite verbs (FV)									
FV as % of IW	26	31	22	30	23	30	22	22	25
% of FV with errors	15	7	9	11	11	44	9	24	16
% of errors corrected	14	24	4	1	25	23	19	14	16
Focus in correction	1.4	1	0.7	0.4	1.4	2	1.9	1.3	1.3
Nouns (N)									
N as % of IW	23	19	24	18	27	30	28	29	25
% of N with errors	16	12	17	24	17	15	11	20	17
% of errors corrected	5	8	2	1	6	6	4	11	5
Focus in correction	0.5	0.6	0.6	0.5	0.5	0.2	0.5	0.3	0.5
Articles (A)									
A as % of IW	18	16	11	15	17	18	17	18	16
% of A with errors	44	21	46	45	28	63	31	42	40
% of errors corrected	7	21	3	3	15	5	6	15	9
Focus in correction	2	3	3	4	2	0.7	2	2	2.3
Personal pronouns (PP)									
PP as % of IW	23	21	18	23	14	12	14	16	18
% of PP with errors	2	1	3	1	2	5	2	2	2
% of errors corrected	12	23	8	0	13	(100)[+]	12	13	12[+]
Focus in correction	0.1	0.2	0.4	0	0.1	(1)[+]	0.3	0.1	0.2[+]

[+] The relatively poor data base for Yo does not justify inclusion in the mean.

inflection. It *might* however signal learner-specific approaches; P employs few inflected forms, and these are 86% correct; K uses many inflected forms, but about one-third of them are wrong. A consideration of the learner's focussing upon the various word classes reveals extreme variations; Yo corrects 1 in 11.3 inflected words (about one-quarter of one-third) and S corrects only 1 in 217.4 inflected words (2% of a little less than one-quarter). In other words, the learners differ tremendously in the extent to which they control their speech. It would be interesting to know what factors are behind the differential 'propensity to self-correction', but the available evidence provides no clues on this. What one cannot fail to note is that the Japanese learners tend to correct themselves more than twice as often as the Americans, and that female learners are nearly three times as critical of their performance as are the male learners. It is left to the reader to interpret this in accordance with his (or her) views on national character and sex. What remains to be said is that there is obviously no interdependence between error rate and self-correction propensity: D, S, and C make about the same percentage of errors but C corrects three times more often than D and six times more often than S.

So far we have considered all inflected words together. An inspection of the various word classes reveals both verbs and nouns to have about the same share among all inflected words (exactly one-third, see last column), and to show about the same error rate (16–17%). There are, however, large variations among the learners, though it would be difficult to identify any trends. One is struck by the 2:1 ratio of errors in verbs among the Japanese learners as compared with the Americans, but the value for Yo (44%) may be misleading, as it is based on relatively few data (still, 324 verbs, 143 of them wrong). What is of some interest is the finding that verbs are, on average, subject to corrections about three times as often as nouns. This is reflected in the consistently low focussing upon nouns, as against much higher values for verbs. Only one speaker, S, who seems to have practically no control of his production (while committing very many errors!) scores consistently low on all verb classes. We cannot offer any explanation for these differences in focussing.

Finally, let us take a look at the two remaining word classes, articles and personal pronouns. Their share in all inflected words is about the same (16% and 18%), but the error rate is very different: for articles it is 40%, for personal pronouns it is marginal. The learner's correction propensity varies considerably in both word classes, the value for both D and S being again very low. Averaging across learners, we find that the two classes are not far apart (9% and 12%, excluding Yo). This closeness is misleading however, because in the case of articles the percentage of errors is very high, so the 9% of corrections testify to a relatively close monitoring of the article. A clear picture emerges from the focussing values, where the corrections are counted in reference to all corrections: personal pronouns attract little attention, the learners being fairly well in command of them. In contrast, articles, where errors are relatively frequent, come from the most carefully controlled class. In contradistinction to what we found for nouns and verbs, this points to a close link between scale of difficulty (error rate) and focussing in self-correction (correction rate). But this matter, like so many others, calls for further investigation.[11]

CONCLUSION

Research on second language acquisition has too short a history to supply conclusive evidence on any important question. However, my impression is that in some areas there are the indications of a firm foundation upon which we can build. In other areas we have little more than clouds under our feet. There are three concluding comments to be made.

One: From among the three groups of factors, namely propensity, language faculty (or language processor), and access, which determine the structure, the speed, and the end state of language acquisition, we have after all come to speak of only the last two (in Part II). This may partly reflect my own interests; but I feel that little can be said about the factors of propensity and their influence upon second language acquisition beyond what has been included in section 2.2. The rather extensive psychological research on motivation presents itself more favourably from a distance than in the kind of close-up required for working out suitable applications to second language learning. That is not to suggest that there is no need to investigate the factors of propensity in second language acquisition.

Two: It does not seem to me that second language research has supplied enough scientific evidence to serve as a solid foundation for second language instruction. But I do think that it will eventually be able to accomplish this task and that on some points it has made progress in this direction. Rather than repeating the arguments presented in chapter 3, I would like to make a more general point here: scientific research should indeed be useful (although one must be happy these days if it does no harm). But although it should be guided towards usefulness, the ferret must also, sometimes, be let off the leash.

Three: Any introduction to an area of research is bound to deal with its subject matter from one particular perspective, the perspective of the writer. This cannot be avoided, but the reader should know that he can avail himself of those means whereby this bias may be corrected. After all, this book has an extensive bibliography.

NOTES

1 Some forms of language acquisition, some fundamental facts, some focal issues, some well-known theories

1 One such case was thoroughly studied recently; see Curtiss (1977). There is also a rich literature on the language of Kaspar Hauser, probably the most studied 'wild child'; see, for example, Hörisch (1979).

2 Lamendella (1977) suggested, quite plausibly, replacing 'first language acquisition' by 'primary acquisition' – as opposed to 'non-primary acquisition', which latter should include the acquisition of a second, third, fourth . . . language. Some authors have taken his lead, but this terminology, whilst quite sensible, is still rather uncommon; it is therefore not adopted here.

3 This case will not be considered; but it exists, of course. Let me add a more general remark here. In a number of cases, it is not difficult to find exceptions to some of the general statements and descriptions which will be made in this chapter. Similarly, there are a number of cases and possibilities which will be ignored. To mention all possible special cases and exceptions and to elaborate on all sorts of side issues would totally obliterate the main line of the argument and, in this introductory overview, it is more important to make this main line clear than to take into account anything and everything. Or to quote Aristotle (in the *Nikomachian ethics*): It distinguishes the real scholar not to be more precise than the occasion requires.

4 I hate abbreviations of this sort, but sometimes they are simply economic; some will therefore be used occasionally but not systematically. SLA and 'second language acquisition' will thus be used interchangeably.

5 The need to investigate the different types of language acquisition in parallel has been repeatedly stressed by Wode (specifically, 1981); see also section 1.5.1.

6 Among the comprehensive overviews of first language acquisition let us mention the classical work by Brown (1973), the clear exposition of Dale (1976), and the collections by Fletcher and Garman (1979) and Gleitman and Wanner (1982) which review the state of research in a number of areas. A comprehensive view of European work is offered in Levelt, Karmiloff-Smith, and Mills (1981).

7 The relationship between cognitive and linguistic development has given rise to a vast literature (cf. the volumes edited by Moore, 1973; and Brainerd and Pressley, 1982); its importance is stressed in particular by the Piagetians.

8 This question has been investigated principally by Bühler (1934); cf. also Wun-

derlich (1971), Fillmore (1971), and, on deixis in various languages, Weissen-born and Klein (1982).

9 Scarcely any of the syntactic rules contained in an English grammar apply to Chinese. This is not to say that there are no rules that apply to both English and Chinese, but these are not mentioned in conventional descriptive grammars which deal only with the rules specific to the given language.

10 There are numerous works on bilingualism, both from a sociolinguistic and a psycholinguistic point of view. Hornby (1977) and Beardsmore (1982) give concise treatments. Grosjean (1982) is very comprehensive and particularly interesting because he gives an 'insider's view'. McLaughlin (1978) and Taeschner (1983, chapter 1) review the literature on child bilingualism.

11 See Paradis (1977), Albert and Obler (1978), Paradis and Lebrun (1983) and Peng (1983).

12 For an overview, see McLaughlin (1978, chapter 8); see also Vihman and McLaughlin (1982), Saunders (1982), Porsché (1983), Lüdi and Py (1983).

13 One is reminded of Wode's (1974) provocative question whether learning takes place thanks to or in spite of teaching.

14 The term apparently originates with Wode (1974); but the underlying idea has been expressed by a number of writers.

15 See, for example, the Contrastive Structure Series edited by Ch. A. Ferguson in Chicago from 1962 onwards; for critical reviews see Nickel (1972a) and Bausch and Kasper (1979).

16 The principle aspects of the theory are discussed in Krashen (1981), chapter 8 dealing specifically with its implications for second language teaching. For some empirical support, see Dulay, Burt and Krashen (1982). A well-grounded critique can be found in McLaughlin (1978b).

17 Like other definitions of 'pidgin', the present one has some drawbacks too. For example, we might ask whether pidgins are indeed acquired only by speakers of a subordinate language, or else, what 'subordinate' actually means. The reader is referred to the extensive literature on pidgins, in particular to Hymes (1971), DeCamp and Hancock (1974), and Valdman (1977).

2 Six dimensions of language acquisition

1 For a detailed discussion of 'foreigner talk' (in German in this case) see Heidelberg Research Project (1975, pp. 42–61) and especially Roche (1982); comprehension checks are dealt with in particular by Long (1982) and Perdue (1982, chapter 4.4).

2 The morpheme order studies have been heavily criticized on methodological grounds, e.g. because they were initially not longitudinal, or in view of some inadequacies in the so-called bilingual syntax measure, etc. (cf. Rosansky, 1976; Hatch, 1983, chapter 5). However, our reservations apply irrespective of any methodological shortcomings in these studies.

3 Originally the term was used by Selinker (1977) to designate one stage within the second language acquisition process, rather than a series of stages. There has been a long and extensive discussion about variability and systematicity of 'interlanguage' and 'interlanguages' since; see, for example, Adjémian (1976), Arditty and Perdue (1979), Gass (1984), Rutherford (1984b).

5 The problem of analysis

1 Syllables are fairly easy to identify in a sound sequence. Subjects who hear sound sequences of a totally unfamiliar language, or a tape-recorded piece of their native language backwards, tend to agree on the *number* of syllables, although they may have difficulties in determining the precise location of the boundaries between the syllables.

2 We give here the translation of SP-35 in place of SP-21, for reasons that will become apparent in a moment. The translation rendered by SP-21 was: *En este año no me voy a España* ('this year I don't go to Spain'). The two learners display a similar level of advancement.

3 This observation was made by Mercedes Cano.

6 The problem of synthesis

1 'Invariable' should not be taken literally: one and the same morph may have different phonetic realizations, even in the language variety of a particular learner. For example, the morph for *Arbeit* ('job', 'work', 'labour') may be pronounced either ['arbaɪ], or ['abaɪ], or ['arebaɪ], or ['arbaɪt], or [are'baɪte], or the like (the sign ' precedes the stressed syllable). These variants cannot be counted as consistently differing grammatical variants of a word.

2 In all the data I have looked at so far, there is only consistent *pre*posing. This, however, might be an accident. Such a principle of consistent serialization (either *pre-* or *post-*) is postulated for fully developed languages by Bartsch and Vennemann (1972). Whether the principle applies to the latter is an open question, but it seems highly plausible in the case of learner varieties with limited 'syntactic' structuring. It should be noted that the much-discussed 'pivot-grammar' postulated by Braine (1963) for first language acquisition can be viewed as a borderline case in the application of the principle. In either case there is a crucial problem with this idea – namely, where to draw the boundary between the two word classes.

3 Phonetically, the learner's speech production differs vastly from any standards for German. Since we disregard the phonetic aspects of the utterances, the chosen sample is presented in normal spelling. For an exact phonetic transcription the reader is referred to the appendix of the Heidelberg Research Project (1979). To catch the flavour of this speech, here is the first utterance in IPA:

i 'kinda ni fi:l mon'eða 'espanje

4 Apparently, questions like 'you see' can appear everywhere: at the end of the setting as well as the focus. We will not consider them here (they are (a) formulaic (b) not part of the story).

5 This sentence can also mean, 'At four, when my dad died, my grandma came to live with me'. The context does not unambiguously tell us which of the two interpretations is right, but the latter clearly appears less plausible.

6 Felix (1982, p. 20, my translation) writes: 'It cannot be denied that the learner is unable to acquire all structures he is confronted with at one time. Hence his first step must be to make a selection from what he is offered. This could be performed according to one of two principles. The learner might select at first from among a set of different clause structures (e.g. copula clause, full

verb clause, passive, imperative, interrogative clause, etc.) just one or perhaps two clauses and employ it or them in his own production; he might, for instance, pick up imperatives before copula clauses. This selection principle has in fact been observed in the acquisition of clause types' (he then refers to his own studies). This raises the question, how does the learner know that some particular sound-wave hitting his ear is a full verb clause in active mood rather than, say, an imperative clause? To accomplish this, he must be able to distinguish active from passive, full verb from copula, imperative from indicative, etc. A learner in command of all this would be described as rather advanced. This does not gainsay the fact that acquisition sequences such as those found by Felix do indeed occur. But the reason is not that the learner performs a selection from what is offered to him in the described fashion, but rather that the results of his own organizational principles are seen – by the analyst – as corresponding to some TL structure type.

7 In response to Jordens' comments (Jordens, 1980), Hyltenstam (1982) has taken a critical stance to this interpretation, arguing that it does not account for the strong inherent variation in the data. He does not deny, however, that the four types follow each other in this order, though not in sharply delimited stages, but through finely graded shifts in balance. This reservation applies to all 'stages' discussed so far.

7 The embedding problem

1 This is not only a popular view, it has also given rise to an important trend in second language research known as 'error analysis'; cf. Corder (1967), Nickel (1972b), Richards (1974), Kielhöfer (1975), Cherubim (1980).

2 These terminological distinctions should not be overrated. Clearly, a good terminology can be of much help, but it also seems that the clarity of a terminological system has sometimes proved an obstacle in research work: strictly defined notions are not necessarily adequate notions, and the web spun from our concepts has often captured the least valuable constructs.

3 Strictly speaking, personal pronouns *in anaphoric usage*, because a pronoun like *he* can also be used *deictically* in that it refers to a person who, without being mentioned earlier, is perceived in the given situation (in connection, for example, with a pointing gesture).

4 Parentheses are used here to indicate an approximate specification of the word's contribution – i.e. the strictly 'lexical meaning' of the term – to the overall utterance information. The particular referent of the term in a given utterance is further contingent on the situational information; on this, cf. Kratzer and Stechow (1979).

5 The functions of deixis can be presented here only in outline; for a more detailed presentation see Klein (1978).

6 It is dangerous to indulge in the illusion that ungrammatical speech or errors in the application of certain forms and constructions invariably jeopardize communication. The fact is that they are frequently not even noticed. In English, the surface form of the perfect tense is very similar to that in German, although it functions somewhat differently. An English speaker learning German is likely to follow his native language in this respect. His 'errors' in German, however,

may escape the attention of all but the most inquisitive minds; to pinpoint them, special tests would have to be used.

7 There is a similar rule (in German or English) applying to coordinative sequences, as in *He entered the house*, (*he*) *climbed the stairs, and* (*he*) *unlocked the door*. This does not apply, however, to other ways of introducing precedent information: *What is he doing? – (He) is working*, where the pronoun cannot be omitted.

8 The inspiration for such examples apparently derives from Hermann Paul (cf. Paul, 1882, p. 218).

9 There are many other effects of context, for instance in the elimination of lexical ambiguities or in the delimitation of lexically vague expressions. If we can employ ambiguous terms such as *fan* in *I hate fans*, it is because it follows from the concomitant knowledge whether the utterance refers to fanatics or to instruments. This is commonly known; what is less well-known is the way in which this contextual effect comes into being and how it could be accounted for in detail (cf. Kratzer, 1979). One of the few studies which makes allowances for the role of context in second language acquisition (in the development of modal verbs) is that by Dittmar (1980).

10 The data were recorded as part of the Heidelberg Research Project for Pidgin German (1975); see also Klein and Dittmar (1979). For a most comprehensive study of temporality in narratives (of Turkish workers learning German), see von Stutterheim (1984). Her study also includes a detailed discussion of the concept of temporality and the influence of conceptual structure on language acquisition.

11 In contrast to literary narration of fictive events; on this in general see Haubrichs (1976, 1977, 1978); specifically on oral accounts of real series of past events see Labov (1972), Quasthoff (1980), Ehlich (1980); and on accounts by foreign workers see Wildgen (1978), Dittmar and Thielicke (1979).

12 The form *Ich weiß net* (instead of the standard *Ich weiß nicht*) follows the rules of the target language by having the verb correctly inflected. From the way the expression is used by other learners at about the same level of advancement it would appear that it functions as a 'rote form', which is acquired as an entity, and not analysed (see section 5.3).

8 The matching problem

1 There are apparently discrepancies – sufficiently small to pass unnoticed – due to differences in modes of language processing between the second-language learner and the native speaker; on this, see the interesting research by Bates *et al.* (1982).

2 For measures of distance in syntax see Klein and Dittmar (1979, p. 93) and Wildgen (1977).

3 The importance of this distinction has been pointed out by Kellerman (1979), though in respect of the differences between first language and second language rather than between learner variety and target variety.

4 The role of language awareness in first language acquisition has attracted some attention in recent years; cf. the volumes by Jarvella, Levelt, and Sinclair

(1978); Hakes (1980); Böhme (1982); and Tunmer, Pratt and Herriman (1984). No comparable work is yet available for second language acquisition.

5 See, for example, Berthoud (1980, 1982), Véronique and Faita (1982), the comments by Mittner and Kahn (1982), and Perdue (1982, section 6.3).

6 In contrast, a lively discussion is in progress on the role of explicit corrections in first language acquisition; see, for example, Käsermann (1980) or Anders (1980) for further references.

7 Cf. in this context the remarks by Labov and Labov (1978, p. 38):

> It is not difficult to see the analogy between the child as language learner and the researchers we have projected. Both pay close attention to the speech of those around them, though they are not so foolish as to abandon their own system every time they hear another one. But in the course of time, they redraft their theory until it is closer and closer to the model that the every-day world provides, since they find that world is richer, more rewarding, and more intricately put together than anything they could have imagined. Those who have been fortunate enough to bring their analyses into close contact with the every-day world will agree that this is indeed the case.

8 For a discussion of this problem (with numerous references) see 'Disorders of language and speech' (1981, Part II, sections 2.2 and 4.3).

9 There is a comprehensive literature on these phenomena (cf. Cutler, 1981), but only a fraction of it deals with second language acquisition; see, for example, Fathman (1980).

10 The investigation was supervised by Rainer Dietrich. The report comprises four closely interrelated papers; my account is based on the whole volume rather than on a particular paper.

11 In a case study of three of the eight speakers it was found that the speaker's focus in self-correction tended to reflect the state of his syntactic development; for details see Carroll, Dietrich, and Storch (1982, pp. 113–39).

REFERENCES

Adjémian, Ch. (1976): On the nature of interlanguage systems. In: *Language Learning* 26, 297–320.

Albert, M. L. and Obler, L. K. (1978): *The bilingual brain.* New York: Academic Press.

Anders, K. (1980): Von Worten zur Syntax: Spracherwerb im Dialog. Universität Frankfurt: Ph.D. thesis.

Andersen, R. W. (1981): Two perspectives on pidginization as second language acquisition. In: Andersen, ed. (1981), 165–95.

Andersen, R. W., ed. (1981): *New dimensions in second language acquisition research.* Rowley, Mass.: Newbury House.

Andersen, R. W. (1983a): Transfer to somewhere. In: Gass and Selinker (1983), 177–201.

Andersen, R. W. (1983b): A language acquisition interpretation of pidginization and creolization. In: Andersen (1983c), 1–56.

Andersen, R. W., ed. (1983c): *Pidginization and creolization as language acquisition.* Rowley, Mass.: Newbury House.

d'Anglejean, A. (1978): Language learning in and out of classrooms. In: Richards (1978), 218–37.

Arditty, J. and Perdue, C. (1979): Variabilité et connaissances en langue étrangère. In: *Encrages*, Numéro Spécial, 32–43.

Baker, L. L. and McCarthy, J. A., eds. (1982): *The logical problem of language acquisition.* Cambridge, Mass.: MIT Press.

Barkowski, H., Harnisch, U. and Kumm, S. (1980): *Handbuch für den Deutschunterricht mit ausländischen Arbeitern.* Königstein/Ts.: Scriptor.

Barton, O. (1978): *The role of perception in the acquisition of phonology.* Indiana University Linguistics Club.

Bartsch, R. and Vennemann, Th. (1972): *Semantic structures.* Frankfurt: Athenäum.

Bates, E., McNew, S., MacWhinney, B., Devescovi, A. and Smith, S. (1982): Functional constraints on sentence processing: A crosslinguistic study. In: *Cognition* 11, 245–99.

Bäuerle, R. (1977): *Temporale Deixis, temporale Frage.* Tübingen: Narr.

Bausch, K. R. and Kasper, G. (1979): Der Zweitspracherwerb: Möglichkeiten and Grenzen der großen Hypothesen. In: *Linguistische Berichte* 64, 3–35.

Bausch, K. R. and Raabe, H. (1978): Zur Frage der Relevanz von kontrastiver

Analyse, Fehleranalyse und Interimsprachenanalyse für den Fremdsprachenunterricht. In: *Jahrbuch Deutsch als Fremdsprache* 4, 56–78.

Beardsmore, H. B. (1982): *Bilingualism: Basic principles*. Clevedon, Avon: Tieto.

Becker, A. and Klein, W. (1979): Eine Gesprächsanalyse. In: Heidelberger Forschungsbericht (1979), 125–73.

Becker, A. and Perdue, C. (1982): Ein einziges Mißverständnis. In: F. Januschek and W. Stölting, eds., *Handlungsorientierung im Zweitspracherwerb von Arbeitsimmigranten*. Osnabrücker Beiträge zur Sprachtheorie 22, 85–121.

Behaghel, O. (1923): *Deutsche Syntax*. Heidelberg: Winter.

Berthoud, A. C. (1980): Rôle de la métalangue dans l'acquisition de la déixis spatiale. In: *Encrages* Numéro Spécial, 109–17.

Berthoud, A. C. (1982): La relative fiabilité du discours métalinguistique des apprenants. In: *Encrages* 8/9, 139–42.

Bickerton, D. (1981): *Roots of language*. Ann Arbor: Karoma Publishers.

Bickerton, D. (1984): The language bioprogram hypothesis and second language acquisition. In: Rutherford (1984a), 141–61.

Bloom, L. (1970): *Language development. Form and function in emerging grammars*. Cambridge, Mass.: MIT Press.

Bodemann, Y. M. and Ostow, R. (1975): Lingua franca und Pseudo-Pidgin in der Bundesrepublik: Fremdarbeiter und Einheimische im Sprachzusammenhang. In: *Zeitschrift für Literaturwissenschaft und Linguistik* 18, 122–46.

Böhme, K. (1982): Children's understanding and awareness of possessive pronouns. Universiteit Nijmegen: Ph.D. thesis.

Bot, C. de (1982): Visuele feedback van intonatie. Universiteit Nijmegen: Ph.D. thesis.

Bowerman, M. (1983): How do children avoid constructing an overly general grammar in the absence of feedback about what is not a sentence. In: *Papers and Reports on Child Language Development* (Stanford University, Department of Linguistics) 22.

Braine, M. (1963): The ontogeny of English phrase structure: The first phase. In: *Language* 39, 1–13.

Braine, M. (1971): On two types of models of the internalization of grammar. In: D. Slobin, ed., *The ontogenesis of grammars*. New York: Academic Press, 153–86.

Brainerd, Ch. J. and Pressley, M., eds. (1982): *Verbal processes in children*. Berlin: Springer.

Brown, R. (1973): *A first language: The early stages*. Cambridge, Mass.: Harvard University Press.

Bühler, K. (1934): *Sprachtheorie*. Jena: Fischer.

Bühler, U. B. (1972): *Empirische und lernpsychologische Beiträge zur Wahl des Zeitpunkts für den Fremdsprachenunterrichtsbeginn*. Zürich: Orell Füssli.

Burke, S. H. (1974): Language acquisition, language learning and language teaching. In: *International Review of Applied Linguistics in Language Teaching* 12, 53–68.

Burt, M. K. and Dulay, H. C. (1980): On acquisition orders. In: Felix (1980), 265–327.

Butzkamm, W. (1973): *Aufgeklärte Zweisprachigkeit*. Heidelberg: Quelle und

References

Meyer.

Campbell, R. N. and Schumann, J. (1981): Hypnotism as a tool in second language research. In: Andersen, ed. (1981), 80–91.

Cancino, H., Rosansky, E. J. and Schumann, J. (1978): The acquisition of English negatives and interrogatives by native Spanish speakers. In: Hatch (1978), 207–30.

Carroll, M., Dietrich, R. and Storch, G. (1982): *Learner language and control.* Frankfurt: Lang.

Cazden, C., Cancino, H., Rosansky, E. J. and Schumann, J. (1975): *Second language acquisition sequences in children, adolescents, and adults.* Final Report, Dept. of Health, Education and Welfare.

Cherubim, D. (1980): *Fehlerlinguistik. Beiträge zum Problem der sprachlichen Abweichung.* Tübingen: Narr.

Chomsky, C. (1969): *The acquisition of syntax in children from 5 to 10.* Cambridge, Mass.: MIT Press.

Chomsky, N. (1959): Review of B. F. Skinner. Verbal behavior. In: *Language* 35, 26–58.

Chomsky, N. (1965): *Aspects of the theory of syntax.* Cambridge, Mass.: MIT Press.

Chomsky, N. (1975): *Reflections on language.* New York: Pantheon Books.

Chomsky, N. (1981): *Lectures on government and binding.* Dordrecht: Foris.

Chun, J. A. F. (1981): Second language acquisition in a natural setting. Stanford University: Ph.D. thesis.

Clark, E. (1970): How young children describe events in time. In: G. B. Flores d'Arcais and W. J. M. Levelt, eds., *Advances in psycholinguistics.* Amsterdam: North Holland, 275–84.

Clark, E. (1978): From gesture to word: On the natural history of deixis in language acquisition. In: S. J. Bruner and A. Garton, eds., *Human growth and development: Wolfson College Lectures 1976.* Oxford: Oxford University Press, 85–120.

Clark, H. and Clark, E. (1977): *Psychology and language: An introduction to psycholinguistics.* New York: Harcourt Brace Jovanovitch.

Clyne, M. (1968): Zum Pidgin-Deutsch der Gastarbeiter. In: *Zeitschrift für Mundartforschung* 35, 130–39.

Clyne, M., ed. (1982): Foreigner talk. *International Journal of the Sociology of Language* 28. Den Haag: Mouton.

Corder, P. (1967): Significance of learners' errors. In: *International Review of Applied Linguistics* 5, 162–9.

Corder, P. (1973): *Introducing applied linguistics.* Harmondsworth: Penguin.

Cromer, R. F. (1968): The development of temporal reference during the acquisition of language. Harvard University: Ph.D. thesis.

Culioli, A. (1976): *Recherche en linguistique: théorie des opérations énonciatives.* Transcriptions du séminaire de D.E.A., Université de Paris VII.

Cummins, J. (1976): The influence of bilingualism on cognitive growth: A synthesis of research findings and explanatory hypotheses. In: *Working Papers in Bilingualism* 9, 1–43.

Curtiss, S. (1977): *Genie. A psycholinguistic study of a modern-day wild child.* New York: Academic Press.

Cutler, A., ed. (1981): *Slips of the tongue and language production.* Amsterdam: Mouton (special issue of *Linguistics*).

Dale, Ph. S. (1976): *Language development. Structure and function.* New York: Holt, Rinehart and Winston.

Day, R. R., Chenoweth, N. A., Chun, A. E. and Luppescu, S. (1984): Corrective feedback in native–nonnative discourse. In: *Language Learning* 34, 19–45.

De Camp, D. and Hancock, J. F., eds. (1974): *Pidgins and Creoles. Current trends and prospects.* Washington, D.C.: Georgetown University Press.

Dechert, H., Möhle, D. and Raupach, M., eds. (1984): *Second language productions.* Tübingen: Narr.

Dechert, H. and Raupach, M., eds. (1980): *Towards a crosslinguistic assessment of speech production.* Frankfurt: Lang.

Dechert, H. and Raupach, M., eds. (1985): *Transfer in production.* New York: Plenum Press.

Denny, J. P. (1978): Locating the universals in lexical systems for spatial deixis. In: D. Farkas *et al.*, eds., *Papers from the parasession on the lexicon.* Chicago: Chicago Linguistic Society, 7, 1–84.

Disorders of language and speech (1981): Nijmegen: Max-Planck-Institut für Psycholinguistik (MS).

Dittmar, N. (1980): Fremdsprachenerwerb im sozialen Kontext. Das Erlernen von Modalverben – eine lexikalisch–semantische Analyse. In: *Zeitschrift für Literaturwissenschaft und Linguistik* 33, 84–103.

Dittmar, N. (1982): 'Ich fertig arbeite – nicht mehr spreche Deutsch'. Semantische Eigenschaften pidginisierter Lernervarietäten des Deutschen. In: *Zeitschrift für für Literaturwissenschaft und Linguistik* 45, 9–34.

Dittmar, N. and Thielicke, E. (1979): Der Niederschlag von Erfahrungen ausländischer Arbeiter mit dem institutionellen Kontext des Arbeitsplatzes in Erzählungen. In: H. G. Soeffner, ed., *Interpretative Verfahren in den Sozial- und Textwissenschaften.* München: Fink, 1979, 65–103.

Dulay, H. and Burt, M. (1974): Natural sequences in child second language acquisition. In: *Language Learning* 24, 37–53.

Dulay, H., Burt, M. and Krashen, S. (1982): *Language two.* New York: Oxford University Press.

Ehlich, K., ed. (1980): *Erzählungen im Alltag.* Frankfurt: Suhrkamp.

Ekstrand, L. H. (1979): *Replacing the critical period and optimum age theories of second language acquisition with a theory of ontogenetic development beyond puberty.* Malmö/Lund: Malmö School of Education/Lund University, Dept. of Educational and Psychological Research.

Els, Th. van and Oud-Glas, M., eds. (1983): *Research on foreign language needs.* Augsburg: Universität Augsburg.

Els, Th. van *et al.* (1984): *Applied linguistics and the learning and teaching of foreign languages.* London: Edward Arnold.

Ervin, S. and Osgood, Ch. E. (1954): Second language learning and bilingualism. In: *Journal of Abnormal and Social Psychology* 49, Supplement, 139–46.

Ervin-Tripp, S. (1969): Sociolinguistics. In: *Advances in Experimental Social Psychology* 4. New York: Academic Press, 91–165.

Ervin-Tripp, S. (1974): Is second language learning like the first? In: *TESOL*

References

Quarterly 8, 111–27.

Faerch, C., Haastrup, K. and Philipson, R. (1984): *Learner language and language learning.* Clevedon, Avon: Multilingual Matters.

Faerch, C. and Kasper, G., eds. (1983): *Strategies in interlanguage communication.* London: Longman.

Fant, G. and Tatham, M. A., eds. (1975): *Auditory analyses and perception of speech.* New York: Academic Press.

Fathman, A. K. (1980): Repetition and correction as an indication of speech planning and execution processes among second language learners. In: Dechert and Raupach (1980), 77–85.

Felix, S. (1978): *Linguistische Untersuchungen zum natürlichen Zweitspracherwerb.* München: Fink.

Felix, S., ed. (1980): *Second language development: Trends and issues.* Tübingen: Narr.

Felix, S. (1982): *Psycholinguistische Aspekte des Zweitspracherwerbs.* Tübingen: Narr.

Felix, S. and Simmet, A. (1982): L'acquisition des pronoms personnels en milieu scolaire. In: *Encrages* 8/9, 33–41.

Ferguson, Ch. (1977): Simplified registers, broken language and Gastarbeiterdeutsch. In: C. Molony, H. Zobl and W. Stölting, eds., *Deutsch im Kontakt mit anderen Sprachen.* Kronberg Ts.: Scriptor, 1977, 25–39.

Ferguson, Ch. and de Bose, C. E. (1977): Simplified registers, broken language and pidginization. In : Valdman (1977), 99–125.

Ferguson, Ch. and Slobin, D., eds. (1973): *Studies of child language development.* New York: Holt, Rinehart and Winston.

Fillmore, Ch. (1971): Santa Cruz lectures on deixis. University of California, Santa Cruz (available at Indiana University Linguistic Club).

Fletcher, P. and Garman, M., eds. (1979): *Language acquisition.* Cambridge: Cambridge University Press.

Foppa, K. (1965): *Lernen, Gedächtnis, Verhalten, Ergebnisse und Probleme der Lernpsychologie.* Köln: Kiepenheuer und Witsch.

Friederici, A. D. (1983): *Neuropsychologie der Sprache.* Stuttgart: Kohlhammer.

Fromm, E. (1970): Age regression and unexpected reappearance of a repressed childhood language. In: *International Journal of Clinical Experimental Hypnosis* 18, 79–88.

Galloway, L. and Krashen, S. D. (1980): Cerebral organization in bilingualism and second language. In: Scarcella and Krashen (1980), 74–80.

Gardner, R. C. and Lambert, W. E. (1972): *Attitudes and motivation in second language learning.* Rowley, Mass.: Newbury House.

Gaskill, W. H. (1980): Correction in native speaker–nonnative speaker conversation. In: Larsen-Freeman (1980), 125–37.

Gass, S. (1984): A review of interlanguage syntax: Language transfer and language universals. In: *Language Learning* 34, 115–31.

Gass, S. and Selinker, L., eds. (1983): *Language transfer in language learning.* Rowley, Mass.: Newbury House.

Genesee, F. *et al.* (1978): Language processing in bilinguals. In: *Brain and Language* 5, 1–12.

Givón. T. (1979): From discourse to syntax. Grammar as a processing strategy. In: T. Givón, ed., *Discourse and syntax* (Syntax and Semantics 12) New York: Academic Press, 81–111.

Givón, T. (1984a): *Syntax. A functional–typological introduction.* Amsterdam: Benjamins.

Givón, T. (1984b): Universals of discourse structure and second language acquisition. In: Rutherford (1984a), 109–36.

Gleitman, L. R. and Wanner, E., eds. (1982): *Language acquisition: The state of the art.* Cambridge: Cambridge University Press.

Gold, E. (1967): Language identification in the limit. In: *Information and Control* 16, 447–74.

Greenberg, J. H. C. (1978): *Universals of human language.* Stanford: Stanford University Press.

Grégoire, A. (1937): *L'apprentissage du langage: Les deux premières années.* Liège: Bibliothèque de la Faculté de Philosophie et de Lettres.

Grewendorf, G. (1982): Zur Pragmatik der Tempora im Deutschen. In: *Deutsche Sprache* 10, 213–36.

Grosjean, F. (1982): *Life with two languages: An introduction to bilingualism.* Cambridge, Mass.: Harvard University Press.

Guiora, A. Z. *et al.* (1972): The effects of benziodiazepine (Valium) on permeability of language ego boundaries. In: *Language Learning* 30, 351–63.

Gumperz, J. and Roberts, C. (1978): *Developing awareness skills for inter-ethnic communication.* Southall: National Centre for Industrial Language Training.

Hahn, A. (1982): Fremdsprachenunterricht und Spracherwerb. Universität Passau: Ph.D. thesis.

Hakes, D. T. (1980): *The development of metalinguistic abilities in children.* Berlin: Springer.

Hakuta, K. (1974): Prefabricated patterns and the emergence of structure in second language acquisition. In: *Language Learning* 24, 287–97.

Halliday, M. A. K. and Hasan, R. (1976): *Cohesion in English.* London: Longman.

Hatch, E. M., ed. (1978): *Second language acquisition. A book of readings.* Rowley, Mass.: Newbury House.

Hatch, E. M. (1983): *Psycholinguistics. A second language perspective.* Rowley, Mass.: Newbury House.

Haubrichs, W., ed. (1976, 1977, 1978): *Erzählforschung* I–III. Göttingen: Vandenhoeck.

Heckhausen, H. (1981): *Motivation und Handeln.* Berlin: Springer.

Heidelberger Forschungsprojekt 'Pidgin-Deutsch' (Heidelberg Research Project) (1975): *Sprache und Kommunikation ausländischer Arbeiter.* Kronberg/Ts.: Scriptor.

Heidelberger Forschungsprojekt 'Pidgin-Deutsch' (Heidelberg Research Project) (1976): *Untersuchungen zur Erlernung des Deutschen durch ausländische Arbeiter.* (Arbeitsbericht III), Germanistisches Seminar der Universität Heidelberg.

Heidelberger Forschungsprojekt 'Pidgin-Deutsch' (Heidelberg Research Project) (1977): *Die ungesteuerte Erlernung des Deutschen durch spanische und italienische Arbeiter.* Osnabrücker Beiträge zur Sprachtheorie, Beiheft 2.

179

References

Heidelberger Forschungsprojekt 'Pidgin-Deutsch' (Heidelberg Research Project) (1979): *Studien zum Spracherwerb ausländischer Arbeiter.* (Arbeitsbericht V), Germanistisches Seminar der Universität Heidelberg.

Heike, G. (1969): *Suprasegmentale Analyse.* Marburg: Elwert.

Henrichson, L. E. (1984): Sandhi-Variation: A filter of input for learners of ESL. In: *Language Learning* 34, 103–26.

Hörisch, J., ed. (1979): *Ich möchte ein solcher werden wie . . . Materialien zur Sprachlosigkeit des Kaspar Hauser.* Frankfurt: Suhrkamp.

Hornby, P. A., ed. (1977): *Bilingualism.* New York: Academic Press.

Hornstein, N. and Lightfoot, D. (1981): *Explanation in linguistics. The logical problem of language acquisition.* London: Longman.

Huebner, Th. (1983): *A longitudinal analysis of the acquisition of English.* Ann Arbor: Karoma Publishers.

Hüllen, W. and Jung, L. (1979): *Sprachstruktur und Spracherwerb.* Düsseldorf: Bagel.

Hyltenstam, K. (1977): Implicational patterns in interlanguage syntax variation. In: *Language Learning* 27, 383–411.

Hyltenstam, K. (1978): *Variation in interlanguage syntax.* Working Papers Nr. 8, Dept. of General Linguistics, Lund University.

Hyltenstam, K. (1982): On descriptive adequacy and psychological plausibility: A reply to Jordens. In: *Language Learning* 32, 167–73.

Hymes, D., ed. (1971): *Pidginization and creolization of language.* Cambridge: Cambridge University Press.

Isačenko, A. and Schädlich, J. (1966): Untersuchungen über die deutsche Satzintonation. In: *Studia Grammatica* VII. Berlin: Akademie Verlag, 7–67.

Jacobs, J. (1982): *Syntax und Semantik der Negation im Deutschen.* München: Fink.

Jakobovits, L. A. (1970): *Foreign language learning – a psycholinguistic analysis of the issues.* Rowley, Mass.: Newbury House.

Jakobson, R. (1960): Linguistics and poetics. In: Th. A. Sebeok, ed., *Style in language.* Cambridge, Mass.: MIT Press, 350–77

Jarvella, R. and Klein, W., eds. (1982): *Speech, place, and action.* Chichester: Wiley.

Jarvella, R., Levelt, W. J. M. and Sinclair, A., eds. (1978): *The child's conception of language.* Berlin: Springer.

Jordens, P. (1980): Interlanguage research: Interpretation of explanation. In: *Language Learning* 30, 195–207.

Kainz, F. (1959): *Psychologie der Sprache.* Vol. II. Stuttgart: Enke (2nd edition).

Karmiloff-Smith, A. (1979): *A functional approach to child language: A study of determiners and reference.* Cambridge: Cambridge University Press.

Käsermann, M.-L. (1980): *Spracherwerb und Interaktion.* Bern: Huber.

Kellerman, E. (1979): The problem with difficulty. In: *Interlanguage Studies Bulletin* 4, 27–44.

Kellerman, E. and Sharwood-Smith, M., eds. (1985): *Crosslinguistic influence in second language acquisition.* Oxford: Pergamon Press.

Kielhöfer, B. (1975): Fehlerlinguistik des Fremdspracherwerbs. Kronberg/Ts.: Scriptor.

180

Kintsch, W. (1977): *Memory and cognition*. New York: Wiley.

Klein, W. (1977): Einige wesentliche Eigenschaften natürlicher Sprachen und ihre Bedeutung für die linguistische Theorie. In: *Zeitschrift für Literaturwissenschaft und Linguistik* 23/24, 11–31.

Klein, W. (1978): Wo ist hier? Präliminarien zu einer Untersuchung der lokalen Deixis. In: *Linguistische Berichte* 58, 18–40.

Klein, W. (1979): Temporalität. In: Heidelberger Forschungsprojekt 'Pidgin-Deutsch' (1979), 87–104. (Reprinted as 'Der Ausdruck der Temporalität im ungesteuerten Spracherwerb'. In: G. Rauh, ed., *Essays on deixis*. Tübingen: Narr, 1983, 149–68.)

Klein, W. (1981): Some rules of regular ellipsis in German. In: W. Klein and W. J. M. Levelt, eds., *Crossing the boundaries in linguistics. Studies presented to Manfred Bierwisch*. Dordrecht: Reidel, 1981, 51–78.

Klein, W. (1984): Bühler Ellipse. In: T. Hermann and F. J. Graumann, eds., *Bühlers Axiomatik*. Frankfurt: Klostermann, 117–41.

Klein, W. and Dittmar, N. (1979): *Developing grammars*. Berlin: Springer.

Klein, W. and Rieck, B.-O. (1982): Der Erwerb der Personalpronomina im ungesteuerten Spracherwerb. In: *Zeitschrift für Literaturwissenschaft and Linguistik* 45, 35–71.

Kleinmann, H. H. (1978): The strategy of avoidance in adult second language acquisition. In: Ritchie (1978), 157–74.

Knapp-Potthoff, A. and Knapp, K. (1982): *Fremdsprachenlernen und -lehren*. Stuttgart: Kohlhammer.

Kohler, K. J. (1977): *Einführung in die Phonetik des Deutschen*. Berlin: Schmidt.

Königs, F. G. (1983): *Normenaspekte im Fremdsprachenunterricht*. Tübingen: Narr.

Krashen, S. O. (1981): *Second language acquisition and learning*. Oxford: Pergamon Press.

Kratzer, A. (1979): *Semantik der Rede*. Kronberg/Ts.: Scriptor.

Kratzer, A. and Stechow, A. von (1979): Äußerungssituation und Bedeutung. In: *Zeitschrift für Literaturwissenschaft und Linguistik* 23/24, 98–130.

Kuno, S. (1982): Principles of discourse deletion. Case studies from English, Russian and Japanese. In: *Journal of Semantics* 1, 61–93.

Labov, W. (1972): *Sociolinguistic patterns*. Philadelphia: Pennsylvania University Press.

Labov, T. and Labov, W. (1976): Das Erlernen der Syntax von Fragen. In: *Zeitschrift für Literaturwissenschaft und Linguistik* 22/23, 47–82.

Labov, W. and Labov, T. (1978): Learning the syntax of questions. In: R. N. Campbell and P. T. Smith, eds., *Recent advances in the psychology of language*. Vol. II. New York: Plenum Press, 1–44.

Lado, R. (1957): *Linguistics across cultures: Applied linguistics for language teachers*. Ann Arbor: University of Michigan Press.

Lambert, D. R. (1977): Learning to recognize foreign speech sounds. University of California, San Diego: Ph.D. thesis.

Lambert, W. (1969): Psychological studies of the interdependencies of the bilingual's two languages. In: J. Puhvel, ed., *Substance and structure of language*. Berkeley: University of California Press, 99–126.

References

Lambert, W. and Freed, B. (1982): *The loss of language skills.* Rowley, Mass.: Newbury House.

Lamendella, J. (1977): General principles of neurofunctional organization and their manifestation in primary and non-primary language acquisition. In: *Language Learning* 27, 155–96.

Larsen-Freeman, D., ed. (1980): *Discourse analysis in second language research.* Rowley, Mass.: Newbury House.

Lehiste, I. (1970): *Suprasegmentals.* Cambridge, Mass.: MIT Press.

Leischner, A. (1979): *Aphasien und Sprachentwicklungsstörungen.* Stuttgart: Thieme.

Lenneberg, E. (1967): *Biological foundations of language.* New York: Wiley.

Leopold, W. F. (1939–49): *Speech development of a bilingual child: A linguist's record.* Evanston: Northwestern University Press.

Levelt, W. J. M. (1974): *Formal grammar in linguistics and psycholinguistics.* Den Haag: Mouton.

Levelt, W. J. M. (1983): Monitoring and self-repair in speech. In: *Cognition* 13, 41–104.

Levelt, W. J. M., Mills, A. and Karmiloff-Smith, A., eds. (1981): *Child language research in ESF countries – an inventory.* Strasbourg: European Science Foundation.

Lewis, D. (1979): Scorekeeping in a language game: In: R. Bäuerle, U. Egli and A. von Stechow, eds., *Semantics from different points of view.* Berlin: Springer, 172–87.

Lindner, K. (1983): *Sprachliches Handeln bei Vorschulkindern.* Tübingen: Niemeyer.

Lindsay, P. H. and Norman, D. A. (1977): *Human information processing.* New York: Academic Press.

Long, M. H. (1982): Adaption an den Lerner. In: *Zeitschrift für Linguistik und Literaturwissenschaft* 45, 100–19.

Lüdi, G. and Py, B. (1984): *Être bilingue.* Bern: Lang.

Macnamara, J. (1970): Bilingualism and thought. In: *Monograph Series of Language and Linguistics* 23, 25–40.

Marshall, J. and Morton, J. (1978): On the mechanics of Emma. In: A. Sinclair, R. Jarvella and W. J. M. Levelt, eds., *The child's conception of language.* Berlin: Springer, 225–39.

Mazurkiewicz, I. (1984): The acquisition of the dative alternation by second language learners and linguistic theory. In: *Language Learning* 34, 91–109.

McLaughlin, B. (1978a): *Second language acquisition in childhood.* Hillsdale, N.J.: Earlbaum (second revised version 1984).

McLaughlin, B. (1978b): The monitor model: Some methodological considerations. In: *Language Learning* 28, 309–32.

Meisel, J. (1975): Ausländerdeutsch und Deutsch ausländischer Arbeiter. Zur möglichen Entstehung eines Pidgin in der BRD. In: *Zeitschrift für Literaturwissenschaft und Linguistik* 18, 9–53.

Meisel, J. (1983): Transfer as a second language strategy. In: *Language and Communication* 3, 11–46.

Meisel, J., Clahsen, H. and Pienemann, M. (1981): On determining developmental stages in natural second language acquisition. In: *Studies in Second Language Acquisition* 3, 109–35.

Mittner, M. and Kahn, G. (1982): Réflexions sur l'activité métalinguistique des apprenants adultes en milieu naturel. In: *Encrages* 8/9, 67–75.

Moore, T. E. (1973): *Cognitive development and the acquisition of language.* New York: Academic Press.

Müller, K. E., ed. (1980): The foreign language syllabus and communicative approaches to teaching. Special issue of: *Studies in Second Language Acquisition* 3, 1980.

Neufeld, G. (1979): Towards a theory of language learning ability. In: *Language Learning* 29, 227–41.

Neufeld, G. (1980): On the acquisition of prosodic and articulatory features in adult language learning. In: Felix (1980), 137–49.

Nickel, G. (1972a): *Reader zur kontrastiven Linguistik.* Frankfurt: Athenäum.

Nickel, G. (1972b): *Fehlerkunde. Beiträge zur Fehleranalyse, Fehlerbewertung und Fehlertherapie.* Berlin: Cornelsen.

Nooteboom, S., Brokx, J. P. L. and de Rooij, J. J. (1978): Contributions of prosody to speech perception. In: W. J. M. Levelt and G. B. Flores d'Arcais, eds., *Studies in the perception of language.* Chichester: Wiley, 75–107.

Oller, J. W. Jr. (1981): Research on the measurement of affective variables. In: Andersen, ed. (1981), 14–27.

Paradis, M. (1977): Bilingualism and aphasia. In: H. and H. A. Whitaker, eds., *Studies in neurolinguistics* 3. New York: Academic Press, 65–121.

Paradis, M. and Lebrun, Y. (1983): La neurolinguistique du bilinguisme. Paris: Larousse (*Languages* 72).

Paul, H. (1882): *Prinzipien der Sprachgeschichte.* Leipzig: Niemeyer.

Penfield, W. and Roberts, L. (1959): *Speech and brain mechanisms.* Princeton: Princeton University Press.

Peng, F. C. L., ed. (1983): *Neurology of language: A first approximation.* London: Earlbaum.

Perdue, C., ed. (1982): *Second language acquisition by adult immigrants. A field manual.* Strasbourg: European Science Foundation. (Reprinted 1984, Rowley, Mass.: Newbury House.)

Piaget, J. (1946): *Le développement de la notion de temps chez l'enfant.* Paris: Presses Universitaires de France.

Piepho, H. E. (1974): *Kommunikative Kompetenz als übergeordnetes Lernziel im Englischunterricht.* Dornburg-Frickhofen: Frankonius.

Pinker, S. (1979): Formal models of language learning. In: *Cognition* 7, 217–83.

Porsché, D. C. (1983): *Die Zweisprachigkeit während des primären Spracherwerbs.* Tübingen: Narr.

Quasthoff, U. M. (1980): *Erzählungen in Gesprächen.* Tübingen: Narr.

Quest, J., Bolton, S. and Lauerbach, G. (1981): *Fremdsprachen für Erwachsene.* Berlin: Cornelsen.

Raabe, J. (1974): *Trends in kontrastiver Linguistik* I. Tübingen: Narr.

Raabe, J. (1976): *Trends in kontrastiver Linguistik* II. Tübingen: Narr.

Rauh, G. (1982): *Essays in deixis.* Tübingen: Narr.

Raupach, M. (1984): Formulae in second language speech production. In:

References

Dechert, Möhle and Raupach (1984), 114–37.

Richards, J. C., ed. (1974): *Error analysis: Perspectives on second language acquisition*. London: Longman.

Richards, J. C., ed. (1978): *Understanding second and foreign language learning: Issues and approaches*. Rowley, Mass.: Newbury House.

Ritchie, W. C., ed. (1978): *Second language acquisition research*. New York: Academic Press.

Roche, J. (1982): Merkmale des foreigner talk im Deutschen. Universität München: MA thesis.

Rohrer, Ch., ed. (1980): *Time, tense, and quantifiers*. Tübingen: Narr.

Ronjat, J. (1913): *Le développement du langage observé chez un enfant bilingue*. Paris: Champion.

Rosansky, E. J. (1976): Methods and morphemes in second language acquisition research. In: *Language Learning* 26, 409–25.

Rösel, P. (1980): *Perzeption und Imitation kontextgebundener Vokale durch deutsche Englischlerner*. Tübingen: Narr.

Rutherford, W. E., ed. (1984a): *Language universals and second language acquisition*. Amsterdam: Benjamins.

Rutherford, W. E. (1984b): Description and explanation in interlanguage syntax: State of the art. In: *Language Learning* 34, 127–55.

Sag, I. (1979): *Deletion and logical form*. MIT: Ph.D. thesis.

Saunders, G. (1982): *Bilingual children: Guidance for the family*. Clevedon, Avon: Tieto.

Saussure, F. de (1916): *Cours de linguistique générale*. Paris: Payot.

Scarcella, R. C. and Krashen, S. D., eds. (1980): *Research in second language acquisition*. Rowley, Mass.: Newbury House.

Scherer, K. R. and Wallbott, H. G., eds. (1979): *Nonverbale Kommunikation: Ausgewählte Forschungsberichte zum Interaktionsverhalten*. Weinheim: Beltz.

Schmidt, M. (1980): Coordinate structures and language universals in interlanguage. In: *Language Learning* 30, 397–416.

Schumann, J. (1978a): *The pidginization process*. Rowley, Mass.: Newbury House.

Schumann, J. (1978b): Social and psychological factors in second language acquisition. In: Richards (1978), 163–78.

Scovel, Th. (1981): The effects of neurological age on nonprimary language acquisition. In: Andersen, ed. (1981), 33–42.

Seliger, H. W. (1978): Implications of a multiple critical period hypothesis for second language learning. In: Ritchie (1978), 11–20.

Selinker, L. (1972): Interlanguage. In: *International Review of Applied Linguistics* 10, 209–31.

Sgall, P., Hajičová, E. and Benešová, E. (1973): *Topic, focus, and generative semantics*. Kronberg/Ts.: Scriptor.

Sharwood-Smith, M. (1983): On first language loss in the second language acquirer: Problems of transfer. In: Gass and Selinker (1983), 222–31.

Skinner, B. F. (1957): *Verbal behavior*. Englewood Cliffs: Prentice Hall.

Slobin, D. (1971): *Psycholinguistics*. Glenview, Ill.: Scott, Foresman and Co.

Slobin, D. (1973): Cognitive prerequisites for the development of grammar. In: Ferguson and Slobin (1973), 175–208.

References

Smith, L. E., ed. (1983): *Readings in English as an international language.* Oxford: Pergamon Press.

Snow, C. A. and Ferguson, Ch. (1977): *Talking to children – language input and acquisition.* Cambridge: Cambridge University Press.

Snow, C. A. and Hoefnagel-Höhle, M. (1978): Age differences in second language acquisition. In: Hatch (1978), 333–44.

Solmecke, G., ed. (1983): *Motivation im Fremdsprachenunterricht.* Paderborn: Schöningh (2nd edition).

Solmecke, G. and Boosch, A. (1983): *Affektive Komponenten über Lernerpersönlichkeit und Fremdsprachenerwerb.* Tübingen: Narr.

Stauble, A. M. E. (1981): A comparative study of Spanish-English and Japanese-English second language continuum: Verb phrase morphology. University of California, Los Angeles: Ph.D. thesis.

Stutterheim, Ch. von (1981): When language barriers become mind blocks. Max-Planck-Institut für Psycholinguistik, Nijmegen (MS).

Stutterheim, Ch. von (1984): Der Ausdruck der Temporalität in der Zweitsprache. Max-Planck-Institut für Psycholinguistik, Nijmegen: Ph.D. thesis.

Szulc, A. (1976): *Fremdsprachendidaktik. Konzeptionen – Methoden – Theorien.* Warschau: Panstwowe Wydawnictwo Naukowe.

Taeschner, T. (1983): *The sun is feminine. A study on language acquisition in bilingual children.* Berlin: Springer.

Tanz, Ch. (1980): *The acquisition of deictic terms.* Cambridge: Cambridge University Press.

Tarone, E., Frauenfelder, U. and Selinker, L. (1976): Systematicity/variability and stability/instability in interlanguage systems. In: H. D. Brown, ed., *Papers in second language acquisition.* Ann Arbor: University of Michigan Press, 93–134.

Tarone, E., Frauenfelder, U. and Selinker, L. (1978): The phonology of interlanguage. In: Richards (1978), 15–33.

Trévise, A. (1979): Spécificité de l'énonciation didactique dans l'apprentissage de l'anglais par des étudiants francophones. In: *Encrages* Numéro Spécial, 44–52.

Tropf, H. (1983): Variation in der Phonologie des ungesteuerten Spracherwerbs. Universität Heidelberg: Ph.D. thesis.

Tunmer, W. E., Pratt, C. and Herriman, M. (1984): *Metalinguistic awareness in children: Theory research and implications.* Berlin: Springer.

Ullmer-Ehrich, V. (1982): *Da* and the system of spatial deixis in German. In: Weissenborn and Klein (1982), 43–63.

Valdman, A., ed. (1977): *Pidgin and Creole linguistics.* Bloomington: Indiana University Press.

Véronique, D. and Faita, D. (1982): Sollicitation de données syntaxiques auprès d'un groupe de travailleurs maghrébins. In: *Encrages* 8/9, 47–56.

Vihman, M. M. and McLaughlin, B. (1982): Bilingualism and second language acquisition in preschool children. In: Brainerd and Pressley (1982), 35–58.

Wales, R. (1979): Deixis. In: Fletcher and Garman (1979), 241–60.

Wandruszka, M. (1974): *Die Mehrsprachigkeit des Menschen.* München: Piper.

Weinreich, U. (1953): *Languages in contact. Findings and problems.* New York:

References

Humanities Press.

Weinrich, H. (1964): *Tempus. Besprochene und erzählte Welt*. Stuttgart: Kohlhammer.

Weir, R. (1962): *Language in the crib*. Den Haag: Mouton.

Weissenborn, J. and Klein, W., eds. (1982): *Here and there. Crosslinguistic studies in deixis and demonstration*. Amsterdam: Benjamins.

Wexler, K. und Culicover, P. W. (1980): *Formal principles of language acquisition*. Cambridge, Mass.: MIT Press.

White, L. (1983): *Markedness and parameter setting: Some implications for a theory of adult second language acquisition*. Paper presented at the 12th Annual University of Wisconsin Linguistics Symposium, March 1983.

Wildgen, W. (1977): *Differentielle Linguistik: Entwurf eines Modells zur Beschreibung und Messung semantischer und pragmatischer Variation*. Tübingen: Narr.

Wildgen, W. (1978): Zum Zusammenhang von Erzählstrategie und Sprachbeherrschung bei ausländischen Arbeitern. In: Haubrichs (1978), 380–411.

Winkler, P. (1980): Über die perzeptiv-psychologische Realität der distinktiven Merkmale von R. Jakobson. In: *Linguistische Berichte* 65, 1–8.

Wode, H. (1974): Natürliche Zweitsprachigkeit. Probleme, Aufgaben, Perspektiven. In: *Linguistische Berichte* 32, 15–36.

Wode, H. (1981): *Learning a second language. An integrated view of language acquisition*. Tübingen: Narr.

Wode, H. (1983): *Papers on language acquisition, language learning, and language teaching*. Heidelberg: Groos.

Wolfson, N. (1982): On tense alternation and the need for analysis of native speaker usage in second language acquisition. In: *Language Learning* 32, 53–68.

Wong-Fillmore, L. (1976): The second time around: Cognitive and social strategies in second language acquisition. Stanford University: Ph.D. thesis.

Wunderli, P., Benthin, K. and Karasch, A. (1978): *Französische Intonationsforschung*. Tübingen: Narr.

Wunderlich, D. (1970): *Tempus und Zeitreferenz im Deutschen*. München: Hueber.

Wunderlich, D. (1971): Pragmatik, Sprechsituation, Deixis. In: *Zeitschrift für Literaturwissenschaft und Linguistik* 1/2, 151–90.

INDEX OF NAMES

187

Index of names

INDEX OF SUBJECTS

matching problem, 62, 138–66
mesolang, 99
metalinguistics, 17, 28–9, 141–2
  see also reflection
modal verb, 74–7
monitoring, 142–4
monitor theory, 17, 20, 28–9
morph, 81
morpheme order studies, 24, 49
morphological matching, 160–1
motivation
  instrumental *vs* integrative, 37
  see also propensity

narrative, 132–7
nasilang, 99
negation, 95–109
negative evidence, 151–2
neurolinguistics, 10, 12

origo, 117, 125

parallel information, 59–60, 66, 70–1
phonological matching, 157–60
pidginization, 30–2
position (in an utterance), 68–9
pragmatic mode, 83–4
prefabricated pattern, *see* formulaic speech
primary language acquisition, 3
principle
  of utterance structure, 82–4
  of natural order (PNO), 82, 127–9, 135–6
proficiency, 54–5
  active *vs* passive, 42
pronoun, 71–4, 188–9
propensity, 33–9, 167
prosody, *see* intonation

re-acquisition, 3, 22–3
reflection (on language), 142, 145

règle
  de Pitres, 23
  de Ribot, 23

salience, 68–70
second language acquisition (SLA), 1–2,
  15–22, 43, 50
  guided, 15, 19–21, 28, 50
  spontaneous, 15–19, 21, 50, 146–7
setting, 85–9, 109
social factor, *see* development, social, *and
  also* identity, social and personal
strategy, 17, 29
structure of acquisition, 34, 47–50
synchronization, 47–9
syntactic matching, 161–3
syntactic mode, 83–4
synthesis problem, 60–1, 79–110

teaching, 18–22, 46–7, 53–5
tempo of acquisition, 35, 50
temporality, 4, 123–37
test
  repetition, 71–4
  translation, 74–7
test rule, *see* critical rule
theme *vs* rheme, 82–3
time reference, 124
  see also temporality
transfer, 13, 25–9

universal grammar, 6–8
universals, 63–4

variability
  of acquisition process, 49–50
  of target language, 54–5, 138–40

wolf child, 3
word class, 80–2, 90
word order, 80–9, 122–3